Northern Ireland: Crisis and Conflict

John Magee

Department of History,
St Joseph's College of Education,
Belfast

LONDON AND BOSTON

ROUTLEDGE & KEGAN PAUL

First published in 1974
by Routledge & Kegan Paul Ltd
Broadway House, 68–74 Carter Lane
London EC4V 5EL and
9 Park Street,
Boston, Mass. 02108, USA
Set in Baskerville
and printed in Great Britain by
Willmer Brothers Limited, Birkenhead
© John Magee 1974
ISBN 0 7100 7946 X (c)
ISBN 0 7100 7947 8 (p)
Library of Congress Catalog Card No. 74–81316

Contents

	page
GENERAL EDITOR'S PREFACE	xi
VOLUME EDITOR'S PREFACE	xiii
ACKNOWLEDGMENTS	xv
GLOSSARY	xvii
INTRODUCTION	1
Suggested Exercises	28

SELECT DOCUMENTS

PART I: THE GENESIS OF THE ULSTER QUESTION

1. Extracts from 'The treatment of the native population under the scheme for the plantation in Ulster', by T. W. Moody (*Irish Historical Studies*, vol. 1, no. 1, March 1938) — 31
2. Extracts from *A Short History of Ireland*, by J. C. Beckett (Hutchinson, 3rd ed., 1966) — 34
3. Extracts from *Orangeism in Ireland and Britain, 1795–1836*, by Hereward Senior (Routledge & Kegan Paul, 1966) — 38
4. Extracts from *Orangeism: A New Historical Appreciation*, by M. W. Dewar, J. Brown and S. E. Long (Grand Orange Lodge of Ireland, 1967) — 38
5. Extracts from 'Belfast', by Emrys Jones (*Ulster since 1800*, 2nd series, edited by T. W. Moody and J. C. Beckett, BBC, 1957) — 42
6. Extracts from Isaac Butt's speech on Home Rule, House of Commons, 30 June 1874 (*Parliamentary Debates*, series 3, ccxx, cols 700–17) — 45
7. Extracts from a speech by Charles S. Parnell at Cork, 21 January 1885 (*Freeman's Journal*, 22 January 1885) — 46
8. Extracts from a speech by Sir Edward Carson at Belfast, 23 September 1911 (quoted in *Ulster's Stand for Union*, by Ronald McNeill, John Murray, 1922) — 47
9. Extracts from a speech by Sir Edward Carson at Blenheim, 27 July 1912 (*The Complete Grammar of Anarchy*,

Maunsel, Dublin, 1918)   48

10. Ulster's Solemn League and Covenant, 28 September 1912 (Ulster Unionist Council Papers, NIPRO, D1327/3/21)   50

11. Letter of Hugh de F. Montgomery, of the Ulster Unionist Council, to his son, 22 June 1916, explaining acceptance of partition (Montgomery papers, NIPRO, D627/429)   50

12. Extracts from the Government of Ireland Act 1920 (10 and 11 Geo. V, ch. 6, 7)   52

13. Extracts from Articles of Agreement for a Treaty between Great Britain and Ireland, 6 December 1921 (Saorstat Eireann, General Public Acts, 1922)   54

PART II: THE CONSTITUTION AND POLITICAL INSTITUTIONS OF NORTHERN IRELAND

14. Extracts from *Constitutional Law in Northern Ireland*, by Harry Calvert (Stevens & Sons and *Northern Ireland Legal Quarterly*, 1968)   59

15. Extracts from speech by the Home Secretary, Mr Roy Jenkins, in the House of Commons, 25 October 1967   61

16. Extracts from *The Government of Northern Ireland*, by Nicholas Mansergh (Allen & Unwin, 1936)   64

17. Extracts from *Ulster 1969: The Fight for Civil Rights in Northern Ireland*, by Max Hastings (Gollancz, 1970)   64

18. Extracts from *The Future of Northern Ireland: A Paper for Discussion* (London, HMSO, 1972)   66

19. Extracts from *Whitehall Diary*, Vol. III, by Thomas Jones, edited by Keith Middlemas (Oxford University Press, 1971)   68

20. Extracts from *Disturbances in Northern Ireland*, Report of the Cameron Commission, 1969 (Belfast, HMSO, Cmnd 532)   69

21. Extracts from *Disturbances in Northern Ireland*, Report of the Cameron Commission, 1969 (Belfast, HMSO, Cmnd 532)   72

22. Extracts from *Violence and Civil Disturbances in Northern Ireland in 1969*, Report of the Scarman Tribunal, 1972 (Belfast, HMSO, Cmnd 566)   74

23. Extracts from *Disturbances in Northern Ireland*, Report

of the Cameron Commission, 1969 (Belfast, HMSO, Cmnd 532)   80

PART III: ULSTER UNDER HOME RULE

24. Extracts from *Whitehall Diary*, Vol. III, by Thomas Jones, edited by Keith Middlemas (Oxford University Press, 1971)   88
25. Text of the Agreement Amending and Supplementing the Articles of Agreement for a Treaty between Great Britain and Ireland, signed on December 3rd, 1925   90
26. Extracts from an interview with Lord Brookeborough (*Irish Times*, 30 October 1968)   92
27. Extracts from *Northern Ireland: Fifty Years of Self-Government*, by Martin Wallace (David & Charles, 1971)   96
28. Extracts from 'The political scene in Northern Ireland 1926–1937', by J. L. McCracken, in *The Years of the Great Test 1926–39*, edited by Francis MacManus (Mercier Press, Cork, 1967)   99
29. Manifesto issued by the Irish Republican Army, 12 December 1956   100
30. Extracts from *Ireland Since the Famine*, by F. S. L. Lyons (Weidenfeld & Nicolson, 1971)   101
31. Extracts from *The Government of Northern Ireland: Public Finance and Public Services, 1921–1964*, by R. J. Lawrence (Oxford University Press, 1965)   105
32. Extracts from an address by Mr Terence O'Neill, Prime Minister of Northern Ireland, to the Commonwealth Parliamentary Association, at Westminster, 4 November 1968 (*Ulster at the Crossroads*, ed. John Cole, Faber, 1969)   110

PART IV: REVOLUTION AND CHANGE

33. Extracts from *Disturbances in Northern Ireland*, Report of the Cameron Commission, 1969 (Belfast, HMSO, Cmnd 532)   122
34. Extracts from *Ulster 1969: The Fight for Civil Rights in Northern Ireland*, by Max Hastings (Gollancz, 1970)   123
35. Text of a Communiqué and Declaration issued after a meeting held at 10 Downing Street on 19 August

1969 (London, HMSO, Cmnd 4154)   125

36. Extracts from *Ulster*, by the *Sunday Times* 'Insight' Team (Penguin Books, 1972)   128

37. Extracts from *States of Ireland*, by Conor Cruise O'Brien (Hutchinson, 1972)   130

38. Extracts from *How Stormont Fell*, by Henry Kelly (Gill & Macmillan, Dublin, 1972)   133

39. Extracts from a statement issued by the Social Democratic and Labour Party, 16 July 1971   138

40. Extracts from *Ulster*, by the *Sunday Times* 'Insight' Team (Penguin Books, 1972)   142

41. Extracts from the letter of a Belfast girl, aged 11, to the BBC programme 'Your Own Voices' (1971), printed in *Community Forum*, Vol. 3, No. 1, 1973 (The Northern Ireland Community Relations Commission)   143

42. Extracts from *Children in Conflict*, by Morris Fraser, Senior Registrar in Psychiatry at the Royal Belfast Hospital for Sick Children (Secker & Warburg, 1973)   144

43. Extracts from *Report of the enquiry into allegations against the security forces of physical brutality in Northern Ireland arising out of events on the 9th August, 1971*, the Compton Report (London, HMSO, Cmnd 4823)   145

44. Extracts from a speech by the Prime Minister, Mr Edward Heath, to the House of Commons, 24 March 1972   147

45. Extracts from statements made early in 1972 by (a) Sean Mac Stiofáin, Chief of Staff, Provisional IRA, and (b) Cathal Goulding, Chief of Staff, Official IRA (quoted in *On Our Knees*, by Rosita Sweetman, Pan Books, 1972)   153

46. Proposals by political parties in Northern Ireland from *The Future of Northern Ireland, A Paper for Discussion* London, HMSO, 1972)   157

47. Extracts from *The Future of Northern Ireland, A Paper for Discussion* (London, HMSO, 1972)   161

48. Extracts from *Report of the Commission to consider legal procedures to deal with terrorist activities in Northern Ireland*, the Diplock Report, 1972 (London, HMSO, Cmnd 5185)   168

49. Extracts from *Northern Ireland Constitutional Proposals*, 1973 (London, HMSO, Cmnd 5259)   172

CONTENTS

50. Statement by the Prime Minister, Mr Edward Heath, to the people of Northern Ireland, on a visit to Belfast, 29 August 1973 (*Irish Times*, 30 August 1973)   180

POSTSCRIPT   186
SELECT BIBLIOGRAPHY   189
INDEX   192

Maps

---

1 Northern Ireland   xix
2 Inner Belfast   116

General Editor's Preface

The World Studies Series is designed to make a new and important contribution to the study of modern history. Each volume in the Series will provide students in sixth forms, Colleges of Education and Universities with a range of contemporary material drawn from many sources, not only from official and semi-official records, but also from contemporary historical writing from reliable journals. The material is selected and introduced by a scholar who establishes the context of his subject and suggests possible lines of discussion and inquiry that can accompany a study of the documents.

Through these volumes the student can learn how to read and assess historical documents. He will see how the contemporary historian works and how historical judgments are formed. He will learn to discriminate among a number of sources and to weigh the evidence. He is confronted with recent instances of what Professor Butterfield has called 'the human predicament' revealed by history; evidence concerning the national, racial and ideological factors which at present hinder or advance man's progress towards some form of world society.

Readers of this volume will hear the authentic sound of 'the four, deep, tragic notes in Irish History' (Yeats, 'Four Bells'). They will also find massive and reliable evidence on which to base their own judgments regarding that delicate, tripartite relationship of government between Belfast, Dublin and London. This is given its appropriate, global setting in the following sentence from the British Government's discussion paper, quoted by Mr Magee himself on page 107 of his book:

In a world of growing inter-dependence, where even the

aspirations of major sovereign powers can only be fully met by their participation in wider associations and communities, a small area such as Northern Ireland cannot, without the gravest consequences for its own citizens, make its way alone.

JAMES HENDERSON

Volume Editor's Preface

Less than a decade ago it was possible for British historians to regard the Government of Ireland Act 1920 and the Anglo-Irish Treaty of 1921 as a final answer to the Irish Question. 'Lloyd George conjured it out of existence', wrote A. J. P. Taylor in 1965. According to C. L. Mowat, 'it simply disappeared as a major factor in British politics'. The tragic history of Northern Ireland since 1969 has illustrated the superficiality of such judgments, and the Irish Question is in the forefront of British politics again. A senior cabinet minister replaced the Government of Northern Ireland, thousands of troops are engaged in security duties there, and the United Kingdom Government has embarked on the difficult and dangerous task of making a new Irish settlement. Because they are more directly involved than at any time in recent history, the British people have been forced to come to grips with 'the Ulster problem' and to try to understand it.

The purpose of this book is to provide students with evidence and information on some of the basic questions, and the fact that it has to go back to the seventeenth century to find the roots of the conflict indicates how complex and intractable a problem it is. The book suggests answers to a number of questions. Why are there two separate communities in Northern Ireland and why are they so bitterly divided? When and how did Ulster Unionism develop as a strong political force? Why has there been no *rapprochement* between the north and south of Ireland during the past fifty years? How much fault for the present conflict is attributable to the Churches? to the schools? to the history taught in the schools? These last questions particularly interest the volume editor but they would require a separate book.

The final section of Part IV deals in some detail with the new constitutional arrangements proposed for Northern Ireland and with the prospects of establishing some kind of all-Ireland institution. The volume editor can only hope that what he has had to say will not be overtaken and disproved by events.

The words 'Protestant' and 'Catholic' are used throughout the book in the sense in which they are used in Northern Ireland to represent the majority and minority communities, and no offence is intended to members of religious denominations who feel they are as much entitled to use the term 'Catholic' as are members of the Roman Catholic Church.

I wish to thank Mrs Amanda Crichton, who undertook the typing of the manuscript at short notice; Mr Gerard Cleary of the Geography Department of St Joseph's College of Education, Belfast, who prepared the maps; and also my wife for her help and encouragement while the book was being written, and for sacrificing a vacation so that it might be finished on time.

Acknowledgments

The author and publishers wish to thank the following for kind permission to print in this volume extracts from the works cited:

The Deputy Keeper for use of material in the Public Record Office for Northern Ireland

The Social Democratic and Labour Party for the statement of 16 July 1971

George Allen & Unwin Ltd for *The Government of Northern Ireland* by N. Mansergh

Penguin Books Ltd for *Ulster* by the *Sunday Times* 'Insight' Team, copyright © Times Newspapers Ltd, 1972; and Random House Inc. for *Northern Ireland: A Report on the Conflict* by the London *Sunday Times* 'Insight' Team, copyright © Times Newspapers Ltd, 1972

Hutchinson Publishing Group Ltd for *A Short History of Ireland* by J. C. Beckett

Oxford University Press for *Whitehall Diary: Volume III Ireland 1918-1925* by Thomas Jones, edited by Keith Middlemas

Mercier Press for J. L. McCracken's essay 'The political scene in Northern Ireland, 1926-1937' in *The Years of the Great Test 1926-37*, edited by Francis MacManus

Weidenfeld (Publishers) Ltd and Charles Scribner's Sons for *Ireland Since the Famine* by F. S. L. Lyons

M. Wallace for *Northern Ireland: Fifty Years of Self-Government*, David & Charles, Newton Abbot, 1971

Emrys Jones for 'Belfast' in *Ulster since 1800, II*, edited by T. W. Moody and J. C. Beckett, BBC Publications, 1957

Rosita Sweetman and Pan Books for *On Our Knees*

Her Majesty's Stationery Office for Statutes, Treaties, Official

Reports, *Hansard* and *The Future of Northern Ireland* (by permission of the Controller of HMSO)

Faber & Faber for *Ulster at the Crossroads* by Terence O'Neill, edited by J. Cole

Gill & Macmillan Ltd for *How Stormont Fell* by Henry Kelly

The Irish Times for interview with Lord Brookeborough, by Dennis Kennedy

R. J. Lawrence for *The Government of Northern Ireland: Public Finance and Public Services 1921–1964* © 1965 Oxford University Press, and by permission of The Clarendon Press, Oxford

The Northern Ireland Community Relations Commission for extracts from *Community Forum* vol. 3, no. 1, 1973

Routledge & Kegan Paul and Humanities Press Inc. for *Orangeism in Ireland and Britain, 1795-1836* by Hereward Senior

Secker & Warburg Ltd for *Children in Conflict* by Morris Fraser, reprinted by permission of A. D. Peters & Company

The Grand Orange Lodge of Ireland for *Orangeism: A New Historical Appreciation* by M. W. Dewar, J. Brown and S. E. Long

Max Hastings for *Ulster 1969: The Fight for Civil Rights in Northern Ireland*, Gollancz, 1970

The editor and proprietors of *Irish Historical Studies*, vol. 1, no. 1, March 1938 for 'The treatment of the native population under the scheme for the plantation in Ulster' by T. W. Moody

Conor Cruise O'Brien for *States of Ireland*, Hutchinson, 1972

Harry Calvert for *Constitutional Law in Northern Ireland*, Stevens & Sons and *Northern Ireland Legal Quarterly*, 1968

Glossary

Apprentice Boys—Protestant Orange society based in Derry, dedicated to commemorating the action of Protestant apprentices who, in 1688, secured the city for the Williamite cause by closing the gates against the forces of James II

Ardoyne—Catholic district of Belfast

Ballymurphy—Catholic housing estate in Belfast

Bogside—Catholic area in Derry

Dail Eireann (the Dail)—parliament of the Irish Republic

Dail Uladh—'Ulster Parliament'—hypothetical institution envisaged by certain sections of the IRA as an alternative government for the province of Ulster

Falls—Falls Road and surrounding area—Catholic area of Belfast

feiseanna—festivals and competitions of traditional music and dance

GOC Northern Ireland—the General Officer Commanding British Armed Forces in Northern Ireland

IRA—Irish Republican Army

IRB—Irish Republican Brotherhood

NILP—Northern Ireland Labour Party

NIPRO—Northern Ireland Public Record Office

PR—the proportional representation system of voting

Ribbonmen—nineteenth-century clandestine agrarian groups

RIC—Royal Irish Constabulary

RUC—Royal Ulster Constabulary

Saorstat Eireann—Irish Free State

SDLP—Social Democratic and Labour Party

Shankill—Shankill Road and surrounding area—Protestant area of Belfast

STV—Single Transferable Vote system of proportional representation

Taoiseach—the Prime Minister of the Irish Republic

TD—*Teachta Dála*—Deputy of the Dail

Threshers—nineteenth-century clandestine agrarian societies

UDA—Ulster Defence Association

UDI—Unilateral Declaration of Independence

UDR—Ulster Defence Regiment

Ulster—the traditional province consists of the counties of Londonderry, Antrim, Down, Armagh, Tyrone, Fermanagh, Monaghan, Cavan and Donegal. Northern Ireland consists of the first six of these counties, and the remaining three now form part of the Republic of Ireland

USC—Ulster Special Constabulary

UVF—Ulster Volunteer Force

UWC—Ulster Workers Council

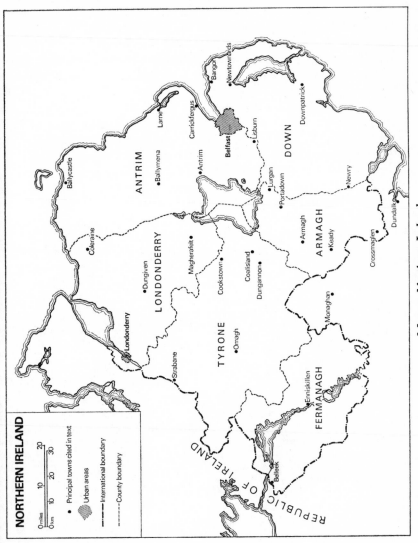

Map 1 Northern Ireland

Introduction

It is impossible to write about the current situation in Northern Ireland without frequent use of the terms 'Protestant' and 'Catholic', for it is difficult to find more accurate labels to identify the two communities locked in conflict there. The media reinforce the impression these terms create by publishing statistics of Catholics and Protestants who have been killed or maimed by violence, alongside pictures of churches and schools which the terrorists have destroyed. Because of this, the Northern Ireland problem is seen in many parts of the world as an anachronistic survival of the seventeenth-century religious wars in which two groups of Christians are apparently prepared to kill one another for the love of God. A cartoon in an Australian newspaper showed a bedraggled British lion in an arena, with wild Irishmen behind gates waiting to get at him. The caption read: 'What nobler end for a lion than to be thrown to Christians?' Irish churchmen of all denominations are incensed by this interpretation of a highly complex human situation, and point out that the men of violence, whose activities have attracted so much publicity, are not fighting about points of theological difference and are concerned solely with political, social and economic issues. But while the Northern Ireland conflict may not be a 'holy' war, it would be unrealistic not to recognize the importance of religion as a factor in the situation. Religion is the foundation upon which the constitutional, political and social structures of the state have been built, and almost every problem has a sectarian dimension.

People from outside Northern Ireland do not always realize how clear-cut this division on religious lines is, mainly because they find it incomprehensible that anything so outmoded as sectarianism can shape a country's politics in the modern world. The origins of the Protestant/Unionist and Catholic/Nationalist brand of Ulster politics can be traced back to the English and Scottish settlement in the province at the beginning of the seventeenth century. Earlier settlers in Ireland had been easily assimilated and within a short time their descendants were indistinguishable from the native population. But in the plantation of Ulster religious difference was a barrier to integration, and the two peoples lived side by side but very much apart in separate and almost self-contained communities. Occasionally they came into conflict and started the terrible cycle of communal warfare that has marked the history of Ulster over the past three hundred years. In 1641 the Catholics attempted to exterminate the Protestants, only to be harried themselves by the parliamentary forces and eventually to lose most of their lands. Half a century later, the attempt by the Catholic army of James II to starve the Protestants of Derry into surrender was followed in 1690 by William III's victory at the Battle of the Boyne. Because of their seventeenth-century experiences the Ulster Protestants developed an almost pathological fear of the Catholics as a threat to their existence and to their property. The penal laws were to some extent a defence mechanism, and it was hoped that, if they were strictly administered, the degraded and impoverished Catholics would never be in a position to rise again. Especially in Ulster, where Protestants were most numerous, religion became the criterion whereby a man's civil rights and economic opportunities were determined. Catholics were excluded from respectable society.

At the end of the eighteenth century an attempt was made to break out of this situation, when a group of Belfast Presbyterians affected by the Enlightenment rejected the concept of a Protestant ascendancy as a relic of a barbarous age. It was not that they had lost their traditional detestation of 'popery', but rather that they found it difficult to reconcile the liberal ideas they professed with the blatant discrimination practised against the majority of the Irish population by a privileged minority. Their attitude was not entirely one of self-abnegation; the Presbyterians also suffered from disabling laws and hoped with Catholic assistance to undermine the monopoly of the Established Church. This attitude never gained much support from the rank and file of Ulster Presbyterians, and it received almost a mortal blow with the formation of the Orange Order (1795), the collapse of the 1798 rebellion and the passing of the Act of Union (1800).

A number of subsequent developments ensured the permanent polarization of the Irish population on Catholic/Protestant lines and the eventual separation of Northern Ireland from the rest of the country. The first of these was the evangelical movement which brought Anglicans and Presbyterians closer together and reduced the likelihood of denominational rivalry, thereby giving Ulster Protestantism a greater homogeneity than it had possessed at any time since the seventeenth century. A second development was the industrialization of north-east Ulster, financed and controlled by the Protestant section of the population which also provided nearly all of the skilled operatives. The menial tasks were performed by the poorer and less educated Catholics, whose rapid growth in numbers in Belfast reactivated Protestant fears that were never far below the surface. The despised 'papists' retreated from a hostile society to find security in the ghettos that grew up around their churches and schools. Protestant fears were further intensified by the admission of Catholics to full political rights and the gradual extension of the franchise. When in the 1880s Charles Stewart Parnell organized the most effective mass movement in the history of Catholic Ireland, Ulster Unionists fell back on an argument that brought all Protestants together: 'Home Rule is Rome Rule'. In the last resort they were prepared to resist under arms any attempt to put them under what they saw as a Catholic parliament. Faced with this dilemma, the United Kingdom Government compromised: if Protestants and Catholics could not live together in a unitary state, then it might be better if they were given separate administrations. Thus the Government of Ireland Act 1920 made provision for a northern parliament to legislate for the six counties of Antrim, Down, Armagh, Tyrone, Fermanagh and Londonderry, which taken together had a Protestant majority, though with a substantial Catholic minority; and a southern parliament to legislate for the remainder of the country. The state of Northern Ireland came into existence in 1921.

3

From the outset Northern Ireland was a confessional state. The first Prime Minister, Lord Craigavon, made this clear: 'I am an Orangeman first and a member of this parliament afterwards. . . . We are a Protestant Parliament and a Protestant State.' The ethos of the state was Protestant, with public houses, cinemas, even children's playgrounds, closed on Sundays and with the Protestant churches exercising a very considerable influence, particularly in the field of education. There were institutional links between the ruling Unionist Party and the Orange Order, and the national holiday chosen for the new state was 12 July, the anniversary of William III's victory over the Catholics at the Battle of the Boyne, 1690. On that day all industry and business in Northern Ireland comes to a halt, and in working-class areas arches are erected, flags are flown and kerbstones are painted red, white and blue, often for the full length of a street. The celebrations held throughout the province on that day are partly Protestant religious service and partly Unionist political rally, in which government ministers and clergymen occasionally exchange roles. Thus the religious division of society corresponds exactly with the political division, and Protestant solidarity is little weakened by class or sectional rivalry.

The Catholics must bear some of the blame for the kind of political and social apartheid that developed in the province in its early years. They regarded partition as an injustice and looked outwards to their co-religionists in the south whom they one day hoped to join. Their attitude to the regime was ambivalent, ranging from outright rejection on some occasions to reluctant acceptance of it as a *fait accompli*. On their behalf it may be said that little attempt was made to win their allegiance, and a prominent member of the Unionist Party said of them: 'It is difficult to see how a Roman Catholic with the vast differences in our religious outlook could either be acceptable within the Unionist Party or for that matter bring himself unconditionally to support its ideals.' Lord Brookeborough was even more explicit: 'Catholics are out to destroy Ulster with all their might and power. They want to nullify the Protestant vote, to take all they can out of Ulster and then see it go to hell.' It is incredible that a statesman should speak of one-third of his subjects as potential traitors, without any distinction or qualification, and simultaneously expect them to believe in the impartiality of the regime (see Documents 26–8). As so often happens, Unionists' fears became self-fulfilling predictions, for, during the whole of the regime's existence, a substantial section of the Catholic population withheld allegiance from it. That does not mean that many Catholics sympathized with the tactics pursued by the IRA, but almost to a man they rejoiced when the United Kingdom Government prorogued Stormont in March 1972 and embarked on a new settlement of the Irish Question.

Religion runs through the whole fabric of Ulster life and has created two separate social systems. The basic information people look for in relation to those they meet is their religion, and they have developed sensitive antennae to pick up the faintest signals which help them to identify and categorize the most perfect strangers. In most parts of the province Catholics and Protestants have little intercourse beyond that required in their business and professional lives. Societies and clubs are usually church-related, and even where not are frequently patronized by one religion only. A town may have as many badminton teams or indoor bowling clubs as there are church congregations, and they are more likely to play against Protestant or Catholic teams in adjacent areas than with their neighbours of a different religion. Catholics and Protestants play association football, but even this can, on occasion, be a divisive rather than a unifying experience, for certain teams (such as Linfield and Glasgow Celtic) have become symbols of the religious tribes and their supporters provocatively goad opponents with flags and slogans. Only Catholics play hurling and Gaelic football, and it is unusual to find Protestants who have an interest in the Irish language or in traditional music and dancing. In following pop stars and show bands the young display a more ecumenical spirit than their parents, but even in this the Protestant attitude towards frivolous Sunday amusements is an inhibiting factor.

Segregation of the communities is most marked in urban areas, and the majority of towns have districts where Protestants and Catholics tend to congregate. In very segregated areas each religious group has its own doctors, solicitors, tradesmen and shops; and as the children are educated separately, there is little opportunity for personal friendships to be formed across the religious divide. Before the present troubles started, segregation of this kind had begun to break down, especially in the new housing estates of Belfast and Craigavon, but attitudes and prejudices acquired over three centuries are hard to discard, and the study by Barritt and Carter, *The Northern Ireland Problem: a Study in Group Relations* (Oxford University Press, 1962) indicates that the breakdown of the old moulds caused disquiet in some quarters:

> Where the segregation of Catholics begins to break down, this is regarded by many Protestants with alarm (however friendly they may be with individual Catholic neighbours): 'they are getting in' is the phrase one hears, and it is evident that in general a 'mixed' area in the towns is regarded by Protestants as one which is going downhill. In consequence a Protestant landlord is unfaithful both to his own 'side' and perhaps to his long term business interest if he sells or lets part of his property to a Catholic. In some town or country areas, sales to those of the other religion may upset the delicate balance of voting, and change the representation of the district in local government. There is naturally strong social pressure to prevent any landlord doing such a thing, though it is not always effective in withstanding economic inducements.

The trends to which Barritt and Carter referred have been reversed by the present troubles, and the tendency is now for working-class areas in Belfast, Derry, Portadown and other towns to be totally segregated on religious lines.

Unemployment, and the poverty and frustration which accompany it, are at the root of much community tension (see Part III, section iii, and Document 31). Protestants and Catholics compete for too few jobs, and in this kind of situation Catholics are at a disadvantage, for most of the older industries are owned and controlled by Protestants. There are complaints, too, that new industries, introduced with government assistance, were not located in the west and south of the province where there was a high percentage of Catholics, but were directed to areas where Protestant workers predominated. Trade union leaders have done their utmost to keep sectarianism out of workshops and factories, but the religious ghettos in which many of the industries are situated make it easy for foremen and supervisors to ensure that only 'the right sort' are employed.

Poverty and unemployment cause many Catholics to emigrate, so that, although the Catholic birthrate at 28·3 per thousand is 40 per cent higher than that of Protestants, the religious balance of the population with which the state began has not been significantly altered. In general, Protestants feel superior to Catholics and ascribe the poverty of the latter to their lack of the virtues of thrift and hard work. They believe them to be improvident and lazy, to have too many children and to expect the state to do everything for them. Lord O'Neill, in a radio interview a few days after his resignation as Prime Minister, provided a classic example of this kind of condescension:

> The basic fear of the Protestants in Northern Ireland is that they will be outbred by the Roman Catholics. It is frightfully hard to explain to a Protestant that if you give the Roman Catholics a good job and a good house, they will live like Protestants, because they will see neighbours with cars and television sets. They will refuse to have eighteen children. But if the Roman Catholic is jobless and lives in a most ghastly hovel, he will rear eighteen children on the National Assistance. It is impossible to explain this to a militant Protestant because he is so keen to deny civil rights to his Roman Catholic neighbours. He cannot understand, in fact, that if you treat Roman Catholics with due consideration and kindness, they will live like Protestants in spite of the authoritative nature of their Church.

Both communities disapprove of mixed marriages, and they have been so rare that a social scientist has concluded that Protestants and Catholics 'can be considered as two endogamous societies'. Where they do occur, the Catholic partner nearly always insists that the conditions of the *Ne Temere* decree should be observed: the ceremony takes place in a Catholic church before a priest and all the children of the marriage are baptized and brought up in the Catholic faith. Mixed marriages consequently add to the other tensions and cause great distress to the families of the young people involved.

The education of the two communities is almost completely separate, except in the technical colleges and at the universities. In recent times denominational schools have come in for much criticism and are said to 'perpetuate the socialising of children into the values and prejudices of their religious beliefs'. In a survey conducted for the *Belfast Telegraph* before the present disturbances, 65 per cent of the youth of both communities favoured educating Protestant and Catholic children together; but it is not clear what either the questioner or the respondent meant by 'integrated' education. The United Kingdom Government's White Paper, *Northern Ireland Constitutional Proposals* (HMSO, 1973, Cmnd 5259), was cautious in its comment on the subject, for it was obvious that any hint of pressure at this time would only increase social tensions and worsen relations between the two communities:

> The re-creation of inter-communal confidence is bound to be a long and slow affair. There is no single means by which it can be accomplished. But the Government is convinced that, if the tragic events of recent times are not to recur, means must be found to create a greater sense of community in the minds of the rising generation. One of the obvious factors in the situation is the high degree of educational segregation. This is not of itself in any way peculiar to Northern Ireland. The importance which, in the United Kingdom and in many other countries, certain of the Churches place upon their own school systems stems from deep conviction about the need for an underlying religious basis to all teaching. While, in Northern Ireland, it is the Roman Catholic Church which maintains a separate system, it is by no means to be assumed that, in practice, all Protestant parents would be happy to see a completely integrated school system, involving as it would the teaching of Protestant children by Roman Catholic teachers, some of them members of religious orders. To make the educational system itself the scapegoat for all the ills of Northern Ireland would be to obscure problems whose origins are of a much more complex character.

At the present time, when Catholics and Protestants of Belfast and Derry seek shelter and security in huge 'reservations' confined exclusively to people of their own faith, and children of the different religious denominations occasionally attack each other on their way to and from school, the question of integrated education can be of little more than academic interest. The point can be made, however, that separate schooling over the past fifty years has reinforced the cultural differences already existing between the two communities, and has contributed to the confusion about their national identity which bothers so many young Protestants today. Catholic children study Irish history, learn the Irish language, play Gaelic games and compete in the local *feiseanna*. Schools attended by Protestant children have tended to concentrate on British history and to inculcate a British consciousness, with the result that the impression has been created that Gaelic culture is something that belongs to 'the other side'. This has begun to change, but in the past many Ulster children grew up with no knowledge of the history and traditions of the country to which they themselves were attached by every human feeling. A study carried out by James L. Russell for the Northern Ireland Community Relations Commission and published as *Some Aspects of the Civic Education of Secondary Schoolboys in Northern Ireland* (1972) found that three-quarters of the Catholics felt themselves to be Irish; Protestants were equally split between a British and an Ulster identity. In a question about who they thought were 'people like us', most Protestant children identified with England and most Catholic children with the Republic of Ireland. Since the suspension of the Stormont Parliament in March 1972, there has been an interesting vogue for displaying the Ulster Flag instead of the Union Jack in Protestant working-class districts. This may be only a temporary phase arising from the frustration most right-wing Unionists feel about Westminster's mishandling of the situation. But the increased sense of an 'Ulster' identity may be of some significance if it leads to a more rational approach to the future relationship of the province to the rest of the island of Ireland.

(ii) NORTHERN IRELAND: RELATIONS WITH WESTMINSTER

The general election of December 1918 gave a landslide victory to the Sinn Fein candidates in every part of Ireland outside the Protestant counties of Ulster. Some weeks later they set up their own parliament (Dail Eireann) in Dublin and issued a declaration of Irish independence. It was clear that some form of Irish self-government would have to be conceded, and consequently the Ulster Unionist MPs who had been elected demanded that the province should continue to be ruled from Westminster. Partition was seen by the Prime Minister, Lloyd George, as a way out of this impasse, and the Government of Ireland Act 1920 set up two Home Rule parliaments in Ireland, one for the six north-eastern counties and one for the rest of the country. There was also provision for a Council of Ireland to act as a bridge between the two parts of the country, and in view of the present demand for a similar constitutional arrangement something should be said about it. It was to consist of twenty representatives of each parliament, who would meet regularly to discuss matters of mutual concern, and it was to be given certain modest powers of its own. The United Kingdom Government hoped that by co-operating in this way the two parts of Ireland might ultimately be united by the consent of the two regional parliaments. With hindsight, one can see that the scheme had great merits, and had it been introduced a decade earlier the subsequent history of Ireland might have been different. But in 1920 it was too late. Sinn Fein had raised the expectations of Nationalists and they would be satisfied with nothing short of independence. Consequently, as far as southern Ireland was concerned, Lloyd George's scheme was virtually ignored and it was soon superseded by the Anglo-Irish Treaty of 1921.

Northern Ireland was therefore one part of a compromise which failed, and as a result has always been in an anomalous position. Like Scotland and Wales it was an integral part of the United Kingdom and the authority of the Westminster Parliament was as full and complete there as in any other part of Great Britain; but unlike the other parts of the United Kingdom it had its own form of regional administration. The system of government provided for Northern Ireland is described in detail in Part II, but in the light of the situation half a century later, the following additional observations may be of interest.

1   The Unionists had never demanded a parliament of their own. In a letter to Lloyd George, Sir James Craig (later Lord Craigavon) made this clear. 'In order that you may correctly understand the attitude we propose to adopt,' he wrote, 'it is necessary that I should call to your mind the sacrifices we have so recently made in agreeing to self-government and in consenting to the establishment of a Parliament for Northern Ireland. Much against our wish but in the interests of peace we accepted this as a *final settlement* of the long outstanding difficulty with which Great Britain has been confronted.'

With the passing of time the attitude of the Unionist Government changed, for the Unionists discovered that there were advantages in having a parliament of their own, in which they were assured of a permanent majority. Their control of the day-to-day administration of the province and of the police gave them an opportunity to create the kind of state they wanted, without having to pay too much attention to the fluctuation of party politics in Great Britain. Even before the building of Stormont it was clear that any attempt to integrate the province within the United Kingdom would be extremely unpopular. In 1936 the Ulster Unionist Council declared:

> The cry 'Back to Westminster' is a subtle move fraught with great danger. Had we refused to accept a Parliament for Northern Ireland and remained at Westminster there can be little doubt that by now we would be either inside the Free State or fighting desperately against incorporation. Northern Ireland without a Parliament of her own would be a standing temptation to certain British politicians to make another bid for a final settlement with Irish Republicans.

This continued to be the policy of Ulster Unionists up to 1972, and they feared that the prorogation of Stormont might prove to be a step on the road to a United Ireland. Recently the cry of 'Back to Westminster' has been raised again by right-wing Unionists such as Mr West and Mr Taylor, by Mr Craig of the Ulster Vanguard and by the Rev. Ian Paisley, leader of the Democratic Unionist Party. They fear that the obligation imposed upon Unionists, by the Constitution Act 1973, of sharing political power with the representatives of the Catholic minority, and the proposal to establish a Council to provide a link between the two parts of Ireland, must eventually lead to the political unity of the country. So they wish to return to the position before 1920, with Northern Ireland as an integral part of the United Kingdom.

2 Ultimate authority in Northern Ireland rested with Westminster, but in practice the sovereign parliament devoted very little time to the affairs of the province. In one period of just over a year—from October 1934 to November 1935—the time spent on Northern Ireland business was one hour and fifty minutes, and, until the present troubles started, that seems to have been about the average. After 1922 United Kingdom governments were so relieved to be free at last from apparently insoluble Irish problems that their policy was to have as little as possible to do with the internal affairs of Northern Ireland. Consequently a parliamentary convention grew up that Westminster would not legislate for the province in respect of matters for which Stormont had been given responsibility, unless it was invited to do so by the Northern Ireland Government. A second convention made it impossible for questions to be asked at Westminster in respect of 'transferred matters', because there was no minister in a position to provide the information required. Thus the oversight over Northern Ireland affairs envisaged for the United Kingdom Government by the 1920 Act early fell into disuse. The result was the growth among Ulster Unionists of an independent spirit which resented any interference, even by the United Kingdom, in their domestic affairs. In *The Ulster Debate* (Bodley Head, 1972) Professor Beckett wrote:

> The very use of the term 'Ulster' as equivalent to 'Northern Ireland', which was common among Protestants, though it was often no more than a sacrifice of accuracy to convenience, could carry significant overtones. It gave the new state a kind of continuity with the past; it implied that it represented a recognised and well-established territorial division; and it associated Northern Ireland with those stirring seventeenth-century events that were always alive in the folk-memory of Ulster Protestants. Here we have already a kind of embryonic nationalism; or, at the least,

a state of mind out of which a sense of national, rather than merely regional, distinctiveness might, in certain circumstances, emerge.

These developments caused many Catholics to believe that the safeguards against religious discrimination provided for in the 1920 Act were in fact of little value. After the 1964 general election a number of Labour MPs at Westminster, notably Paul Rose, Stanley Orme and Kevin McNamara, attempted to initiate debates on allegations made by Catholics against local authorities in respect of housing and public appointments, but their efforts were invariably frustrated by the Speaker's ruling that these matters were not the concern of the United Kingdom Parliament. Carefully documented evidence about the manipulation of electoral boundaries and the effects of a restricted franchise in local government elections, as well as allegations of discrimination against Catholics in the matter of jobs and houses, were forwarded to both Labour and Conservative home secretaries without result, so that, in the words of the Government's Green Paper, *The Future of Northern Ireland*, 'many members of the minority felt that they could not expect redress of grievance through Parliament or through the constitutional safeguards which had been written into the Act of 1920'.

Two results followed. First, the inability of the Catholic minority to have their complaints investigated by the British Government was undoubtedly a contributory cause of the early disturbances. Second, when in August 1969 the United Kingdom Government began to push the Northern Ireland Government in the direction of reform, there was understandable irritation in Unionist Party circles at what was regarded as a serious departure from established procedures. Mr Callaghan, who was Home Secretary at the time, has revealed in his book *A House Divided: The Dilemma of Northern Ireland* (Collins, 1973) the difficulty he had in convincing the Stormont administration that Westminster was the supreme authority that had to be obeyed:

Cairncross, the Under-Secretary at the Home Office, had been having talks which continued throughout the day with Harold Black, and reported that while the Northern

Ireland Cabinet were likely to agree to consider my proposed programme of reforms, they were showing an unwillingness to commit themselves to a specific examination of the various items, on the grounds that they might prove to be impractical and would savour of dictation from Westminster. I said that was not good enough. I was in no particular mood at that stage to be put off by a group of people who seemed to have no conception of how close they were to disaster. I instructed Cairncross to get hold of Black, even if it meant getting him out of bed, and tell him that I would not be satisfied unless the Cabinet would agree to commit themselves to a specific programme. I also asked Cairncross to draft a communiqué during the night on the assumption that at the conclusion of the talks there would be basic disagreement between Northern Ireland Ministers and myself. In the draft communiqué he should set down, and he should tell Black that he was doing so, the reforms that I had put to the Cabinet for examination and which they were unwilling to accept. In the absence of agreement I would make it public . . . .

It was clear that the semi-independence which the United Kingdom Government had given to Stormont over the years made its task very difficult now, when it was forced by the pressure of world opinion to remove some of the causes of communal strife in Northern Ireland.

The outside observer may feel that the leaders of both communities in Northern Ireland were equally short-sighted: the Unionists for having made no serious effort over the years to obtain Catholic support for the regime or to offer them a share in the running of the state; the Nationalists for not accepting the settlement of 1920 and putting forward a comprehensive political programme attractive to Protestants with a view to providing an alternative government. Such criticism displays a fundamental misunderstanding of the situation. Northern Ireland emerged because Catholics and Protestants found it impossible to live peaceably together in Ireland as a whole. It was created as a separate entity, within the United Kingdom, for the purpose of calming Protestant fears by giving them a state of their own. But included within Northern Ireland was a substantial Catholic minority, which did not accept partition and refused to participate in the institutions of the state. A meeting of the Catholic hierarchy at Maynooth, in October 1920, condemned a settlement in which 'all Ireland must be coerced for the sake of the North-East' and individual bishops ignored the Unionist administration whenever possible. Paradoxically, Ulster Protestants who had been given their own state, within the United Kingdom, felt more threatened than ever. The claim of the Dublin Government that Northern Ireland was *de jure* part of the Irish state intensified these fears and ensured Protestant solidarity behind the Unionist Party. Catholics were also affected, and from the time that the anti-partition campaign began in the 1930s the hope was kept alive, especially in the traditionally republican areas of south Armagh, Tyrone and south Derry, that the unification of Ireland would sooner or later be achieved. In these circumstances normal politics were impossible. For Protestants the maintenance of the state became the central issue of politics and every election was a plebiscite on 'the Border'. Catholics were seen as a threat to the regime, and the Protestant who practised or tolerated discrimination against them was not motivated solely by religious bigotry but also by the fear that his enemies might get the upper hand and that he would be absorbed into a Catholic Republic of Ireland. However one may dislike this situation or the circumstances which produced it, it is the essence of the Northern Ireland problem.

(iii) NORTHERN IRELAND: RELATIONS WITH THE SOUTH

The second state of Ireland, occupying the greater part of the country, came into existence when the Anglo-Irish Treaty was signed on 6 December 1921, but its boundaries were exactly those of 'southern Ireland' as defined by the 1920 settlement. None of the Irish signatories of the Treaty were happy about partition, but they placed great trust in Articles 11 and 12 which provided that, if Northern Ireland exercised the option open to it of retaining the status it had secured in 1920, a Boundary Commission would be appointed to determine the boundaries between Northern Ireland and the Irish Free State (Document 19). The Irish delegates appear to have believed that the

Boundary Commission would transfer to the Irish Free State Fermanagh, Tyrone, south Armagh, south Down and Derry City, all of which had large Nationalist majorities, and that the area left under the jurisdiction of the Northern Ireland Parliament and Government would be unable to exist separate from the rest of Ireland. Even those who opposed the Treaty did not regard the partition of Ireland as its most important defect, but concentrated instead on the limitations placed on the new state's sovereignty and on the symbolism of the oath of allegiance. De Valera's modification of the Treaty—Document 2—made no alteration in the terms relating to Northern Ireland, and this suggests that he, too, believed that the Boundary Commission would reduce the size of Northern Ireland so drastically that it could not survive alone.

Michael Collins and Arthur Griffith had signed the Anglo-Irish Treaty in the belief that it was the best settlement they could get. Collins told De Valera that the settlement gave Ireland 'freedom, not the ultimate freedom that all nations desire and develop to, but freedom to achieve it'. De Valera and his supporters were not satisfied that dominion status provided that kind of opportunity, but they failed in their attempt to have the Treaty rejected by the Dail. A civil war between them, which lasted until May 1923, ended with victory for the pro-Treaty side. The two groups then formed were the progenitors of the main political parties in the Republic of Ireland today: Fine Gael led by Mr Cosgrave (pro-Treaty) and Fianna Fail led by Mr Lynch (anti-Treaty).

While the civil war was still going on, the Irish Free State came into existence officially on 6 December 1922. On the following day Northern Ireland exercised its right of opting out of the new dominion and retaining the status it had been given by the Government of Ireland Act 1920. The civil war delayed the establishment of the Boundary Commission until October 1924. The Northern Ireland Government would not accept that the boundaries of the state were negotiable and refused to nominate a member to the Commission. Eventually the United Kingdom Government appointed a member to act on its behalf, but the delay had made any rectification of the boundaries difficult. It had also put a severe strain on the relations between Protestants and Catholics of the border areas, and the enmities created between the two communities at that time have continued to the present day. The Prime Minister, Sir James Craig, tried to calm Unionist fears in the interest of peace; he told a meeting at Brookeborough, on 13 October 1923:

> Regarding the counties of Fermanagh and Tyrone, I recall the days of the Buckingham Palace Conference. That Conference broke down simply and solely because Carson and myself refused to budge one inch on the subject of Fermanagh and Tyrone. We are now in 1923, all square on the six counties, and as far as that is concerned, not one loyalist within the boundary of the six counties will be transferred into the Free State with my will, unless the loyalists themselves so desire it.

In the autumn of 1925 the Commission was preparing to present its report, when, on 7 November, the *Morning Post* published a 'forecast', accompanied by a map, to the effect that the only significant change contemplated was the transfer of east Donegal to Northern Ireland. If the report were published it would have the force of law and, in order to prevent this, the Dublin Government in a hastily arranged treaty accepted the existing border with Northern Ireland as a permanent arrangement. As part of the agreement the Council of Ireland was abolished, thereby ending the only formal political link between the two parts of the country (Document 25).

Under the Treaty the Irish Free State had become a self-governing dominion within the British Empire, where it enjoyed the same status as Canada. Over the following decade the government of William T. Cosgrave set about enlarging the freedom of action which it had been given by the Treaty. It co-operated with South Africa and Canada to have the equality of the dominions with the United Kingdom recognized. The final stage in this development was the Statute of Westminster (1931), which provided that 'the parliament of a dominion shall have power to repeal or amend any existing or future Act of Parliament of the United Kingdom in so far as the same is part of the law of the dominion'. In the Commons debate on the Statute, Winston Churchill pointed out that it was now possible for Dail Eireann to repudiate every clause of the Anglo-Irish Treaty which it had ratified only a decade before.

In the following year the Fianna Fail party headed by De Valera came into office, and proceeded to do just that. Fianna Fail had been founded in 1926 from amongst those who had opposed the Treaty and it was determined to use the powers conferred by the Statute of Westminster to remove the Treaty's more objectionable features. The oath of allegiance was abolished, the office of governor-general was degraded and a separate Irish citizenship was created. The British Government was indignant but was powerless to intervene, for De Valera was acting within his legal rights. In 1937 a new constitution, enacted by plebiscite, made the twenty-six-county state a republic in all but name, and repudiated the recognition given Northern Ireland by the Cosgrave Government in 1925. Article 2 of the Constitution declared the national territory to be 'the whole island of Ireland, its islands and the territorial seas', and De Valera made it clear that he intended to re-unify the country as quickly as possible. Meanwhile he refused to pay the land annuities to Britain: these were moneys owed as a result of advances made to tenants to enable them to pur-chase their farms, and their repayment had been guaranteed in the Treaty. The United Kingdom retaliated by imposing tariffs on imports from Ireland and an economic war ensued which did great damage to the Irish economy. This was ended in 1938 by an agreement between Neville Chamberlain and De Valera, which, among other things, handed over to the Irish Government the three naval bases that had been occupied by the British forces under the terms of the Anglo-Irish Treaty.

Ever since the civil war De Valera had been used by Unionist politicians as a convenient bogeyman to keep their supporters in line. But, when he showed signs of directly involving him-self in the affairs of Northern Ireland by contesting and winning the South Down seat at Stormont in the general election of 1933, the fears displayed by the Protestant community were real and not feigned. Thereafter each year brought its own stage in the deterioration of relations between north and south, culminating in the Constitution of 1937, which, as we have seen, laid claim to the six-county area as part of 'the national territory'. Eire's neutrality in the war (benevolent though it was to Great Britain and her allies) and the activities of the IRA in Northern Ireland, where it carried on a guerrilla war against the security forces, generated hatreds and tensions that had not been equalled in Ireland since the 1920s. What added to Unionists' fears was the realization that the United Kingdom might be tempted to do a deal with De Valera, at the expense of Northern Ireland, in order to obtain the use of Irish bases on the Atlantic coast. British cabinet papers released for public inspection some years ago show that such an attempt was made after the collapse of France. On 26 June 1940 the United Kingdom Government intimated to De Valera that, if he were prepared to enter the war, it would issue a declaration 'accepting the principle of a United Ireland' and would set up a committee including representatives of both Irish governments 'to work out the constitutional and other practical details of the Union of Ireland'. Nothing came of the offer for De Valera was unwilling to abandon neutrality, but it is easy to see here a justification for the suspicion with which Ulster Unionists have always treated the promises of a British government.

In 1948, after sixteen years in office, Fianna Fail was replaced by a coalition government dominated by the old pro-Treaty party, now Fine Gael. It was this coalition government which in 1949 passed the legislation turning Eire into the Republic of Ireland and thereby taking it out of the British Commonwealth. The British Labour Government, led by Attlee, immediately responded with the Ireland Act which gave a solemn guarantee that 'in no event will Northern Ireland or any part thereof cease to be part of the United Kingdom without the consent of the parliament of Northern Ireland'. It was only at this point that many people in the Republic began to realize that partition was unlikely to be ended in the foreseeable future. Nevertheless the 'reunification of our national territory' became one of the great clichés of Irish politics, about which party spokesmen invariably talked but without really expecting much to be achieved. The truth was that outside a few of the northern counties, notably Donegal, Cavan, Monaghan and Louth, few people in the Irish Republic knew anything about Northern Ireland—except that 'it was ours and should be handed back'. They believed, or pretended to believe, that sectarianism was fomented and kept alive there by politicians for their own ends. Break the connection with Britain, and bigotry of this kind would come to an end. After 1949 an All-Party Committee was formed in Dublin which sponsored the distribution of anti-partition literature, and De Valera went on a world tour with a view to putting international pressure on Britain to withdraw. The only result of this campaign was to infuriate Northern Ireland Protestants and to ensure that few concessions were made to Catholics who were seen as a fifth column in their midst. The IRA raids across 'the Border' between 1956 and 1962, in the course of which a number of RUC men lost their lives, raised the political temper in Northern Ireland and generated a good deal of bitterness against the south. This was scarcely justified, for the government of the Republic pursued the IRA as relentlessly as did the Stormont authorities, and internment without trial was introduced in both parts of the country.

Before the IRA campaign ended De Valera had retired and was succeeded as Taoiseach by Sean Lemass, one of the most dynamic of Irish politicians. A few weeks after he came to office on 23 June 1959, in an interview with the *Belfast Telegraph*, he said:

I have no illusions about the strength of the barriers of prejudice and suspicion which now divide the people, but given good will nothing is impossible. Meanwhile better relations can be fostered by practical co-operation for mutual benefit in the economic sphere . . . Even at present, and without reference to any wider issue, we would be prepared to consider and discuss proposals as to how policy might be directed so as to ensure that the economic progress of both parts of the country will be impaired as little as possible by the existing political division.

This was the most constructive attitude to the problem of partition that had yet emerged, and it was gradually followed by increased co-operation between the Dublin and Belfast governments in matters of transport, electricity, tourism, etc. Of partition itself, Mr Lemass told the Oxford Union in October 1960 that he was aware of the very real cultural and religious differences which separated Northern Protestants from the rest of Irishmen and which made them afraid of being absorbed into a Catholic republic. He did not formally drop the claim to unity but suggested it might be considered on a federal basis: 'the suggestion seems eminently reasonable and should effectively dispose of the apprehensions of the North of Ireland Protestant population about the consequences of re-unification which they seem most to fear'. These statements represented a new and more realistic approach to north–south relations and were based on a belief that contact between Irishmen from both sides of 'the Border' was the only thing that could dispel traditional fears and misunderstandings. It was against this background that the now famous O'Neill–Lemass meeting took place at Stormont on 14 January 1965.

Sean Lemass portrayed fairly accurately the changed attitudes in the Republic of Ireland as far as Northern Ireland was concerned. The majority of the population had come to regard the twenty-six counties as their country and showed little inclination to adjust the system under which they lived to make it more attractive to Ulster Protestants. Under the Constitution, the state recognized 'the special position of the Holy Catholic Apostolic and Roman Church as the guardian of the Faith professed by the great majority of the citizens' and Roman Catholic teachings on divorce and contraception were reflected in the laws of the state. This was understandable in a country whose population was 95 per cent Catholic, but difficult to reconcile with the frequently repeated invitation to the one million northern Protestants to sink their identity in a United Ireland. Deeds did not match words, because re-unification had become for most people in the south a matter of slogans. In the 1960s many Catholics in the north came to realize this. They decided to leave the issue of partition on one side for the time being and to concentrate on more proximate grievances such as discrimination in housing and employment. On these issues they found their most effective allies in London rather than in Dublin.

The stages by which the demands of northern Catholics advanced from 'British standards of Justice' to the abolition of Stormont and finally to national re-unification are dealt with later in the book. Here it is necessary to underline the fact that the terrible bloodshed and destruction in the province in the summer of 1969 brought the Dublin Government and the southern Irish people face-to-face with reality. Rhetoric of the old kind was now dangerous, as the Protestant reaction to Mr Lynch's speech of 13 August demonstrated; but apart from the IRA no one in the Republic seemed to know what to do. When in the autumn there was a lull from violence in Northern Ireland, the Taoiseach made a more conciliatory speech at Tralee on 23 September. 'We are not seeking to overthrow by violence the Stormont Parliament and Government,' he said, 'but rather to win the agreement of a sufficient number of people in the North to an acceptable form of re-unification.' Although they were reluctant to admit it, most people in the south did not want their relatively comfortable lives disturbed and there was little support for armed intervention. In May 1970 the Dublin magazine *This Week* found that only 17 per cent of those interviewed in an opinion poll favoured the sending of the Irish Army over 'the Border' if the pogrom of August 1969 should be repeated. Gradually the Lynch Government was forced back upon the Lemass line, but not before a serious crisis forced the Taoiseach to dismiss a number of his senior ministers for alleged complicity in gun-running for the IRA. Thereafter, although incidents such as internment and 'Bloody Sunday' raised strong emotions in the Republic, the Government kept a firm grip on the situation and 'national honour' was vindicated by appeals to the United Nations, to the Court of Human Rights at Strasbourg and to the United Kingdom Government.

At the outset the United Kingdom Government would not admit Dublin's right to interfere in what it regarded as an internal matter. Mr Lynch was not likely to be impressed by that argument as thousands of refugees sought shelter in the Republic and the leaders of the Catholic community turned to him for help. After a bitter public wrangle between Mr Heath and himself, the Taoiseach announced the beginning of an international campaign to force Westminster to dismantle the Stormont regime and to replace it by an administration that would give equal representation to the two communities in Northern Ireland. This was the first expression of the concept of power-sharing, which in a modified form was included by

Westminster in the Constitution Act 1973. In time Westminster abandoned its policy of refusing to discuss Northern Ireland's internal affairs with the Republic's government, and after the prorogation of Stormont in March 1972 there was continuous consultation between London and Dublin while a new form of government for the province was being devised. The contact became even closer after Mr Cosgrave replaced Mr Lynch as Taoiseach early in 1973. Relations between the United Kingdom and the Republic of Ireland are now probably more friendly than at any time over the past fifty years. Both governments are committed to a peaceful solution of the Irish question and have agreed that in no circumstances will Northern Ireland be coerced into the Republic against the wishes of the majority of its inhabitants. The promotion of the 'Irish Dimension' will require from them unusual powers of persuasion and patience; and the price of Northern Ireland's acceptance may well be the *de jure* recognition of the state. Paradoxically, before there can be any progress in reconciling the two parts of Ireland, it may first be necessary to recognize them as separate states.

(iv) THE IRA

Something must be said about the IRA, the guerrilla movement which has carried on a relentless war against the British forces in Northern Ireland over the past three years. It is not a powerful political movement (for it has never gained the support of more than a minority of the population), but it does symbolize the odd mixture of idealism and terror which has characterized much of Irish history over the past hundred years. The origins of the IRA can be traced back to the Fenians (founded in 1858) whose aim was the separation of Great Britain and Ireland by force of arms and the establishment of an Irish republic. Their first attempt to do so in 1867 was something of a fiasco, but the movement lingered on to undergo a revival and play a significant part in the Easter Rising of 1916 and the subsequent Anglo-Irish war. It became the army of Dail Eireann, the assembly set up in Dublin by the successful Sinn Fein candidates at the 1918 election who refused to take their seats at Westminster. Sinn Fein had been founded by

Arthur Griffith, but it was only after 1916 that it took over the leadership of the Irish Nationalist movement.

The IRA consisted of small guerrilla bands under local leaders, and they carried on a surprisingly successful campaign against the British forces, until a cease-fire was agreed upon on 11 July 1921 for the purpose of negotiating a settlement between the United Kingdom Government and Dail Eireann. The IRA split when the militantly republican section of Sinn Fein led by Eamon de Valera refused to accept the Treaty and precipitated a civil war. They were defeated but they continued to give their support to De Valera until he decided to enter the Dail in 1926. At that stage they appropriated the name IRA, and it has ever since been used by irregular forces at war with the established governments in both parts of Ireland.

It was against Northern Ireland that the IRA first directed its attention, very often provoking Protestant retaliation in which Catholics were killed or lost their homes. But its most determined efforts were made from 1938 onwards, and on 12 January 1939 an ultimatum was issued to the Foreign Secretary, Lord Halifax, demanding the withdrawal of British forces from Irish soil. A week later attacks were made on military installations in the north, and in England there was a spate of bombings which reached their climax in the summer of 1939, when five people, one of them a man of eighty-one, were killed in Coventry. These incidents achieved nothing, except to arouse strong anti-Irish feeling in Britain. On the outbreak of the European war, De Valera, knowing that efforts were being made to establish links between the IRA and the Nazis, dealt severely with the movement. Internment camps and military courts were set up and a number of IRA men died on hunger-strike or were shot after being condemned to death by army officers sitting as judges. This period saw the decline in popular support among Catholics for physical force organizations.

The extent of the decline was revealed in 1956 when, after the issue of a proclamation obviously based on that of 1916 (Document 29), 'Operation Harvest' was launched on the north. It lasted for six years and cost the lives of six members of the RUC and eleven republicans, as well as causing damage estimated at £1 million. There was little or no support for it from Catholics in the north; and the government in the Republic contributed to its defeat by re-introducing internment and making it impossible for the IRA to recruit or train members there. Yet two of those who lost their lives, Sean South and Fergal O'Hanlon, were given the biggest funerals in living memory and ballads were composed in their honour.

After the campaign collapsed there was dissension in the ranks of the IRA. The physical-force men had been beaten and a new leadership of left-wing intellectuals took their place. They rejected the old idea of absorbing Northern Ireland into the Republic, and declared that their aim was to secure the support of the Protestant and Catholic working class in the creation of an Irish socialist state of thirty-two counties. Tomas Mac Giolla became President of Sinn Fein (the political wing of the movement) and Cathal Goulding Chief of Staff of the IRA; but the most influential of the new leaders was Roy Johnston, a young Marxist computer scientist, who has been described as the movement's 'education officer-cum-political commissar'. Without ruling out the use of force entirely, they decided from now on to concentrate mainly on social issues such as housing, working conditions, land leagues and fishing rights. The Northern Ireland Civil Rights Association provided them with exactly the sort of opportunity they wanted and they were involved in it from the start. Their intention was not to use it as a front for military organization; they were genuinely committed to the aims of the civil rights movement and valued its non-sectarian character. But as soon as republicans were known to be involved, Protestant suspicions were aroused, and Unionist ministers, like Mr William Craig, used the Special Powers Act to curtail its activities.

Some traditional republicans had never gone along with the socialist ideas of the IRA leaders and gradually dropped out of the movement. When the inter-communal riots erupted in the working-class areas of Belfast the new-style IRA were taken by surprise. They had no weapons and few people able to use them. Veteran republicans were furious as the slogans 'IRA—I Ran Away' were daubed on the walls along the Falls Road. They rejected the leadership of the organization and broke away to form their own 'provisional' council. There were now two rival republican armies—the 'Officials' and the 'Provisionals', each with its own political front in Dublin, Sinn Fein (Gardiner Place) and Sinn Fein (Kevin Street). The Chief of Staff of the 'Provisionals' was Sean Mac Stiofáin, an Englishman who lived in the south, but the overwhelming majority of the rank and file belonged to Northern Ireland.

The 'Provisionals' maintained that their primary aim was the defence of the Catholic ghettos should another attack be made on them. But those now in control were ardent republicans of the traditional kind, who would find it difficult to resist the temptation of attacking 'the forces of occupation' whom the Catholics had welcomed to their areas in 1969. For the next twelve months the 'Provisionals' were busy organizing support and building up a supply of arms, so that, apart from an unexpected and unwanted clash with the British Army in the summer of 1970, they did not really adopt their new role of urban guerrillas until 1971. From then on they were responsible for most of the attacks on the military and for the bombings of shops, offices and public buildings. Their strategy appears to have been to draw the army into the Catholic ghettos, where their searchings and interrogations would gain the movement general support from the population. The introduction of internment was probably their most successful achievement, for they calculated that the wholesale arrest of members of the minority, many of whom were not involved in subversive activities, would stir up great resentment and provide them with ideal conditions under which to operate. They also appear to have set their sights on forcing direct rule from Westminster, in the belief that the alienation of Protestants from the United Kingdom might provide an opportunity for an alliance between the Protestant and Catholic working class. They certainly blundered here, for the main result of their activity to date has been to polarize the two communities in Northern Ireland and to make a sectarian civil war a distinct possibility.

The attitude of the 'Officials' towards violence has been ambivalent. On the one hand they have accused the 'Provisionals' of stirring up sectarian hatred between Protestants and Catholics in the poorer areas of Belfast and other industrial areas by their indiscriminate shooting and bombing. But they have also admitted responsibility for the murder of Senator Barnhill, the attempted murder of a Unionist Minister, Mr John Taylor, and the Aldershot explosion of February 1972 when seven innocent people were killed. The activities of both kinds of IRA from 1971 onwards are dealt with in Part IV (see Document 45).

The IRA tradition is one of physical force and political separatism. It is not an intellectual movement, but draws its inspiration from folk memory, ballads, commemorations and a selective and emotionally taught version of Irish history. In recent times there has been much criticism of history teaching and Professor Hayes-McCoy has condemned some of the textbooks used in the schools of the Republic of Ireland:

> Such are the books that, forty years after, still trumpet forth the revolution, as though nothing had happened but the work of Tone, the Young Irelanders, the Fenians and the IRB, and as though that century could go on for ever, with its passions, and its suffering, and its heroism and its mistakes. Such one fears are the books which, in the years after leaving school, have helped to send some of their readers to the Border.

More recently a Roman Catholic bishop, Cathal Daly, has said:

> In each generation since independence many young men of twenty have gone out again to kill and to die because they loved Ireland, but knew no other way of loving her, had been taught and shown no other way but the way of the patriotic songs.

There are signs that the romantic glorification of physical force which has been an integral part of Irish nationalism is being rejected by an increasing number of people who realize that when the guns fall silent and the bombs cease to explode, the work of reconstruction and reconciliation must be resumed. Mr John Robb, a surgeon who has seen violence stripped of its glamour in a Belfast hospital, believes that there is now an opportunity of making a fresh start in Northern Ireland:

> The time has come for the men of Ulster to stride forth, not just to create an alliance of Catholics and Protestants

27

for temporary peace nor to create an artificial unification in response to despair, but rather to inspire ideas which will fertilize a new society with a fresh philosophy.

1. Examine the distribution of legislative power between the parliaments of the United Kingdom and of Northern Ireland under the Government of Ireland Act 1920. How effectively did the United Kingdom exercise its powers?

2. To what extent is the structure of the political parties in Northern Ireland cause or consequence of the religious and social divisions? Why was the Labour Party so slow to develop?

3. Are Northern Ireland's objections to a United Ireland religious, political, cultural or economic?

4. On whom would you place responsibility for the outbreak of violence in 1968?

5. Are there limits beyond which a democratic government should not go in dealing with groups that use violence for political ends? What role should courts play in such a situation? Should power to imprison without trial be part of the permanent legislation?

6. Devolution has taken one form in Northern Ireland. In Scotland it has taken another. Which do you prefer? Would anything of value be lost if Northern Ireland were governed directly from Whitehall instead of Stormont?

7. What are the arguments for and against 'power-sharing' as provided for in the Northern Ireland Constitution Act 1973? Suggest means whereby greater participation of the Catholic minority in public life might be obtained.

8. What do you see as the functions of a Council of Ireland? Could a structure such as that envisaged in the Government of Ireland Act 1920 be revived, and, if so, should it operate at inter-governmental or inter-parliamentary level? Should it have links with the United Kingdom?

9. What amendments should the Republic of Ireland make to the Constitution of 1937 with all the people of Ireland in mind? Are Articles 2 and 3 consistent with the assertion

of all political parties in the Republic that Irish unity can come only by consent?

10. Do you see Northern Ireland remaining within the United Kingdom indefinitely?

PART I

The Genesis of the Ulster Question

The historical roots of the modern Ulster problem can be traced to the early seventeenth century, when the province was first brought under English control and colonized by Protestant settlers. Under the Tudors, other parts of Ireland had gradually been reduced to some semblance of order and obedience, but anglicization stopped short at the mountains and lakes which separated Ulster from the rest of the country. Beyond that were great Gaelic chieftains, like the O'Neills and the O'Donnells, whose subjects followed a way of life that had scarcely changed for a thousand years. But the Ulster lords believed that their turn must come next, and when Hugh O'Neill, Earl of Tyrone, and his allies took up arms in 1594, it was in a desperate attempt to preserve their archaic political and social system. They failed, and, when O'Neill submitted to Lord Deputy Mountjoy in 1603, English authority extended for the first time to every part of Ireland.

Queen Elizabeth had died six days before O'Neill's submission, and it was left to James I to arrange terms of peace. At first it seemed as if O'Neill and O'Donnell were prepared to accept the new order: they promised to encourage their people to adopt the English language, customs and dress, and to allow government officials and judges to move freely about their territories. In return they were given English titles and confirmed in the possession of their estates, covering between them the greater part of the province of Ulster. But they found it difficult to live as noblemen where they had formerly been rulers and, after four restless years, they sailed from Lough Swilly into exile in Europe.

The 'flight of the earls' in September 1607 was regarded by the government as proof of their treason, and the estates over which they had exercised or claimed jurisdiction were declared forfeit to the Crown. These territories consisted of the six counties of Donegal, Coleraine (modern Londonderry), Armagh, Tyrone, Fermanagh and Cavan. There was now an ideal opportunity of changing the distinctively Gaelic character of Ulster life, and plans were prepared for introducing English and Scottish settlers (Document 1). The idea of 'planting' loyal subjects in Ireland was not new: Leix and Offaly had been colonized in the 1550s and Munster in the 1580s, but the projects had only a limited success and brought little in the way of political gains to their sponsors. The plantation of Ulster was to be more thorough: in each of the escheated counties there were certain areas from which the natives were to be cleared, so that a network of Protestant communities could be created in the province. In the years after 1609 the colony gradually took shape, and Ulster developed a character that was different from that of the rest of Ireland. But the natives were not driven out, for not enough settlers came in to take up the available land.

The result was that the towns and farms of the English and Scottish immigrants were surrounded by the native Irish, who scratched a living from the poorer lands and nursed a bitter hatred of those who had dispossessed them (Document 1).

DOCUMENT 1. EXTRACTS FROM 'THE TREATMENT OF THE NATIVE POPULATION UNDER THE SCHEME FOR THE PLANTATION IN ULSTER', BY T. W. MOODY (*Irish Historical Studies*, VOL. I, NO. I, MARCH 1938)

The plantation scheme provided for the demarcation of the land of each of the six counties into three main categories: (a) land to be granted to English and Scottish 'undertakers', (b) land to be granted to servitors of Ireland and to 'deserving' natives, and (c) church-land. Land in the first category was subdivided into large estates, which were assigned under strict conditions to a comparatively small number of British proprietors. One of the most important conditions was that these estates were to be entirely inhabited by British colonists, to whom the proprietors were to grant favourable tenancies according to explicit rules. Land of the second category was to be subdivided and allocated on the same basis, but while the servitors were offered low rents if they 'planted' with British tenants, both servitors and native grantees were free to have natives as tenants. Land of the third category, the greater part of which was annexed to bishoprics, fell outside the scope of the plantation, and here the native inhabitants might legally remain.

The intention of the state was thus, in general to create all over the escheated counties islands of territory from which the native Irish were to be wholly expelled and which were to be inhabited entirely by British colonists, both as landlords and tenants. The expelled natives were transferred to the lands of the servitors, of native freeholders, and of the church. This segregation of the incoming settlers from the native population was to ensure that the colony should take firm root, that the islands of British territory would serve as the leaven of 'civility and religion' which would leaven the whole lump of native Irish 'barbarism' and 'superstition'. The plan undoubtedly meant a transference of native inhabitants on a considerable scale within each county, but it did not mean either that they were to be expelled wholesale from the escheated counties or that they were to be driven indiscriminately into the hills and bogs. Absolute expulsion, it is true, was the fate intended for the 'swordsmen' or kernes, the armed followers of Irish lords, who were the only active sources of resistance to the plantation. They were to be removed to the barren regions of Connaught and Munster or transported for service in continental armies. Several hundreds of kernes were actually rounded up and despatched to Sweden, but a far larger number eluded capture and maintained themselves as outlaws in the fastnesses with which Ulster then abounded.

It is essential to bear in mind that the three classes of grantees, British undertakers, servitors, and natives, consisted of landlords, numbering in all only a few hundred persons; that 'British undertakers' must be distinguished from 'British tenants', and 'native grantees' from 'native inhabitants'. So far as ownership of land in the six escheated counties was concerned, the plantation introduced catastrophic changes. In each county, only a small number of individual natives, reckoned by the government to be 'deserving', received land, and the total area thus assigned was only a small fraction of the land previously under Irish ownership. But in regard to the occupation of the soil, the plantation made little difference to the native inhabitants. For the plantation scheme did not materialize in what was considered by its authors as a cardinal point—the removal of the natives from the lands allotted to British undertakers. Whether in fact there was room enough on the 'permitted' territory for the natives intended to be transferred from the 'forbidden territory', is uncertain. The extent of the former was very much greater than is commonly supposed, because the church-land accounted for a substantial proportion of the total area of each county. Moreover, the whole of Ulster, and especially the escheated counties, was then very sparsely inhabited. But the practicability of the plantation scheme from this point of view was never tested. For the pertinacity of the natives in clinging to the places of their birth, and the anxiety of British colonists, in their own economic interests, to retain them as tenants, created an obstacle to their removal that the government found insuperable . . . .

The natives for the most part remained on their former lands, but degraded from the status of proprietors to that of tenants-at-will. The process by which they were driven out of the more fertile land and their places taken by British colonists was a gradual one, and was the product of economic forces rather than of any deliberate act on the part of the state.

*

The Ulster Protestants assumed that the dispossessed Irish would one day attempt to recover their property, and the colonists' situation has been compared with that of 'white farmers in Kenya watching their Kikuyu workers and thinking of the midnight advent of the Mau-Mau'. When the rising eventually occurred in 1641 the Catholic peasantry took vengeance upon the Protestant settlers. In Ulster the undefended colonists were massacred and only military intervention from Scotland saved the plantation from extinction. The colonists' experiences in 1641 deepened, and seemed to justify the distrust they already had of the native population. On the other hand, the brutality with which Oliver Cromwell crushed the rebellion is still remembered by Irish Catholics, and affects some people's political attitudes today.

Within a generation Protestant fears, and Catholic hopes, were aroused again by the accession of James II, and another struggle for control of Ireland took place. The Siege of Derry and the Battle of the Boyne (12 July 1690) not only ensured William III's succession to the throne of Britain and provided the colonists with their own set of enduring folk memories; they also established in Ireland a Protestant ascendancy which held sway until modern times and is only now coming under challenge in Northern Ireland. If one is to understand the 'siege mentality' of many Ulster Protestants, and the emotive force of slogans such as 'Remember 1690', the experiences of the colonists in the seventeenth century cannot be ignored. The Orange Order, founded in 1795, still keeps their memory alive by its numerous parades and church services, and 12 July, the anniversary of the Battle of the Boyne, is the national holiday of Northern Ireland.

The Catholics paid the penalty of failure in the further confiscation of their property, so that by 1703 less than 15 per cent of the land of Ireland was in their hands. In the province of Ulster more than 95 per cent of the land in eight counties was owned by Protestants, and in the remaining county, Antrim, they owned more than half. Catholics were excluded from political life and were severely hampered in their religious, educational, and economic activities by the penal laws passed during the late seventeenth and early eighteenth centuries. In Document 2 a distinguished Irish historian outlines the scope of this legislation, and comments on the long-term consequences of treating Catholics as disloyal and inferior subjects.

DOCUMENT 2. EXTRACTS FROM *A Short History of Ireland*, BY J. C. BECKETT (HUTCHINSON, 3RD ED., 1966)

These penal laws have been compared with the almost contemporary French laws against the Huguenots, upon which they may have been partly based; but the circumstances in which they were enacted and the ends they served were very different. They were directed against the religion of the great bulk of the population, not against that of a tiny minority; they arose from political fear, not from missionary zeal or an authoritarian desire for uniformity; their general purpose was degradation rather than conversion. The Irish penal code, unlike the French, cannot be regarded as religious persecution in the strict sense of the term, for there was no effort to suppress Roman Catholic worship. An act of 1703 provided for the registration of 'popish priests', and though laws were passed for the expulsion of dignitaries and of regular clergy, they were not enforced. But while their worship was to be tolerated, the Roman Catholics themselves were to be deprived of all political influence. They were excluded not only from parliament but also from the army and the militia, from every branch of the civil service, from municipal corporations and from the legal profession. They were forbidden to send their children abroad to be educated, and efforts were made to keep all education at home under the control of the established church.

All these restrictions bore most heavily upon the gentry, and it was against them that the penal code was really directed. The peasantry were not regarded as dangerous, but the few surviving Roman Catholic proprietors were. For this reason parliament was above all determined that land, the key to political power, should not pass into their hands. They were forbidden to acquire it from a Protestant by purchase, inheritance or gift, nor might they lease it for a longer term than thirty-one years. A Roman Catholic proprietor had no power to leave land at will. On his death it was to be divided among his sons, but if the eldest became a Protestant he was to inherit all. If his conversion took place during his father's lifetime, the latter became merely a life-tenant, without power to alienate any part of the estate. If a Protestant woman, owning land, married a Roman Catholic her land passed at once to the Protestant next-of-kin; if a Roman Catholic wife turned Protestant all her real property was released from her husband's control. Thus the amount of land held by Roman Catholic proprietors could not increase and was almost bound to diminish.

The whole of this penal system was not and could not be rigidly enforced. Children were frequently sent abroad to be educated, and schools were established at home. Bishops and regular clergy moved about the country with some inconvenience, but little danger. Even the land laws could be evaded, and some Roman Catholic families retained their estates entire throughout the whole penal period, usually by the co-operation of friendly Protestants. But in its general purpose the system was successful. The Roman Catholic majority soon ceased to be dangerous; the Jacobite insurrections of 1715 and 1745 produced no disturbance in Ireland; and, until the land purchase schemes of the nineteenth century, the bulk of the land remained in Protestant ownership. The very success of the penal laws had an unforeseen result. The ablest and most active among the Roman Catholic gentry took service abroad, those who remained at home were excluded from public life, and so, in the absence of an intelligent professional middle class to take their place, political leadership passed naturally to the clergy. The great political power of the Roman Catholic Church in modern Ireland can be traced directly to the effectiveness of the eighteenth-century penal code.

(ii)

Much of the discriminatory legislation, known as the penal laws, was enforced also against Presbyterians, and this despite the fact that they had played a significant part in the defeat of James II. In many parts of Ulster they formed a majority of the population and made a substantial contribution to the wealth of the province, but Anglicans monopolized public offices and excluded Presbyterians from the full rights of citizenship. At first there was little sympathy between Presbyterians and Catholics, but late in the eighteenth century, when the impoverished and degraded 'papists' could no longer be regarded as a threat to their security, radical Presbyterians were prepared to accept their help in an attempt to subvert the system of privilege on which the Protestant ascendancy rested. The Society of United Irishmen, founded by Wolfe Tone in Belfast, was largely recruited from this group, and agitated for a fairer and more efficient system of government and for the separation of religion and politics. Frustrated in their efforts, and under the inspiration of the French Revolution, the United Irishmen took up arms in 1798, in a desperate attempt to achieve by force what they had failed to achieve by constitutional agitation. The modern Irish Republican movement derives much of its inspiration from the events of these years, and from Wolfe Tone's declared aims:

> To subvert the tyranny of our execrable government, to break the connection with England . . . and to assert the independence of my country—these were my objects. To unite the whole people of Ireland . . . to substitute the common name of Irishman, in place of the denominations of Protestant, Catholic and Dissenter—these were my means.

This has become part of the nationalist myth and there is a tendency to exaggerate the extent of the *rapprochement* between Catholics and Protestants. The United Irish movement was dictated by expediency as much as by enlightenment, and for many bigotry was laid aside rather than abandoned. In rural Ulster sectarian feeling remained as strong as ever, especially in areas where Catholics and Protestants were evenly divided and in competition for land. It was after a clash between the Protestant Peep O'Day Boys and the Catholic Defenders at a place called the Diamond, in Co. Armagh, that the Orange Order was founded in 1795. In Document 3, a modern historian suggests that the activities of those years, instead of uniting Irishmen as the Presbyterian radicals had hoped, left them more bitterly divided than ever.

The abortive rising of 1798 led directly to the Act of Union, whereby Ireland was merged in the United Kingdom from 1 January 1801. The Government hoped that this arrangement, by incorporating the Ulster 'loyalists' in the permanent Protestant majority of the British Isles, might assuage their traditional fears sufficiently to allow the grievances of Catholics to be dealt with. These hopes were disappointed, for Daniel O'Connell's mass movement which won Catholic Emancipation in 1829, and went on to demand a repeal of the Act of Union, provoked a spirited Protestant reaction. Then the removal of the remaining grievances of Presbyterians, the evangelical movement which was militantly anti-Catholic, and the influence of divines such as Henry Cooke and Hugh Hanna, blurred the

37

sectarian divisions between Episcopalians and Presbyterians and created the concept of political Protestantism. The result was that when the agitation for Home Rule got under way in the 1880s, Ulster Protestants, irrespective of denomination, previous politics or social class, flocked into the Orange Order, which provided the framework of what was to become the Unionist Party (Document 4).

DOCUMENT 3. EXTRACTS FROM *Orangeism in Ireland and Britain, 1795–1836*, BY HEREWARD SENIOR (ROUTLEDGE & KEGAN PAUL, 1966)

Wolfe Tone and the United Irishmen had done their best to direct Irish hatred against Britain, and later republican historians have spoken vaguely about atrocities by British troops. This suited the political purposes of Irish nationalism, but in reality the rebellion of 1798 had as much the character of a civil war as of a war of independence. It had its beginning in an attempt by Belfast radicals to challenge the authority of the Castle, but as the traditional alignment in Irish disputes had been the English government with the Protestant gentry and Ulster Protestants on one side, and the Catholic peasantry and any foreign allies it could find forming the other, whenever politics took a violent turn this pattern re-asserted itself. Ulster radicalism, like the liberalism of the gentry, had matured while the Catholic peasantry was politically dormant. When the peasantry awakened in 1798, this radical sentiment died and Orangeism took its place. Henceforth, Irish nationalism was to be based almost exclusively on the Catholic population.

DOCUMENT 4. EXTRACTS FROM *Orangeism: A New Historical Appreciation*, BY M. W. DEWAR, J. BROWN AND S. E. LONG (GRAND ORANGE LODGE OF IRELAND, 1967)

(a) Most Irish Protestants were deeply afraid of a repetition of the events of 1798, and of the years just before. They tended to consider Roman Catholicism and possible rebellion as almost identical terms. To keep things as they were in Church and State seemed the guarantee of safety. When attempts were made to secure Roman Catholic emancipation, or when

Threshers or Ribbonmen were more than usually active, the Irish Protestant reacted strongly. In the deep South, the landlord, not without the sympathy and aid of his Roman Catholic counterpart, depended on his prestige and his trusted tenants organised as yeomen, and on the military and later police. In the North, where considerable Protestant and Roman Catholic populations bordered on one another in the countryside, and in growing and industrialized centres like Belfast, the Orangeman relied on himself, quite often to the embarrassment of the authorities, and of his own leaders.

What mattered to the ordinary man was to be able to feel that his own position and living, and those of his family were secure. He wanted to go to fairs and markets without being cudgelled there, or waylaid on his return, and to use whatever roads he wished. When reports of disorder, intimidation, and 'agrarian' crime came in from the South, the northern Protestant refused to allow the slightest self-assertion to 'the other side' lest the same occur in his own neighbourhood. On the 12th of July and on other occasions, he marched with his lodge behind its flag and drums and fifes, wearing his regalia (cockade, ribbons, scarf, or sash) and armed with his yeoman gun, to show his strength in the places where he thought it would do most good. Where you could 'walk' you were dominant, and the other things followed . . . .

(b) The Orange Order, founded in 1795, had been very much a labouring and poorer artisan class Protestant movement. It had not gained the support, in size, of the gentry, the clergy, the business and professional men and the farmers until the pressure of a Bill, popularly understood to be aimed at giving over the country to a Dublin government and the control of the Roman Catholic church was mooted. This made Protestant people of unionist loyalties turn to the Order as a likely instrument for maintaining the British connection and preserving the Protestant religion. There was a huge fear because the terms of the Bill appeared to give power to the proposed Irish parliament to grant money to religious bodies and for the erection of chapels.

Lord Cushendun had noted a tendency prior to 1886 for lodge meetings and anniversary celebrations to 'become little better than occasions for conviviality wholly inconsistent with the irreproachable formularies of the Order'. The introduction of Gladstone's Home Rule Bill gave the Order a membership which was to transform it completely, to make it a highly respectable and exceedingly powerful religious political organization.

The whole influence of the Order was to be on the side of continuing union with Great Britain on the existing pattern.

The Orange Institution, in spite of its pre-1886 weaknesses, had a vision and a mission. This was to make reformation easy and a new movement unnecessary. At several meetings from 1880 there had been resolutions deploring the violence and unrest of the country. Much of the trouble had stemmed from the obsession with Home Rule. There had always been expressions of determination to maintain and defend the legislative union between Great Britain and Ireland. Religious uneasiness was uttered at the Grand Lodge meeting at Coleraine, 6 June 1883, when Roman Catholic conspiracies against Protestantism were deplored. The conviction was strengthened that Home Rule would inevitably mean Rome Rule . . . .

The Reform Act of 1884, which extended household franchise to Ireland to more than triple the electorate, had increased the size of the parliamentary Home Rule party to eighty-six members. Sixteen of the thirty-three Ulster members were Home Rulers. This preponderance of Nationalist opinion was an added cause for concern to the Unionists who had reason to fear the power of Charles Stewart Parnell, the Nationalist leader, with the English political parties.

Protestants of different shades of political opinion came together in their determination to maintain the British connection. They formed the Unionist Party and in so doing emphasized the polarization of Unionist Protestant and Nationalist Roman Catholic.

(iii)

If religion sharply divided the population of Ulster into two hostile communities from the establishment of the colony, economic development in the eighteenth century and more especially in the nineteenth century tended to separate the province from the rest of Ireland, so that by 1880 the Belfast area could be fairly accurately described as 'an outpost of industrial Britain', attracting capital, raw materials and skilled labour from England and Scotland, and finding markets for its products in all parts of the world. This divergence had begun after the Cromwellian war, when there was an influx of new settlers from England to the Lagan valley and north Armagh. A considerable number of these immigrants had been textile workers, who, because of their previous industrial training, engaged in spinning and weaving when little work could be done on the land. They were joined later by Huguenot textile workers from France and Flanders, and between them they established the linen industry, which eventually formed the basis of Ulster's prosperity. At the end of the eighteenth century the manufacture began to pass under the control of wealthy bleachers who lived mainly in the Lagan valley, but the prosperity it created was still widely diffused throughout the rural community, and helped to differentiate the north-east of Ireland from the rest of the country.

A herald of the industrial revolution was the extension of the cotton industry to Belfast in the 1780s. Cotton manufacture proved not to be viable, but its decline in the 1830s left a pool of skilled labour which the reorganized linen industry could draw on when its phenomenal growth began in 1850. Cotton also stimulated the engineering industry, which acquired an international reputation, and helped to develop skills put to valuable use in the shipyards of Harland and Wolff, where some of the world's largest ships were built. By the time the Home Rule Bill was introduced in 1886, the Belfast area was part of the industrial complex of north Britain and its prosperity depended largely on its links with the outside world. This industry was almost entirely controlled by Protestants.

With industrialization, the population of Belfast increased rapidly: from 20,000 in 1800 to 100,000 in 1851 and to over 300,000 two generations later. Most of the new inhabitants were Protestants, but there was also a substantial migration to the growing town of Catholics from the south and west of the province, and by the middle of the nineteenth century they formed one-third of the population. Unfortunately the sectarian conflicts of the countryside were transferred to an urban setting, and a pattern of riots developed which has continued to the present day: street fighting, the burning of houses, churches and schools, confrontations with the police, and the frightening of 'the other sort' from their jobs and from their homes. Three times in the course of the nineteenth century rioting was prolonged with serious loss of life. The British Government used the army to restore peace, established commissions of inquiry and reformed the police force, but sectarian violence had become a way of life for many of the inhabitants and the measures taken to preserve order had little success. Document 5 traces the growth of religious ghettos in Belfast, and shows that bitter antagonism existed between Protestants and Catholics in the city before there was any serious threat of Home Rule or the establishment of an Irish Republic.

DOCUMENT 5. EXTRACTS FROM 'BELFAST', BY EMRYS JONES (*Ulster since 1800*, 2ND SERIES, EDITED BY T. W. MOODY AND J. C. BECKETT, BBC, 1957)

One of the fundamental social patterns which were established during the last century was the gradually increasing segregation of catholics and protestants in Belfast. There are too few figures to tell us what relative numbers in each sect were at the beginning of the period; but the catholics were certainly a small minority, small enough to be tolerated by the protestants, many of whom had even striven for their emancipation. But the religious-political climate was changing rapidly in the 1820s and 1830s. The enormous expansion due to industrialization drew its people from a far wider area than Antrim and Down, where protestants were in the majority. Newcomers came from all over Ulster and even beyond, from areas that were predominantly catholic. The famine increased the numbers. By 1850 the proportion of catholics was 35 per cent— alarming to even liberal-minded protestants. Most of these catholics lived along the Falls Road area, in the traditional Irish sector. Others established themselves in Cromac and in the industrial sectors of north Belfast, and in one part of Bally-macarrett. Always they came in at the lowest economic levels; and the lingering effects of the old penal code, one of which was a very high rate of illiteracy, saw to it that few prospered enough to move from these sectors to the better residential areas.

The proximity of two groups of industrial workers of conflicting sects along the Falls Road and the Shankill Road led to periodic conflicts, more particularly around the twelfth of July. People who normally lived in comparative amity flared into rioting moods at the least provocation at this time of the year, and this resulted in a gradual sorting-out process. By the middle of the century the Pound district during 'twelfth' week was no place for a protestant, nor was Sandy Row a congenial place for a catholic. Where there had been some mixing before, these periodic riots gradually imposed the sharp segregation which is familiar today.

(iv)

The Act of Union was the great divide in nineteenth-century Irish politics, for in regard to it there developed the mutually opposed creeds of Unionism and Nationalism. Reference has already been made to Unionism: it had for its aim the preservation of the system of government established for Ireland in 1801, drew most of its supporters from the Protestant section of the population and had close links with the British Conservative Party. Some Unionists supported Gladstone, largely because of his interest in land reform, but when he introduced a Home Rule Bill in 1886 they turned away from him in indignation, and from then on the Liberal Party had few supporters in Ulster.

Nationalism claimed to be non-sectarian and many of its heroes (Tone, Mitchel, Butt and Parnell) were Protestants; but generally speaking Nationalism was, and continues to be, the political creed of most Irish Catholics. Its primary aim was to secure the repeal of the Act of Union so that Ireland might enjoy self-government, but Nationalists did not always agree on the form that self-government should take, or even on the means that might be used to obtain it. Some were separatists, who claimed political descent from Wolfe Tone and the United Irishmen, and wished to establish an independent Irish republic by force of arms. This brand of Irish Nationalism (best represented by the Fenians, the Irish Republican Brotherhood and the present IRA) came under the ban of the Catholic Church and has never been more than a minority movement, but it did become a political force of some consequence for a short period between 1916 and 1921. The majority of Irish Nationalists supported the more moderate demand for Home Rule, i.e. the establishment of a subordinate parliament in Dublin to legislate for purely domestic affairs, leaving important matters such as finance, defence and foreign affairs to Westminster. Isaac Butt, an Ulster Protestant and a former Conservative MP, formulated this policy and established a party to advocate it in Parliament (Document 6). He concerned himself with the social and economic grievances of the country, and hoped to win support from people of both traditions; but, in Ulster, Home Rulers were never really trusted by the Protestant population, and when Parnell, who had succeeded Butt as leader, increased his demands (Document 7) and adopted a more aggressive policy, the loyalists became seriously worried. One Ulster county, Cavan, had been represented by two Home Rulers since 1874, and in 1883 another Home Ruler, Timothy Healy, was returned for Monaghan. The Nationalists were now an effective political force, and when they attempted to organize their supporters in Ulster in preparation for the next general election, the Orange Order adopted a stratagem that has been used many times since, namely the counter-demonstration. Despite their efforts, the Nationalists in 1885 won seventeen of the thirty-three Ulster seats and practically every seat in the other provinces, thereby indicating the over-whelming popular support for Home Rule in the country. Protestant loyalists were thoroughly alarmed, and when Gladstone introduced his Home Rule Bill in 1886 there was an immediate closing of ranks. Every institution of influence came out in defence of the Union, and preparations were made to resist the British Government, if necessary by force of arms. Equally important, the British Conservative Party rallied to the Ulster loyalists' cause, and Lord Randolph Churchill assured them that 'in the dark hour there will not be wanting to you those of position and influence in England who are willing to cast their lot with you, whatever it may be'. Home Rule was defeated by a split in the Liberal Party, but for four months in the summer of 1886 there were fierce sectarian riots in Belfast during which thirty-two people were killed and much property was destroyed. When the Liberals went out of office in 1895 the immediate danger passed, but the loyalists did not relax and in 1905 they formed the Ulster Unionist Council to co-ordinate the activities of the various gun clubs and political associations. Protestants in the other provinces had their organizations as well, but they were neither as militant nor as anti-Catholic as those of the north.

DOCUMENT 6. EXTRACTS FROM ISAAC BUTT'S SPEECH ON HOME RULE, HOUSE OF COMMONS, 30 JUNE 1874 (*Parliamentary Debates*, SERIES 3, CCXX, COLS 700–17)

He proposed no change in the imperial parliament, and if his scheme were adopted, the House would meet next year just as it had done this; there would not be a single change in members or constituencies; there would be the members for Leeds, Glasgow, Dublin and Limerick, the only change would be to take from that assembly some of the duties which it now discharged in reference to Irish business, and to relegate them to another. That being so, he was tempted to ask, whether the removal of the Irish business from that House would be regarded by the honourable members as an intolerable grievance? Some might be of opinion that it would be no great grievance if the Irish members were sent away; but the great majority, he believed, would be of opinion that if the Irish business were transacted elsewhere, more time would be left for the transaction of the legitimate business of the House . . . . He saw no difficulty in the matter. The English parliament could manage English affairs as before the Union; but now the English parliament undertook a duty it was unable to perform, namely, to manage the internal affairs of Ireland to the satisfaction of the Irish people . . . . He was justified in saying that up to now the government of the country had failed, and in asking that the Irish people might have an opportunity of managing their own affairs. He was told that parliament having passed the Land Act and the Church Act, the Irish people were ungrateful in coming forward and demanding Home Rule also. It was even said that such a course was an act of ingratitude towards the individual minister who had been mainly instrumental in passing those acts. All he could say was that such assertions

E

showed the faultiness of the system under which they could be possible. Who ever spoke of the English people being grateful for the passing of a good act? . . . Was there an Englishman in the House who would not be glad to get rid of the opprobium attaching to the government of Ireland? If the wish were really entertained, the way to get rid of it was by allowing the Irish people an opportunity of trying to govern themselves. If they succeeded, great and glorious would be the reward of those who gave the opportunity; if they failed, theirs alone would be the blame. And where was there to be found any valid objection to granting what they asked? The imperial parliament would hold the army, the navy, and all that was connected with affairs purely imperial, and no difficulty would be found in separating from imperial questions those with which an Irish parliament might properly deal. . . . He believed he had devised a plan which would satisfy the just demands of the people without producing a disintegration of the empire; therefore, he had asked the people to give up the madness of revolt and join with him in constitutionally and peacefully making an appeal to England . . . . He believed the Irish people were essentially conservative. It was only mis-government that had driven them into revolt. Give them fair play, and there was no people on earth who would be more attached to the Conservative principles than the Irish nation. The geographical position of Ireland made it her interest to be united with England. They were allied to England by ties of kindred and ties of self-interest which bound them to maintain inviolate the connexion with this country, and the way to maintain that connexion was to give them justice in the management of their own internal affairs.

DOCUMENT 7. EXTRACTS FROM A SPEECH BY CHARLES S. PARNELL AT CORK, 21 JANUARY 1885 (*Freeman's Journal*, 22 JANUARY 1885)

I do not know how this great question will be eventually settled. I do not know whether England will be wise in time and concede to constitutional arguments and methods the restitution of that which was stolen from us towards the close of the last century. It is given to none of us to forecast the future, and just as it is impossible for us to say in what way or by what means the national question may be settled, in what way full justice may be done to Ireland, so it is impossible for us to say to what extent that justice should be done. We cannot ask for less than restitution of Grattan's parliament, but no man has the right to fix the boundary to the march of a nation. No man has a right to say to his country, 'Thus far shalt thou go and no further', and we have never attempted to fix the *ne plus ultra* to the progress of Ireland's nationhood, and we never shall. But, gentlemen, while we leave those things to time, circumstances and the future, we must each one of us resolve in our own hearts that we shall at all times do everything that within us lies to obtain for Ireland the fullest measure of her rights. In this way we shall avoid difficulties and contentions amongst each other. In this way we shall not give up anything which the future may put in favour of our country; and while we struggle today for that which may seem possible for us with our combination, we must struggle for it with the proud consciousness that we shall not do anything to hinder or prevent better men who may come after us from gaining better things than those for which we now contend.

(v)

In 1893 Home Rule had been defeated in Parliament by the absolute veto of the House of Lords. The Parliament Act of 1911 removed that constitutional 'safeguard', and many Ulster Unionists believed that if, as was generally expected, the Liberal Government made yet another attempt to pass a Home Rule Bill, there might be no means of preventing its implementation short of armed resistance. Their new leader, Sir Edward Carson, despite his legal training, was not deterred by that prospect, and the next two documents suggest that he was prepared to defy the will of the people as expressed in Parliament.

DOCUMENT 8. EXTRACTS FROM A SPEECH BY SIR EDWARD CARSON AT BELFAST, 23 SEPTEMBER 1911 (QUOTED IN *Ulster's Stand for Union*, BY RONALD MCNEILL, JOHN MURRAY, 1922)

We must be prepared, in the event of a Home Rule Bill passing, with such measures as will carry on for ourselves the government of those districts of which we have control. We must be prepared—and time is precious in these things—the morning Home Rule passes, ourselves to become responsible for the government of the Protestant province of Ulster. We ask your leave at the meeting of the Ulster Unionist Council, to be held on Monday, there to discuss the matter, and to set to work, to take care that at no time and at no intervening interval shall we lack a government in Ulster, which shall be a government either by the imperial parliament or by ourselves.

DOCUMENT 9. EXTRACTS FROM A SPEECH BY SIR EDWARD CARSON AT BLENHEIM, 27 JULY 1912 (*The Complete Grammar of Anarchy*, MAUNSEL, DUBLIN, 1918)

We will shortly challenge the government to interfere with us if they dare, and we will with equanimity await the result. We will do this regardless of all consequences, of all personal loss, of all inconvenience. They may tell us if they like that this is treason. It is not for men who have such stakes as we have at issue to trouble about the cost. We are prepared to take the consequences, and in the struggle we will not be alone, because we will have all the best in England with us.

*

The Ulster Unionist scarcely needed incitement of this kind. On 28 September 1912, nearly half a million men and women, in towns and villages throughout the province, signed a Solemn League and Covenant binding themselves to resist Home Rule by every means at their disposal (Document 10). A provisional government was formed, a Protestant defence force (the UVF) was enrolled and a consignment of arms was brought in from Germany, with the approval and sometimes the active assistance of Conservative sympathizers in Britain. In face of this opposition, the Prime Minister, Asquith, began to waver, and George V called all parties to Buckingham Palace. The conference failed, and only the outbreak of war in 1914 gave the Government a respite. Parliament passed the Home Rule Act, but there was an understanding that it would not be put into effect until the Ulster problem had been dealt with at the end of the war.

The Easter Rising of 1916 in Dublin changed the situation.

The rebels had proclaimed an Irish republic, and were steadily winning support for their demands in the country. In the hope of achieving a moderate solution, while that was still possible, Lloyd George began negotiations with Redmond and Carson. During the parliamentary debates on the Home Rule Bill, the exclusion of the whole or part of Ulster from the jurisdiction of an Irish parliament had been suggested as a compromise; and, seizing on this, the Ulster Unionist Council agreed to the extension of Home Rule to 'Nationalist' Ireland immediately, provided that the six counties of Londonderry, Antrim, Down, Armagh, Tyrone and Fermanagh were excluded (Document 11). Redmond, in the belief that the exclusion was to be temporary, reluctantly agreed but had difficulty in persuading Ulster Nationalists to go along with him. When the British Government later changed its mind and terminated the negotiations, Redmond was discredited and accused of having agreed to the partition of Ireland.

In the general election of 1918 practically every seat outside Ulster was won by Sinn Fein, which thereupon issued a declaration of independence and set up its own parliament, Dail Eireann, to carry on the administration of the country. A confused period followed, in which two governments claimed jurisdiction over Ireland, and clashes occurred between the British Army and the IRA, as the guerrilla forces of Dail Eireann came to be called. Then Lloyd George, now Prime Minister, passed through Parliament a Government of Ireland Act (1920), which sought a solution by separating the six counties of north-east Ulster from the rest of the country and giving to each part a subordinate government and parliament of the Home Rule type. The scheme was not intended to be a blueprint for partition, and section 2 (1) of the Act created a Council of Ireland to encourage co-operation between 'the two Irelands' in the hope of eventual reconciliation and unity (Document 12).

The Government of Ireland Act was rejected by Sinn Fein, and 'the troubles' continued until 11 July 1921, when a truce was agreed upon for the purpose of negotiating a new settlement. This resulted in the Anglo-Irish Treaty of 6 December 1921, which provided for the whole of Ireland to become a self-governing dominion, but allowed Northern Ireland, if it so wished, to opt out of the settlement and retain the status it had already acquired under the 1920 Act. Within a month the two houses of the Northern Ireland Parliament presented an address to the King for this purpose, thereby putting into operation the provision for the establishment of a Boundary Commission to 'determine in accordance with the wishes of the inhabitants, so far as may be compatible with economic and geographic conditions, the boundaries between Northern Ireland and the rest of Ireland' (Document 13).

DOCUMENT 10. ULSTER'S SOLEMN LEAGUE AND COVENANT, 28 SEPTEMBER 1912 (ULSTER UNIONIST COUNCIL PAPERS, NIPRO, D1327/3/21)

Being convinced in our consciences that Home Rule would be disastrous to the material well-being of Ulster as well as of the whole of Ireland, subversive of our civil and religious freedom, destructive of our citizenship and perilous to the unity of the Empire, we, whose names are under-written, men of Ulster, loyal subjects of His Gracious Majesty King George V, humbly relying on the God whom our fathers in days of stress and trial confidently trusted, do hereby pledge ourselves in solemn Covenant throughout this our time of threatened calamity to stand by one another in defending for ourselves and our children our cherished position of equal citizenship in the United Kingdom, and using all means which may be found necessary to defeat the present conspiracy to set up a Home Rule Parliament in Ireland. And in the event of such a Parliament being forced upon us we further solemnly and mutually pledge ourselves to refuse to recognize its authority. In sure confidence that God will defend the right we hereto subscribe our names. And further, we individually declare that we have not already signed this Covenant. God save the King.

DOCUMENT 11. LETTER OF HUGH DE F. MONTGOMERY, OF THE ULSTER UNIONIST COUNCIL, TO HIS SON, 22 JUNE 1916, EXPLAINING WHY THE COUNCIL IS PREPARED TO ACCEPT THE HOME RULE ACT, WITH THE EXCLUSION OF THE SIX COUNTIES OF NORTH-EAST ULSTER (MONTGOMERY PAPERS, NIPRO D627/429)

It took Carson an hour and a half to explain the situation at the private meeting of the Unionist Council, and I cannot pretend to tell you all he told us; but the main point was this— The Cabinet having unanimously decided that under the pressure of difficulties with America, the Colonies and Parliament (but chiefly with America) they must offer Redmond Home Rule at once; and (not being prepared to coerce Ulster) having authorised Lloyd George to arrange a settlement, Carson, after what had happened at the Buckingham Palace Conference in 1914, could not well refuse to submit to his followers the exclusion of six counties as a basis of negotiation. Carson had satisfied himself, apparently, that he had lost all the ground he and his colleagues had gained in their anti-Home Rule campaign before the war, and that the majority of Unionist members and voters took the same view as the majority of Unionist papers as to the necessity of a settlement. If Ulster Unionists refused to consider such a settlement, the Nationalists and Radicals would hold them up to odium as the people who were preventing a settlement of the Irish question, and they could not hope for any sympathy or support in Great Britain now or hereafter. The Home Rule Act was on the statute book, and now that the Unionist leaders in the Coalition Government had become partners to a proposal to bring it into immediate operation in 26 counties, there was no hope of removing it from the statute book at the end of the war. If we did not agree to a settlement we should have the Home Rule Act coming into operation without the exclusion of any part of Ulster, or subject only to some worthless Amending Act which Asquith might bring in in fulfilment of his pledge, and we should either have to submit to this or fight. To begin fighting here at the end of the Great War would be hopeless and we could not hope for any support. If, in spite of our apparent weakness we succeeded in our fight, we could not possibly hope to get more than we are now offered without fighting, viz. the exclusion of six counties, we should probably get less. We should be in a better position to hold our own and help our friends with only six counties excluded returning 16 unionists and 9 nationalists than we should be with 9 counties excluded returning 17 nationalists and 16 unionists . . . .

Carson holds a letter from Lloyd George stating that the proposed amendment of the Government of Ireland Act is to be a definitive one and not an emergency measure for the duration of the war; but, of course, if the Nationalists refuse to approve of the whole thing tomorrow, even as presented to them by Redmond, that question will not arise. The Ulster Unionists will be more or less on velvet when the matter comes to be finally settled.

The machine is evidently being worked for all it is worth to secure a decision at today's Nationalist convention in favour of agreeing to the Lloyd George settlement; but it seems to me that, if Redmond accomplishes this, his difficulties will be only beginning. I was in Dublin for two or three days last week, and the Southerners I met are all convinced that there will be another rebellion whether the Lloyd George terms are accepted or not. The fact that these terms were suggested has enormously strengthened the Sinn Feiners in the country. The acceptance of the suggestion by the Ulster Unionists has not had much effect on this part of the question. The Unionists' acceptance under protest had only increased Redmond's difficulties, and, as we are given to believe, placed us in the position in the eyes of British public opinion of being reasonable people. If Redmond actually forms a government and tries to rule this country, the rebellion will be directed against him; if he does not, the rebellion will be directed against the existing government: in any case, the country will have to be more or less conquered outside the six counties, and that may possibly be the best way out of all our troubles, which have all their root in a British Prime Minister having brought in a Home Rule Bill.

DOCUMENT 12. EXTRACTS FROM THE GOVERNMENT OF IRELAND ACT 1920 (10 AND 11 GEO. V, CH. 6, 7)

1 (1) On and after the appointed day there shall be established for Southern Ireland a parliament to be called the parliament of Southern Ireland consisting of His Majesty, the Senate of Southern Ireland, and the House of Commons of Southern Ireland, and there shall be established for Northern Ireland a parliament to be called the parliament of Northern Ireland consisting of His Majesty, the Senate of Northern Ireland and the House of Commons of Northern Ireland.

(2) For the purpose of this act, Northern Ireland shall consist of the parliamentary counties of Antrim, Armagh, Down, Fermanagh, Londonderry and Tyrone, and the parliamentary boroughs of Belfast and Londonderry, and Southern Ireland shall consist of so much of Ireland as is not comprised within the said parliamentary counties and boroughs.

2 (1) With a view to the eventual establishment of a parliament for the whole of Ireland, and to bringing about harmonization between the parliaments and governments of Southern Ireland and Northern Ireland, and to the promotion of mutual intercourse and uniformity in relation to matters affecting the whole of Ireland, and to providing for the administration of services which the two parliaments mutually agree should be administered uniformly throughout the whole of Ireland, or which by virtue of this Act are to be so administered, there shall be constituted as soon as may be after the appointed day, a council to be called the Council of Ireland.

(2) Subject as hereinafter provided, the Council of Ireland shall consist of a person nominated by the Lord Lieutenant acting in accordance with instructions from His Majesty who shall be president, and forty other persons, of whom seven shall be members of the Senate of Southern Ireland, thirteen shall be members of the House of Commons of Southern Ireland, seven shall be members of the Senate of Northern Ireland, and thirteen shall be members of the House of Commons of Northern Ireland . . . .

3 (1) The parliaments of Southern Ireland and Northern Ireland may, by identical acts agreed to by an absolute majority of the House of Commons of each parliament at the third reading (hereinafter referred to as constituent acts) establish, in lieu of the Council of Ireland, a parliament for the whole of Ireland . . . .

4 (1) Subject to the provisions of this act, the Parliament of Southern Ireland and the Parliament of Northern Ireland shall respectively have power to make laws for peace, order and good government of Southern Ireland and Northern Ireland with the following limitations, namely, that they shall not have power to make laws except in respect of matters exclusively relating to the portion of Ireland within their jurisdiction, or some part thereof, and (without prejudice to that general

limitation) that they shall not have power to make laws in respect of the following matters in particular: the crown, war and peace, foreign trade, the armed forces, etc. . . .

5 (1)   In the exercise of their power to make laws under this act neither the Parliament of Southern Ireland nor the Parliament of Northern Ireland shall make a law so as either directly or indirectly to establish or endow any religion, or prohibit or restrict the free exercise thereof, or give a preference, privilege or advantage, or impose any disability or disadvantage, on account of religious belief . . . .

75   Notwithstanding the establishment of the Parliaments of Southern and Northern Ireland, or the Parliament of Ireland, or anything contained in this Act, the supreme authority of the Parliament of the United Kingdom shall remain unaffected and undiminished over all persons, matters and things in Ireland and every part thereof.

DOCUMENT 13. EXTRACTS FROM ARTICLES OF AGREEMENT FOR A TREATY BETWEEN GREAT BRITAIN AND IRELAND, 6 DECEMBER 1921 (SAORSTAT EIREANN, GENERAL PUBLIC ACTS, 1922)

11   Until the expiration of one month from the passing of the Act of Parliament for the ratification of this instrument, the powers of the Parliament and the Government of the Irish Free State shall not be exercisable as respects Northern Ireland, and the provisions of the Government of Ireland Act, 1920, shall, so far as they relate to Northern Ireland remain in full force and effect, and no election shall be held for the return of members to serve in the Parliament of the Irish Free State for constituencies in Northern Ireland, unless a resolution is passed by both Houses of the Parliament of Northern Ireland in favour of the holding of such elections before the end of the said month.

12   If before the expiration of the said month, an address is presented to His Majesty by both Houses of the Parliament of Northern Ireland to that effect, the powers of the Parliament and Government of the Irish Free State shall no longer extend to Northern Ireland, and the provisions of the Government of Ireland Act, 1920, (including those relating to the Council of Ireland), shall so far as relate to Northern Ireland, continue

to be of full force and effect, and this instrument shall have effect subject to the necessary modifications.

Provided that if such an address is so presented a Commission consisting of three persons, one to be appointed by the Government of the Irish Free State, one to be appointed by the Government of Northern Ireland, and one who shall be chairman to be appointed by the British Government shall determine in accordance with the wishes of the inhabitants, so far as may be compatible with economic and geographic conditions, the boundaries between Northern Ireland and the rest of Ireland, and for the purposes of the Government of Ireland Act 1920, and of this instrument, the boundary of Northern Ireland shall be such as may be determined by such commission . . . .

14 After the expiration of the said month, if no such address as is mentioned in Article 12 hereof is presented, the Parliament and Government of Northern Ireland shall continue to exercise as respects Northern Ireland the powers conferred on them by the Government of Ireland Act, 1920, but the Parliament and Government of the Irish Free State shall in Northern Ireland have in relation to matters in respect of which the Parliament of Northern Ireland has not the power to make laws under that Act (including matters which under the said Act are within the jurisdiction of the Council of Ireland) the same powers as in the rest of Ireland, subject to such other provisions as may be agreed in manner hereinafter appearing. . . .

16 Neither the Parliament of the Irish Free State nor the Parliament of Northern Ireland shall make any law so as either directly or indirectly to endow any religion or prohibit or restrict the free exercise thereof or give any preference or impose any disability on account of religious belief or religious status or affect prejudicially the right of any child to attend a school receiving public money without attending the religious instruction at the school or make any discrimination as respects state aid between schools under the management of different religious denominations or divert from any religious denomination or any educational institution any of its property except for public utility purposes and on payment of compensation . . . .

*

The Ulster Unionists had thwarted the Liberals' plan of granting Home Rule to Ireland; but the outcome was not the one that Carson had envisaged in 1910 and the partition of Ireland brought him little joy. Apart from that, the methods by which the Unionists had got their way had fatally discredited constitutional Nationalism and opened the way for Sinn Fein. By the Government of Ireland Act 1920, Ulster Unionists were provided with a Home Rule system which they had not sought but which they quickly came to value because of the security it gave them. The rest of Ireland acquired through rebellion a measure of independence far in excess of that denied to Parnell and Redmond. Thus both Northern Ireland and the present Republic of Ireland owe their existence to the threat or to the use of force, and find it difficult to escape from the consequences of that tragic fact.

PART II

The Constitution and Political Institutions of Northern Ireland

---

(i)

The Government of Ireland Act 1920, as amended by subsequent legislation, became the constitution of Northern Ireland, and under its terms a parliament and executive were established which administered the province until 1972. The parliament was given a general power to make laws for 'the peace, order and good government' of Northern Ireland, but it was not a sovereign legislature and certain important matters were excluded from its competence or control. Legislation concerning the Crown, the armed forces, external trade, foreign policy, the levying of income tax and the collection of customs and excise duties were specifically reserved to the Parliament of the United Kingdom. The Lord Chancellor was made responsible for the administration of the Supreme Court of Northern Ireland and for the appointment of its judges and officials. In order that there should be no doubt about the subordinate nature of the new legislature or the competence of the Westminster Parliament to modify or withdraw its powers, section 75 of the Act stated:

Notwithstanding the establishment of the Parliament of . . . Northern Ireland . . . or anything contained in this Act, the supreme authority of the Parliament of the United Kingdom shall remain unaffected and undiminished over all persons, matters and things in [Northern] Ireland and every part thereof [Document 12].

In practice, however, the parliament and government of Northern Ireland were given considerable autonomy in administering the internal affairs of the province, and there

57

developed a convention that Westminster would not legislate, except by invitation, in respect of those matters for which responsibility had been transferred to the Northern Ireland Parliament. Another convention that transferred matters could not be discussed in the United Kingdom Parliament began in 1923, when the Speaker ruled: 'With regard to those subjects which have been delegated to the Government of Northern Ireland, questions must be asked of ministers in Northern Ireland, and not in this House.'

Attempts were made to break those conventions by members who tabled questions on Northern Ireland in the Westminster Parliament, but successive ministers at the Home Office declared that they were not prepared to interfere with transferred matters without the aid of legislation passed by virtue of section 75 of the 1920 Act. Consequently some ambiguity arose about the legal function of the United Kingdom Parliament in relation to matters transferred to Stormont or about its competence to do other than suspend or abolish the Northern Ireland regime (Document 14). Some Unionist politicians claimed that the Northern Ireland Parliament was sovereign, except in respect of those matters reserved to Westminster. The British Home Secretary, Roy Jenkins, sought to clarify the issue in 1967 (Document 15), but a Stormont minister, William Craig, rejected his interpretation and told a Unionist Party meeting in Belfast:

> I would resist any effort by any government in Great Britain, whatever its complexion might be, to exercise that power in any way to interfere with the proper jurisdiction of the Government of Northern Ireland. It is merely a reserve of power to deal with an emergency situation. It is difficult to envisage any situation in which it could be exercised without the consent of the Government of Northern Ireland.

This reasoning was shown to be fallacious when, after the civil disturbances of August 1969, Westminster was forced to interfere directly in the internal affairs of the province. At the request of Stormont the Home Secretary, Mr James Callaghan, provided troops to restore order in Northern Ireland, and, after consultation with Major Chichester-Clark (then Prime

Minister of Northern Ireland) and some of his ministers at
10 Downing Street, the Prime Minister, Mr Harold Wilson,
issued a declaration committing the Northern Ireland Government to an extensive programme of reforms. One of the most
significant passages in the Declaration was an undertaking by
the Stormont Government 'to take into the fullest account at
all times the views of Her Majesty's Government in the United
Kingdom, especially in relation to matters affecting the status
of citizens . . . and their equal rights and protection under the
law'. Thus after fifty years the convention of British non-
involvement in the affairs of Northern Ireland was abruptly
ended, and to indicate the new position a United Kingdom
Representative, Mr Oliver Wright, was appointed to assist the
Stormont Government in implementing the reform programme.

DOCUMENT 14. EXTRACTS FROM *Constitutional Law in Northern
Ireland*, BY HARRY CALVERT (STEVENS & SONS AND *Northern
Ireland Legal Quarterly*, 1968)

The Northern Ireland authorities function within a framework
laid down by the Westminster Parliament. They have no
power to alter that framework: its structure and scope remain
the responsibility of the Westminster Parliament. Responsibility for the exercise of transferred powers, so far as it affects
Northern Ireland, is vested in the Northern Ireland government. But in so far as such exercise produces repercussions
outside Northern Ireland, or provokes reconsideration of the
framework of government of Northern Ireland by United
Kingdom authorities, the responsibility is not vested exclusively
in Northern Ireland authorities, but is shared by the Home
Office which handles Northern Ireland affairs. A former
Secretary of State for the Colonies envisaged his responsibility
for their internal affairs thus: 'before we could undertake to
make special representations on a small point of administrative
detail, we should have to be convinced that there was an
improper state of things justifying such action'. This analogy
is not necessarily precise but merits serious consideration.

This is particularly pertinent to the one question which,
more than any other, has provoked disagreement as to the
propriety of discussing transferred matters—allegations of

religious discrimination in Northern Ireland. Transferred powers cannot be exercised in such a manner as to discriminate on grounds of religion, and it is doubtful to what extent the Northern Ireland Parliament can enact anti-discrimination legislation in this field. The United Kingdom Parliament is not, however, so limited. An attempt to enact discriminatory legislation by the Northern Ireland Parliament would be outside the scope of delegated powers. An isolated example of the discriminatory use of transferred administrative powers would not, by itself, call for interference from Westminster. But a series might well give rise to the conviction that there was an improper state of things justifying action by the Westminster authorities.

There has been considerable vacillation as to exactly what the proper attitude towards discussion of the question of religious discrimination should be. The Chair has, on occasion, been disposed to permit discussion but the Government itself has, usually for inadequate reasons, sought to curtail it. It has been maintained that transferred matters are 'the *sole* responsibility of the Northern Ireland Parliament and Government' which begs the question: and that a remedy is available in the courts, assuming erroneously that Parliament is precluded from considering the matter. The Chair has, nevertheless, acceded to these propositions.

On other occasions, it has been more tolerant. There is, however, a consistent failure to appreciate the distinction between making criticism of the Northern Ireland authorities in respect of individual acts of alleged discrimination, which, it is suggested, would not be in order, and raising the question of the effectiveness of Section 5 of the 1920 Act to deal with a 'state of things'. This latter approach calls into question the adequacy of the constitutional scheme itself, not of the particular exercise of powers under it. It would be relevant to establish the 'state of things' founding the allegation of inadequacy of the constitutional machinery, and hence to instance a series of cases of failure to remedy discrimination. It would not be permissible, under the guise of calling the machinery into question, to harangue the House on particular cases, and the Chair therefore has a very difficult line to draw. But in the final analysis, the adequacy of the constitutional structure to achieve the ends set out for it is in no wise the responsibility of Northern Ireland authorities. It is a responsibility vested at Westminster.

DOCUMENT 15. EXTRACTS FROM A SPEECH BY THE HOME SECRE-TARY, MR ROY JENKINS, IN THE HOUSE OF COMMONS, 25 OCTOBER 1967

Under the Northern Ireland constitution, certain powers and responsibilities are vested in the Parliament and Government of Northern Ireland. Successive Governments here have refused to take steps which would inevitably cut away not only the authority of the Northern Ireland Government but also the constitution of the province. Nevertheless, my right honourable friend and I have not concealed from the Prime Minister of Northern Ireland, with whom we have had continuing discussions, the concern felt here . . . .

I believe that nearly everybody . . . wants to see rapid pro-press. . . . After all, Northern Ireland is part of the United Kingdom. . . . It exists because of its desire to be part of the United Kingdom, but that unity can have little meaning unless we work towards common economic and social standards and common standards in political tolerance and non-discrimination on both sides of the Irish Sea. . . . Provided we can be so satisfied, there is a great deal to be said for not trying to settle the affairs of Northern Ireland too directly from London.

*

Since so many important powers were reserved to the Westminster Parliament, Northern Ireland continued to be represented there by twelve members. Occasionally there has been a demand for an increase in this number, for the Northern Ireland constituencies are very much larger than those in the rest of the United Kingdom; but no party at Westminster seems anxious to give the province representation on an arithmetical basis, in case the Ulster members should at some stage hold the balance of power. Unionists have always held a majority of the Northern Ireland seats, but few have been men of outstanding ability and their contribution to national politics has been small.

(ii)

Superficially the parliamentary system of Northern Ireland closely resembled that of the United Kingdom, with a legislature consisting of the Crown represented by a Governor, a House of Commons of fifty-two members elected for a term not longer than five years, and a Senate of twenty-six members which had little power or influence in the government of the province. The 1920 Act provided that the House of Commons should be elected under a system of proportional representation, apparently with the intention of safeguarding the interests of the Roman Catholic minority (Document 16). From the outset the PR system of voting was opposed by Ulster Unionists, and in 1929 the Prime Minister, Lord Craigavon, abolished it in favour of the British system of single-member constituencies (with the exception of the four university seats). Electoral areas were determined by the Government, and, as set out in the first schedule of the Act, were intended to be permanent and unchanging. Some alleged that the new constituencies were gerrymandered in favour of the Unionist Party, particularly in Fermanagh and Tyrone, but an objective assessment would suggest that Lord Craigavon was more concerned with ensuring that political division in the province should continue to follow traditional sectarian lines, and that parties attempting to bridge the religious chasm should have little chance to emerge. This in fact is what occurred: Protestants voted Unionist almost to a man and kept the Unionist Party in power from 1921 to 1972. In most constituencies the results were a foregone conclusion, and the unhealthy political situation was illustrated by the number of uncontested seats at general elections over the past forty years. Usually 40 per cent of Members of Parliament were returned unopposed, and on occasion this rose to nearly 70 per cent. It is difficult for democracy to flourish in conditions like these (Document 17).

Originally the parliamentary franchise was similar to that in the rest of the United Kingdom, but when plural voting and university representation were abolished for Westminster elections they were retained in Northern Ireland. Over the years there was much criticism of the 'business premises' qualification, whereby the occupant of a business premises of not less than £10 annual valuation was entitled to a personal vote in a constituency other than that in which he resided. This was obviously to the advantage of the Unionist Party, as the professional and business classes were predominantly Protestant, but plural voting and university representation continued in Northern Ireland until 1968.

Executive power was vested in the Monarch and exercised on the Monarch's behalf by ministers who were heads of departments and formed the Government of Northern Ireland. The Cabinet as such is not mentioned in the 1920 Act, but Section 8 (5) provided that:

> The persons who are ministers in Northern Ireland for the time being shall be an executive committee of the Privy Council of Northern Ireland (to be called the Executive Committee of Northern Ireland) to aid and advise the Governor in the exercise of his executive power in relation to Irish services in Northern Ireland.

But in practice British constitutional conventions applied and the Governor exercised his power on the advice of the Government. In 1972 there were ministries of Finance, Home Affairs, Commerce, Education, Development, Health and Social Services, as well as the Department of the Prime Minister. The seat of government was at Stormont, on the outskirts of Belfast, and parliamentary proceedings and ceremonial were modelled on those at Westminster.

There was one striking and fundamental difference between the Northern Ireland parliamentary system and that of the United Kingdom: one party was continuously in office during the whole of its life and the state's survival was thought to depend upon a continuance of that situation indefinitely. There was no possibility of the opposition coming into power or of the government going out: this encouraged irresponsibility on one side and arrogance on the other. Unionist politicians saw no need to obtain Catholic consent for the new institutions and over a period of fifty years they were gradually alienated. The British Government's discussion paper on *The Future of Northern Ireland* recognized this as a fundamental weakness and made it clear that the dominance of one community by the other was harmful to the interests of both (Document 18).

DOCUMENT 16. EXTRACTS FROM *The Government of Northern Ireland*, BY NICHOLAS MANSERGH (ALLEN & UNWIN, 1936)

The value of P.R. in Northern Ireland depended almost entirely upon its political implications. It was inserted in the Act of 1920 as a guarantee for minorities; it gave them both in local and parliamentary elections a reasonably fair representation; its operation—even if cumbersome, as its critics claim— was so obviously equitable in intention as to give a sense of security. The peculiarities of the situation appeared to *demand* some such system of election. The minority, embittered by the partition of the country and resentful of government by their traditional opponents, were naturally sensitive to the smallest infringement of their rights. In such circumstances the Government displayed a frankly aggressive attitude in abolishing P.R. for local government elections in 1922 and for parliamentary elections in 1929. Even if there had been no accompanying injustices of any kind, this action revealed a complete lack of sympathy with the minority outlook. At the worst it was a party manoeuvre; at the best a psychological mistake. A comparison between the electoral returns before and after 1929 reveals that the change has affected neither the accuracy of representation nor the number of the small parties to the extent that was anticipated. It has, however, drawn attention, and added to, the frozen condition of Ulster's political life. This is most clearly indicated by the very large proportion of uncontested seats in local, parliamentary and Imperial elections. When 70 per cent of the members of the House of Commons of Northern Ireland—admittedly the most important legislative body in the province—are returned, as in 1933, without a contest, then indeed there is just occasion for the democrat to fear for the future of representative government.

DOCUMENT 17. EXTRACTS FROM *Ulster 1969: The Fight for Civil Rights in Northern Ireland*, BY MAX HASTINGS (GOLLANCZ, 1970)

When Northern Ireland's first Parliament met in 1921, the Protestant standard bearer was the Unionist Party. From that moment on, for more than forty years, the Unionists have fought with each other within the party, but only a tiny minority of Protestants have ever dared part company altogether with the body that represents the basis of their creed. The Unionists have always enjoyed an unshakeable majority in the Ulster House of Commons. In the handful of constituencies where Catholics can vote in sufficient numbers, Opposition MP's have been elected, but they are few in number, and almost invariably divided among themselves. After the 1969 election, there were still only thirteen opposition members against thirty-nine Unionists. When Sir James Craig, Ulster's first Prime Minister, spoke gleefully of a 'Protestant Government for a Protestant people', he could do so with assurance. In Ulster politics, there are no nation-wide swings at elections such as ring the changes on Governments and Presidents in England and America. When the chips are down, Protestants and Unionists become one at the ballot box. In effect, Ulster politics are Unionist politics. In most Ulster parliamentary constituencies, the election result is a foregone conclusion—a Unionist victory.

This means that the selection of the candidate is the really critical point in the democratic process. He is chosen by vote of the local Unionist association and that association has immense power to discomfit him if, as an MP, he displeases it. A Unionist MP must prove that he is more Unionist than any other Unionist. He must bend his ear sharply when a senior member of the Orange Order indicates that he has something to say to him. And he must never forget that blackmail and intimidation, sometimes of a terrifyingly crude nature, are never far below the surface of Ulster politics. It is a style more familiar in Chicago than in London, and more easily understood if one conceives of Ulster not as a country nor even as a province, but as a village, where all is known and much is used. And since politics tend to become more extreme the further they are removed from the centre of power, so at grass roots level the local Unionists of the constituency associations are the greatest hard-liners of all. The full part the local associations played in influencing the actions and attitudes of MPs in 1969 will never be known, but that which is known is alarming enough. The machinery of the Unionist party is rusty, and until the crisis of 1968 and 1969 it had been unchallenged for more than forty years. In many places it was grossly corrupt, and because of the self-perpetuating nature of the system, immensely difficult to reform. What has been surprising is not how many knaves and fools it produced, but that it brought forth at least a small core of decent, reasonably competent and honourable men. Since Ulster's beginnings, the size of the Protestant majority in the population guaranteed the safety of Unionism.

DOCUMENT 18. EXTRACTS FROM *The Future of Northern Ireland: A Paper for Discussion* (LONDON, HMSO, 1972)

The unbroken dominance of the Northern Ireland House of Commons (and thus of the Government) by the Ulster Unionist Party was based upon an authentic electoral mandate. Although the franchise up to 1968 included provision for a business vote, and electoral boundaries of the Stormont constituencies were not reviewed for many years, neither of these factors had any major bearing on the balance of the parties in the Northern Ireland Parliament.

The alternation of governing Parties which has for so long been a characteristic of the British political system, and which has undoubtedly contributed in a marked degree to the stability of Parliamentary Government in Great Britain, accordingly did not exist in Northern Ireland. It is true that there are other democracies, whether sovereign States or self-governing areas within them, of which this can also be said. The special feature of the Northern Ireland situation was that the great divide in political life was not between different viewpoints on such matters as the allocation of resources and the determination of priorities, but between two whole communities. The 'floating vote' for which rival parties would normally compete was almost non-existent. Thus the relationship between the parties was not fluctuating and uncertain, but virtually fixed from one Election to another. Such a situation was unlikely to foster either sensitivity on the part of the permanent majority, or a sense of responsibility on the part of the permanent minority.

(iii)

Responsibility for law and order was placed unambiguously in the hands of the Northern Ireland Parliament. This provided the Unionist Government with a problem of exceptional difficulty, for it had little hope of winning the allegiance of Catholics for the regime or for the political institutions that were created under the terms of the 1920 Act. The statements of those in authority, with their emphasis on the Protestant character of the new state, did little to improve the situation, and the majority of Catholics were unwilling to recognize the government. The Nationalist and Sinn Fein members returned to the House of Commons in 1921 refused to take their seats, local authorities with Nationalist majorities continued to transact their business with Dublin, and hundreds of teachers refused to recognize the Northern Ireland Ministry of Education or to accept their salaries. Along the border there were IRA attacks from the south, while in the province as a whole there was a mounting wave of communal violence with murder, intimidation and arson on a large scale. To add to the confusion, groups of 'loyalists' formed themselves into an auxiliary police force and armed themselves with what weapons they could find. Some Unionist politicians urged the British Government to legalize these 'special constables', but the authorities hesitated, fearing that the arming of Protestants on a large scale would intensify rather than end the sectarian war. Eventually they gave way, and in October 1920 it was decided to recruit the Ulster Special Constabulary. Originally there were three kinds of 'Specials': A-Specials were generally ex-soldiers, who were willing to do full-time duty and to serve anywhere in Northern Ireland; B-Specials were those willing to do part-time duty in their own districts; C-Specials were a reserve force to be called up in times of grave emergency. In practice the latter were the intelligence wing of 'the Specials'. Control of the USC was handed over to the Northern Ireland Government in 1921. Did the Government of Ireland Act 1920 authorize the Northern Ireland Government to raise and use such a military force? That the British Government had grave doubts on the matter is clear from Document 19; but the question was somehow evaded until the Advisory Committee on Police in Northern Ireland was established in 1969. In his report the Committee's Chairman, Lord Hunt, said that threats to the security of the state from armed incursions and attacks were the direct responsibility of the Westminster Government. He recommended that the Ulster Special Constabulary be disbanded and replaced by a part-time Ulster Defence Regiment under the command of the GOC Northern Ireland.

At one time the Ulster Special Constabulary consisted of 44,000 men, but over the years its numbers were gradually reduced until in 1969 the force comprised 425 full-time and 8,481 part-time members. Each was issued with a uniform and a personal weapon (frequently a sub-machine-gun) which he kept in his home. In city areas 'the Specials' carried out ordinary police duties, but along the border with the Irish Republic they had most of the equipment of a regular army and were engaged primarily in military operations. Until their disbandment the Ulster Special Constabulary remained a Protestant force, and the threat by the Government to mobilize them for full-time duty filled Catholics with fear and apprehension (Document 20).

DOCUMENT 19. EXTRACTS FROM *Whitehall Diary*, VOL. III, BY THOMAS JONES, EDITED BY KEITH MIDDLEMAS (OXFORD UNIVERSITY PRESS, 1971)

17 March 1922, Thomas Jones to Lloyd George

Curtis and I are very disquieted at the position we are moving into in relation to Ulster and a memorandum which is being put up to Mr Churchill will be sent to you in a day or two. Briefly it comes to this:—

(1) It was of the essence of the bargain you made with the South that Northern Ireland was to remain a part of the United Kingdom with a Provisional Government but with powers no greater and no less than under the 1920 Act.

(2) Chamberlain declared explicitly in his reply to Craig's letter in December that 'If Northern Ireland remains part of Great Britain, the British Government will be responsible for the maintenance and control of all military forces which may be needed to support the civil authority in Northern Ireland .... The British Government will not permit the organization of military forces by any other authority'.

(3) We are departing from the spirit of the bargain with the South and will be charged by the world with one more breach of faith if we continue in the present policy of

(a) paying for the Special Constables

(b) making other grants to Ulster

(c) cloaking a military force under the guise of a police force

(d) allowing Henry Wilson to proceed unchallenged to prepare his 'scheme' for which the Northern Parliament is voting £2,000,000 and bringing us back to the position we were in in 1914 with the advantage that the Field-Marshal is making his preparations legally with the money of the British Government and without protest.

(4) Is it not the duty of the British Government to undertake the control of the Border and to remove all justification from the Northern Government for these swollen police forces? I feel strongly that you should not personally be drawn into conniving in the policy clearly hinted at but not expressly stated in Craig's speech . . . .

28 April 1922, Thomas Jones to Sir Maurice Hankey
I find there is little to add about Ireland beyond sending you the enclosed cutting from today's *Morning Post* of another mischievous speech from Henry Wilson. I know how pre-occupied the P.M. is, but both Curtis and I think that he ought to read and make a mental note of this utterance of our distinguished Field-Marshal. A couple of weeks ago his right hand man, General Solly-Flood, had the effrontery to try to get from the Disposals Board a supply of aeroplanes, bombs, etc. for use by the Ulster Specials to be paid for by the British Exchequer. When this was reported to Craig, he agreed in future all such demands should come properly from the Northern Government and not through one of their military officers . . . .

DOCUMENT 20. EXTRACTS FROM *Disturbances in Northern Ireland*, REPORT OF THE CAMERON COMMISSION, 1969 (BELFAST, HMSO, CMND 532)

Another matter of complaint which played a considerable part among the grievances felt particularly among the Catholic section of the community is the continued retention of the USC, commonly known as the ' "B" Specials'. This force, . . . is of long standing and is designed to serve a dual purpose of providing something in the nature of a 'home guard' or defence force and a reserve supplementary to the civil police. The recruitment of this force, for traditional and historical reasons, is in practice limited to members of the Protestant faith. Though there is no legal bar to Catholic membership, it is unlikely that Catholic applications would be favourably received even if they were made. Until very recent years, for drill and training purposes, the Ulster Special Constabulary made large use of Orange Lodges and this, though it may have been necessary for reasons of economy and because of the lack of other suitable premises, tended to accentuate in the eyes of the Catholic minority the assumed partisan and sectarian character of the force.

*

The regular police force of Northern Ireland is the Royal Ulster Constabulary (RUC). Established in 1922, it was closely modelled on the Royal Irish Constabulary, retaining its rank structure, its strict discipline and the general issue of firearms to its members. Like its predecessor it had a dual role and, in addition to ordinary police duties such as crime prevention and the maintenance of public order, it was responsible for security duties of a military nature. At intervals it was engaged in warfare with the IRA, and its chief officer, the Inspector-General, had close contact with the Minister of Home Affairs. Consequently a great deal of the force's time was devoted to the collection of information about opponents of the regime, and County Inspectors were expected to keep the Government fully informed about political activities in their areas. The RIC had extended its surveillance to Irish cultural movements, and the RUC continued this practice, keeping a close watch on organizations such as the Gaelic League and the Gaelic Athletic Association. Membership of these was almost exclusively Nationalist and so it was easy for the criticism to be made that the RUC was an instrument of party government.

The strength of the force was limited by statute to 3,000 men, and it was the Government's intention that one-third of the membership should be reserved for Catholics. But the RUC never succeeded in winning the trust or support of the minority population and in 1969 only 11 per cent of policemen were Catholics. There were a number of reasons for this: the early rejection of the new state by Nationalists and Republicans meant that Catholics joining the force were liable to be ostracized by their friends and neighbours; the close relationship of the RUC with the Ulster Special Constabulary must have been a factor as well; while the decision of the Government to allow constables to form their own Orange Lodge, whose inaugural meeting was addressed by the Minister of Home Affairs, gave the impression of a partisan and sectarian force. Some Catholics did join the RUC and occasionally were able to overcome the hostility of their co-religionists, but in general the force was not welcomed in Nationalist areas. The Cameron Commission, appointed by the Governor of Northern Ireland to report on the disturbances which followed the civil rights march in Londonderry on 5 October 1968, commented on this lack of trust between the RUC and the Catholic community and on the effects which it had on the attitudes and behaviour of individual policemen (Document 21).

The civil rights movement presented an unusual challenge to the RUC. Instead of attacking the regime by force, it massed thousands of people in non-violent demonstrations. The police had little training in crowd control, and their resort to baton-charges and water-cannon were the wrong tactics. As disorder spread throughout the province in the spring and summer of 1969, the RUC broke under the strain, and the British Government assumed responsibility for internal security. Serious charges of police misconduct in Londonderry and Belfast were made, and a tribunal under Lord Justice Scarman was set up to investigate. The tribunal report, from which Document 22 is taken, said that 'the general case of a partisan force co-operating with Protestant mobs to attack Catholic people is devoid of substance, and we reject it utterly', but it recognized that the lack of trust by Catholics in the impartiality of the RUC was a serious problem that would have to be tackled.

Following talks between the British and Northern Ireland governments on 19 August 1969, an Advisory Committee chaired by Lord Hunt was set up 'to examine the recruitment, organisation, structure and composition of the Royal Ulster Constabulary and the Ulster Special Constabulary and their respective functions and to recommend as necessary what changes are required for the efficient enforcement of law and order in Northern Ireland'. The committee recommended that the RUC be relieved of military duties as soon as possible; that the Ulster Special Constabulary be disbanded and replaced by a part-time military defence force under the GOC Northern Ireland; and that there should be a police authority whose membership should reflect the proportions of different groups in the community. The Police Act (NI) 1970 put some of these recommendations into effect but left the Minister of Home Affairs in virtual control of the RUC. Sir Arthur Young, seconded from the City of London Police, worked hard to make the new force acceptable to Catholics, but the RUC's part in the internment and subsequent interrogation of suspected IRA members has made it more unpopular than ever in the Nationalist areas of cities and towns. The creation of a police service that commands the respect and trust of both communities is one of the most essential and difficult tasks remaining to be done.

DOCUMENT 21. EXTRACTS FROM *Disturbances in Northern Ireland*, REPORT OF THE CAMERON COMMISSION, 1969 (BELFAST, HMSO, CMND 532)

One very unfortunate consequence of these breaches of discipline, which occurred in predominantly Catholic areas of Londonderry and were directed against Catholic persons and property, was to add weight to the feeling which undoubtedly exists among a certain proportion of the Catholic community, that the police are biased in their conduct against Catholic demonstrations and demonstrators. Thus it is said that when the police have to interpose themselves between Unionist demonstrators on the one hand and a similar body of Catholic or Civil Rights demonstrators on the other, they invariably face the latter and have their backs to the former. The corollary is that if stones or other missiles are thrown from the Unionist crowd the police do not see who is responsible while they concentrate their attention against the non-Unionists. The fact is undoubted: the reason given for it—that Unionists being loyalists do not attack the police—is not accepted as satisfactory or a sufficient reply to the charge of partisan bias. This complaint however is not confined to the events under investigation but is one of general application and long standing. What in our opinion is perhaps more unfortunate is the criticism, which has been made and which these events illustrate at more than one point, e.g. especially at Dungannon on 23rd November and 4th December, at Antrim on 2nd January, and at Burntollet Bridge and Irish Street, Londonderry, on 4th January, that the police did not take early and energetic action to disperse growing concentrations of persons who were obviously hostile to the Civil Rights demonstrations and were at least likely to resort to violence against them. On the face of the evidence there appears to us force in the criticism. On the other hand the police pointed out that these people were committing no offence which would justify police intervention nor were they carrying arms. In addition, such bodies were usually composed of persons to whom the appellation 'loyalist' was applied and it is easy to appreciate the difficulty which would face any police officer in attempting to disperse or 'move on' individuals or groups of such persons whose conduct at the time was in no sense technically obnoxious to the law. Further, and this is a point of substance, the less police action could be regarded as provocative or likely to lead to dispute or conflict with members of the public the better the chance that the peace might be preserved without a display or use of force by the police . . . .

But there is again no doubt that the appearance of things led many of the Civil Rights demonstrators to infer that the police were not disposed to be unduly solicitous for their safety or protection against missile and other attack from counter demonstrators, who had been permitted under the eyes of the police to concentrate themselves and so be in readiness to attack demonstrations or marches. This inference again did nothing to lower the temperature or to increase confidence among Civil Rights supporters in the impartiality of the police in dealing with these events and their participants. In the case of the Burntollet ambush there was even suspicion—wholly unjustified—among certain of the marchers that they had been led into a trap by the police themselves. Such a suspicion, baseless and indeed ridiculous as it is, could never have arisen at all if there had been such general confidence in police impartiality throughout the community as one would hope and expect to exist.

DOCUMENT 22. EXTRACTS FROM *Violence and Civil Disturbances in Northern Ireland in 1969*, REPORT OF THE SCARMAN TRIBUNAL, 1972 (BELFAST, HMSO, CMND 566)

It is painfully clear from the evidence adduced before us that by July the Catholic minority no longer believed that the RUC was impartial and that Catholic and civil rights activists were publicly asserting this loss of confidence. Understandably these resentments affected the thinking and feeling of the young and irresponsible, and induced the jeering and throwing of stones which were the small beginnings of most of the disturbances. The effect of this hostility on the RUC themselves was unfortunate. They came to treat as their enemies, and accordingly also as the enemies of the public peace, those who persisted in displaying hostility and distrust towards them.

Thus there developed the fateful split between the Catholic community and the police. Faced with the distrust of a substantial proportion of the whole population and short of numbers, the RUC had (as some senior officers appreciated) lost the capacity to control a major riot. Their difficulties naturally led them, when the emergency arose, to have recourse to methods such as baton-charges, CS gas and gunfire, which were ultimately to stoke even higher the fires of resentment and hatred.

There were, in our judgment, six occasions in the course of these disturbances when the police, by act or omission, were seriously at fault.

They were:—

(1) The lack of firm direction in handling the disturbances in Londonderry during the early evening of 12 August. The 'Rossville Street incursion' was undertaken as a tactical move by the Reserve Force commander without an understanding of the effect it would have on Bogside attitudes. The County Inspector did understand, but did not prevent it. The incursion was seen by the Bogsiders as a repetition of events in January and April and led many, including moderate men such as Father Mulvey, to think that the police must be resisted.

(2) The decision by the County Inspector to put USC on riot control duty in the streets of Dungannon on 13 August without

disarming them and without ensuring that there was an experienced police officer present and in command.

(3) The similar decision of the County Inspector in Armagh on 14 August.

(4) The use of Browning machine-guns in Belfast on 14 August and 15 August. The weapon was a menace to the innocent as well as the guilty, being heavy and indiscriminate in its fire: and on one occasion (the firing into St Brendan's block of flats where the boy Rooney was killed) its use was wholly unjustifiable.

(5) The failure to prevent Protestant mobs from burning down Catholic houses:—

(a) in the Conway Street area on the night of 14/15 August: members of the RUC were present in Conway Street at the time, but failed to take effective action;

(b) in Brookfield Street on the night of 15/16 August: a police armoured vehicle was in the Crumlin Road when Brookfield Street was set on fire, but made no move.

(6) The failure to take any effective action to restrain or disperse the mobs or to protect lives and property in the riot areas on 15 August during the hours of daylight and before the arrival of the army.

The conduct we have criticized was due very largely to the belief held at the time by many of the police, including senior officers, that they were dealing with an armed uprising engineered by the IRA. This was what all their experience would have led them to expect: and when, on 13 August, some firing occurred and a grenade was thrown in Leeson Street, Belfast, their expectation seemed to them to have materialized. In dealing with an armed uprising, the usual restraints on police conduct would not be so strong, while more attention would naturally be given to the suppression of the insurgents than to the protection of people's lives and property. In fact, the police appreciation that they had on their hands an armed uprising led by the IRA was incorrect. Direct IRA participation was slight: and there is no credible evidence that the IRA planned or organized the disturbances.

But there was a more fundamental cause for these failures. Police strength was not sufficient to maintain the public peace but the Inspector-General acted in August as though it was.

The Commissioner and Deputy Commissioner for Belfast had learnt the lesson, at the time of the Protestant riots in early August, when they reached the view that, without the aid of the Army, order could not be ensured on the streets of Belfast. But it is clear from the advice given to the Minister of Home Affairs (NI) on the issue whether or not to bar the Apprentice Boys' parade and from his own evidence given to the Tribunal that the Inspector-General did not share this view. It was not until he was confronted with the physical exhaustion of the police in Londonderry on the 14th and in Belfast on the 15th that he was brought to the decision to call in the aid of the Army. Had he correctly appreciated the situation before the outbreak of the mid-August disturbances, it is likely that the Apprentice Boys' parade would not have taken place and the police would have been sufficiently reinforced to prevent disorder arising in the city. Had he correctly appreciated the threat to Belfast that emerged on 13 August, he could have saved the city the tragedy of the 15th. We have no doubt that he was well aware of the existence of political pressures against calling in the Army; but their existence constituted no excuse, as he himself recognized when in evidence he stoutly and honourably asserted that they did not influence his decisions.

The criticisms we have made should not, however, be allowed to obscure the fact that, overall, the RUC struggled manfully to do their duty in a situation which they could not control. Their courage, as casualties and long hours of stress and strain took their toll, was beyond praise; their ultimate failure to maintain order arose not from any lack of professional skill, but from exhaustion and shortage of numbers. Once large-scale communal disturbances occur they are not susceptible to control by police. Either they must be suppressed by overwhelming force, which, save in the last resort, is not acceptable in our society and was not within the control of of the NI Government; or a political solution must be devised.

*

The most controversial legislation enacted by the Parliament of Northern Ireland during the fifty years of its existence was the Civil Authorities (Special Powers) Act, passed in 1922 to deal with the IRA but subsequently made a permanent part of the legal code. The Act gave the Minister of Home Affairs power 'to take all such steps and issue all such orders as may be necessary for preserving the peace and maintaining order', and permitted him to delegate this power to his Parliamentary Secretary or to an officer of the RUC. The Act contains none of the safeguards traditionally regarded as desirable for the preservation of civil liberties, and Section 2 (4) created an almost unprecedented offence:

> If any person does any act of such a nature as to be calculated to be prejudicial to the preservation of the peace or maintenance of order in Northern Ireland and not specifically provided for in the regulations, he shall be deemed to be guilty of an offence against the regulations.

Regulations made, from time to time, under the Act empowered the police to enter and search buildings without a warrant; to stop and search persons and vehicles; to seize property without paying compensation; to close or render impassable roads, paths, ferries or bridges without prior notice; to arrest people without warrant on suspicion of acting, having acted or being about to act in a manner prejudicial to the peace, and to hold such people indefinitely without charge or trial. These powers have been extensively used, and in almost every decade since the establishment of Northern Ireland men have been interned on suspicion of being involved in subversive activities.

Catholics have claimed that 'the Special Powers' have not been invoked impartially, but that the Government has used them to curtail the lawful activities of its political opponents. On the other hand, a constitutional lawyer, Professor Newark, has described the Act as 'a desperate measure taken to deal with a desperate situation', and argued that 'the Special Powers Act should rightly be considered, not as a unique piece of legislation, but as taking its place in that long line of repressive statutes which the unsettled state of Ireland has called forth'.

Whatever view one takes of the legislation, there is no doubt that over the past fifty years it has been, in the words of Lord Cameron, 'a continuing cause of irritation and friction within the body politic' and has 'borne most heavily upon the Roman Catholic part of the population'. Those whose husbands and sons were imprisoned for years without trial were not likely to give much support to the regime. Raids were frequently made on homes during the night or early morning, and children were terrified by the appearance of police carrying torches and guns. The Act was also an embarrassment to the British Government, which had to enter a derogation from the obligations imposed by the European Convention of Human Rights. Consequently the statement of reforms by Captain O'Neill on 22 November 1968 included a promise that 'As soon as the Northern Ireland Government consider this can be done without undue hazard, such of the Special Powers as are in conflict with international obligations will as in the past be withdrawn from current use.'

This hope was not realized and the escalation of community violence over the following two years culminated in the emergence of the Provisional IRA. On 9 August 1971 Mr Faulkner introduced internment without trial and began a 'sweep-up' of suspects in the Catholic ghettos of Belfast and Londonderry. Dr Conor Cruise O'Brien has described the immediate and long-term consequences of internment (*States of Ireland*, Hutchinson, 1972):

> Immediately it produced by far the worst explosion of violence the North had yet known. Twelve people were killed and more than 150 houses burned out on internment day itself. By 12 August, twenty-three people had been killed in four days of internment—as compared with twenty killed in the whole of 1970 . . . .

> The long-term effects of the introduction of internment were even more serious. Violence remained at a high level until, by the end of the year, the death-roll had reached two hundred. The sharply increased use of gelignite bombing against civilian, and mainly Protestant, targets frightened and infuriated the Protestant people until, by the end of the year, Catholic–Protestant relations were worse than at any time in living memory.

> Politically, the post-internment crisis resulted in a complete breakdown of all overt relations between the elected representatives of the two communities. The representatives of the Catholics had indeed walked out *before* internment, but they had not made this irrevocable. Now they were impelled to declare that they would never return to Stormont,

and that they would not even engage in talks about a successor system to Stormont unless—as a precondition—internment without trial was ended, and all internees released. Until then a campaign of civil disobedience, including non-payment of rent and rates, would be kept up.

In March 1972 the United Kingdom Government imposed direct rule on Northern Ireland, and, in an effort to induce Catholics to participate again in the working of the institutions of the state, began to search for an alternative to internment. Large numbers of those detained by Mr Faulkner were unconditionally released, and a commission chaired by Lord Diplock was set up to advise the Government on methods of bringing before the ordinary courts more of those engaged in subversive activities in Northern Ireland. Their report (Cmnd 5185) suggested a number of expedients, such as trial without juries and the admission as evidence of statements made under prolonged police interrogation; but Lord Diplock concluded that in some circumstances there was no alternative to detention of suspects. Even then it was recommended that the Secretary of State for Northern Ireland should refer those held for more than twenty-eight days to an independent judicial body; that the suspect should be informed of the charge under which he was being held and be given an opportunity to refute it. In practice, the procedures introduced by the British Government proved to be unacceptable to either the detainees or their legal representatives and are unlikely to become an acceptable alternative to old-style internment.

(iv)

The most serious accusations levelled against the Unionist majority have been in the field of local government administration. Catholics have claimed that Unionists have flagrantly manipulated electoral divisions and ward boundaries to secure permanent control of counties and towns where they had not a majority of the population; that they used this control to favour their Protestant or Unionist supporters in the making of public appointments and in the allocation of council housing; that they withheld planning permission or caused needless delays where they believed a housing project would be to their electoral disadvantage; and that they retained a household franchise and a system of plural voting which discriminated against the poorer sections of the population, and particularly against Catholics. There is an extensive literature on this aspect of the Northern Ireland problem, because Nationalist politicians and civil rights leaders have concentrated on it in recent years. Document 23, taken from the Cameron Commission Report, is a carefully balanced and objective assessment of the subject by a learned Scottish judge.

DOCUMENT 23. EXTRACTS FROM *Disturbances in Northern Ireland*, REPORT OF THE CAMERON COMMISSION, 1969 (BELFAST, HMSO, CMND 532)

It would be neither possible nor desirable within the compass of this Report to analyse all the representations made to us under the heads of perversion of housing policy to serve political ends, gerrymandering and manipulation of electoral boundaries to achieve and maintain party control of local government, deliberate discrimination in making local administrative appointments at all, but particularly senior levels with a consequence of depriving members of an excluded faith of employment and income from public funds.

We therefore confine our observations in the main to matters directly related to those places in which major disorders and disturbances arose, the City of Londonderry, Armagh, Newry and Dungannon (in both urban and rural areas). In addition, we feel it right to draw attention to certain facts relevant to the same issues . . . in the local administration of the urban district of Omagh and the County of Fermanagh.

The basic complaint in these areas is that the present electoral arrangements are weighted against non-Unionists. In the table . . . [p. 81] we show that the complaint is abundantly justified. In each of the areas with Unionist majorities on their council the majority was far greater than the adult population balance would justify. In Londonderry County Borough, Armagh Urban District, Omagh Urban District and County Fermanagh a Catholic majority in the population was converted into a large Unionist majority on the Councils. In the two Dungannon councils a very small Protestant majority held

Local Area Authority	Population Census 1961					Population Census 1966 (Religion not recorded)		Council Representation as at 30.9.1968		Housing built since 1.6.1944 by local authorities and N.I. Housing Trust as at 30.9.1968	Housing approved by 30.9.1968 but not yet started	Houses being built as at 30.9.1968
	All persons	Total R.C.	Total Others	Adult R.C.	Adult Others	Total	Adults	Non-Unionists	Unionists			
1	2	3	4	5	6	7	8	9	10	11	12	13
Armagh U.D.C.	10,062	5,881	4,181	3,139	2,798	10,997	6,185	9	10	1,334	0	77
Dungannon U.D.C.	6,511	3,276	3,235	1,845	2,041	7,335	4,276	7	14	901	0	20
Dungannon R.D.C.	25,713	13,393	12,320	7,329	7,476	26,680	14,820	6	13 (plus 3 co-opted members)	1,277	115	32
Fermanagh Co. Council	51,531	27,442	24,109	15,884	15,222	49,886	29,910	17	33 (plus 2 co-opted members)	2,176	208	109
Londonderry Co. Borough	53,762	36,073	17,689	18,432	11,340	55,694	30,106	8	12	3,887	66	218
Newry U.D.C.	12,429	10,414	2,015	5,843	1,364	12,208	7,007	12	6	1,855	104	126
Omagh U.D.C.	8,109	4,960	3,149	2,605	1,949	9,989	5,572	9	12	897	45	19

two-thirds or over of the seats on the councils. The most glaring case was Londonderry County Borough, where sixty per cent of the adult population was Catholic but where sixty per cent of the seats on the Corporation was held by Unionists. These results were achieved by the use, for example, of ward areas in which Unionist representatives were returned by small majorities. In Londonderry County Borough there was the following extraordinary situation in 1967:

	Catholic Voters	Other Voters	Seats
North Ward:	2,530	3,946	8 Unionists
Waterside Ward:	1,852	3,697	4 Unionists
South Ward:	10,047	1,138	8 Non-Unionists
Total:	14,429	8,781	20

23,210

The Commission asked several Unionist public representatives from the areas concerned to explain these electoral imbalances. They did not contest the general basis of the figures but argued that the original arrangement of ward boundaries and local government had been based on rateable values as well as population, that population changes had upset arrangements which were originally fair, and that it was quite a frequent democratic situation (e.g. in United Kingdom national politics), for a small majority—or even a minority—to be translated by the electoral system into a large majority.

These arguments however ignore the realities of the local situation in Northern Ireland. It is obvious that local politics in these areas have always turned on questions of sectarian control and influence. There has never been anything resembling electoral swings from Conservative to Labour and back again. This is an important consideration. The electoral arrangement of wards tends inevitably to stereotype political representation without prospect of a change in the balance of political power by the 'swing of the pendulum'. The initial choice of ward areas effectively decided the permanent result of council elections. We note too that there have been times when other electoral systems and boundaries permitted non-Unionist majorities in Omagh Urban District, Armagh Urban District and Londonderry County Borough. Accordingly it is our view that the arguments used to justify the existing arrangements when they were introduced, mainly rationalized a determination to achieve and maintain Unionist electoral control. The Government's dissolution of Londonderry Corporation, and its replacement by a nominated Commission, was thus the most tangible victory of the initial Civil Rights campaign.

In any event there can be no doubt that under modern conditions the electoral arrangements in these areas were producing unfair results. This was not seriously contested by several of the Unionist representatives who appeared before us. On the other hand we accept that any initial imbalances have been greatly worsened by the gradual decline in the relevance of rateable values taken over the whole ward as a determinant of ward boundaries, and by the movements of population which have occurred. We also appreciate that while for some years the government has been proposing to reshape local authorities it has not so far done so. Such considerations do not affect the main issue, which is that the electoral out-turn in these areas was unrepresentative, and was felt to be so by a significant number of people. In such circumstances it is idle to argue that artificial majorities are not unique to Northern Ireland. We feel we must add that, in our opinion, it is essential in the interest of fair representation that such distortions should be kept to a minimum in future, and that there should be periodic independent boundary reviews.

We are satisfied that all these Unionist-controlled councils have used and use their power to make appointments in a way which benefitted Protestants. In the figures available for October 1968 only thirty per cent of Londonderry Corporation's administrative, clerical and technical employees were Catholics. Out of the ten best-paid posts only one was held by a Catholic. In Dungannon Urban District none of the Council's administrative, clerical and technical employees was a Catholic. In County Fermanagh no senior council posts (and relatively few others) were held by Catholics: this was rationalized by reference to 'proven loyalty' as a necessary test for local authority appointments. In that County, among about seventy-five drivers of school buses, at most seven were Catholics. This would appear to be a very clear case of sectarian and political discrimination. Armagh Urban District employed very few Catholics in its salaried posts, but did not appear to discriminate at lower levels. Omagh Urban District showed no clear-cut pattern of discrimination, though we have seen what would appear to be undoubted evidence of employment discrimination by Tyrone County Council.

It is fair to note that Newry Urban District, which is controlled by non-Unionists, employed very few Protestants. But two wrongs do not make a right; Protestants who are in the minority in the Newry area, by contrast to the other areas we have specified, do not have a serious unemployment problem, and in Newry there are relatively few Protestants, whereas in the other towns Catholics make up a substantial part of the population. It is also right to note that in recent years both Londonderry and Newry have introduced a competitive examination system in local authority appointments.

Council housing policy has also been distorted for political ends in the Unionist-controlled areas to which we specially refer. In each, houses have been built and allocated in such a way that they will not disturb the political balance. In Londonderry County Borough a vast programme has been carried out in the South Ward—and Catholics have been housed there almost exclusively. In recent years housing programmes declined because the Corporation refused to face the political effects of boundary extension, even though this was recommended by all its senior officials. In Omagh and Dungannon Urban Districts, Catholics have been allocated houses virtually in the West Wards alone. Conversely Protestants have been rehoused in Unionist wards where they would not disturb the electoral balance. In several of the areas the actual total of new housing has been substantial, and it must be emphasized that both Unionist and non-Unionist Councillors in these areas have until recently been happy to accept the system as they found it.

At the same time there have been many cases where councils have withheld planning permission or caused needless delays, where they believed a housing project would be to their electoral disadvantage. A situation in which individual councillors effectively control the allocation of houses is objectionable in many ways, but in the context of our enquiry it is its political bias which is relevant. We have no doubt also, in the light of the mass of evidence put before us, that in these Unionist-controlled areas it was fairly frequent for housing policy to be operated so that houses allocated to Catholics tended, as in Dungannon Urban District, to go to rehouse slum dwellers, whereas Protestant allocations tended to go more frequently to new families. Thus the total numbers allocated were in rough correspondence to the proportion of Protestants and Catholics in the community; the principal criterion however in such cases was not actual need but maintenance of the current political preponderance in the local government area.

It is in a sense understandable that, given the political history of Northern Ireland, in certain areas in particular, local Unionist groups should seek to preserve themselves in power by ensuring that local authority housing is developed and allocated in ways which will not disturb their electoral supremacy. It is however equally natural that most Catholics and many Protestants should feel that the basis of public administration in such areas is radically unfair. We pause here to note two observations which have been frequently put forward to explain and justify such apparently discriminatory action. The first is that in local government it is the people who pay most rates who should have political power, and that consequently the fairness of ward representation has to be judged upon an overall estimate on rateable values. So judged (it was said), the argument on discrimination disappears. That argument was said to derive support from reference to the terms of the English Local Government Act 1933. But that Act by section 25 (2) required regard to be had both to the number of local government electors for the ward as well as the net annual value of the land in the ward, i.e. of the total valuation of the ward. Such validity as this argument ever possessed is one which is rapidly losing any force which it might have had, because we note that in the recent White Paper called 'The Re-shaping of Local Government' the proportionate contri-bution of rates to local authority finance has substantially fallen in recent years, and that about three-quarters of the necessary resources are found from the Northern Ireland Ex-chequer. In any event universal adult local government suffrage has for long been the rule in the remainder of the United

Kingdom and individual rateable value considerations are not in practice taken into account in the determination of ward boundaries there. The other point, which is constantly made, is that Roman Catholics do not apply for local government appointments in areas which are Unionist-controlled. No doubt that is factually true, but the answering comment which is made with force and supported in evidence, is that from experience it is realised that an application made by a Catholic would stand no real prospect of success.

PART III

Ulster under Home Rule

(i)

The boundaries of Northern Ireland had been chosen to ensure a safe and permanent Protestant majority, but the area also contained a substantial Catholic minority (they constituted one-third of the population), which was utterly opposed to the new regime and did not expect it to last. In the early 1920s some Nationalists pinned their hopes on the IRA which made frequent raids across the Border, but Catholics in general signified their rejection of the regime by refusing to serve on public boards or local authorities. When the Northern Ireland Parliament met for the first time on 22 June 1921, not a single representative of the minority community attended. In these circumstances it was understandable that the Government should look on Catholics as an actual or potential fifth column in their midst and should try to deprive them of political influence.

A more serious worry for Ulster Protestants was the realization that the British Government did not regard the 1920 Act as a final solution of the Irish question, and within a year Lloyd George was already seeking ways of reconciling Northern Ireland's existing constitutional status with Sinn Fein's demand for territorial unity. The first real 'scare' came with the signing of the Anglo-Irish Treaty on 6 December 1921, which recognized the *whole* of Ireland as a self-governing dominion but allowed the Government of Northern Ireland, if it so wished, to opt out of the agreement and retain the status it had already acquired. In that event, Section 12 of the Treaty provided for the establishment of a commission, consisting of one member nominated by each of the Irish Free State and

Northern Ireland governments and a neutral chairman appointed by Britain, 'to determine in accordance with the wishes of the inhabitants, so far as may be compatible with economic and geographic condition, the boundaries between Northern Ireland and the rest of Ireland'. During the Treaty negotiations with the Irish delegation, Lloyd George had encouraged the belief that such a boundary commission would recommend the transfer of extensive areas from Northern Ireland to the Irish Free State and that thereafter the reunification of the country would be only a matter of time. But Sir James Craig, Prime Minister of Northern Ireland, rejected this violation of the Government of Ireland Act, and warned Britain that, rather than yield an inch of their territory, Ulster loyalists would 'go it alone' and declare their independence.

DOCUMENT 24. EXTRACTS FROM *Whitehall Diary*, VOL. III, BY THOMAS JONES, EDITED BY KEITH MIDDLEMAS (OXFORD UNIVERSITY PRESS, 1971)

15 December 1921, Sir James Craig to Austen Chamberlain

I understood that when Ulster's interests were touched upon my colleagues and I would be invited to take part in a Conference once an All-Ireland Parliament was turned down and got out of the way.

I now find myself in the position of having to decide upon a course of action, which will be to the best interest of Ulster, Great Britain and the Empire. That course of action will depend entirely upon assurances from the British Government on several most vital points:

(i) In the event of the Boundary Commission finding that an area shall be excluded from Northern Ireland and incorporated in the Irish Free State, and the Loyalists within that area refusing to owe allegiance to the Irish Free State, will the British Government against their reiterated pledges use British troops to compel them to do so?

(ii) In the event of the British Government maintaining its determination not to coerce the people of Ulster, will they withdraw entirely from the area concerned and allow the

Government of Northern Ireland to stand by the Loyalists in resisting coercion by the Irish Free State?

(iii) As the Government permitted the Sinn Feiners to organise and arm themselves during the Truce whilst Ulster loyally acquiesced in the Government's plans to take no action in that direction, will the Government permit Ulster to arm herself forthwith for the purpose of protection against the Sinn Feiners now so well armed and organised?

(iv) What attitude will the British Government adopt if the Government of Northern Ireland finds it necessary to call upon their friends and supporters—more especially the members of the Loyal Orange Institution—to come to their assistance by means of arms, ammunition and money from Great Britain, the Dominions and other parts of the world where people of Ulster descent are in strength and desirous of helping?

(v) In the event of the British Government being unable to modify the Treaty, although they find no difficulty in tearing up an Act, and being unable to give satisfaction regarding these most momentous questions, and the people of Ulster take the matter into their own hands in order to prevent any Act being placed on the Statute Book which would prejudice their position as citizens within the Empire, will the British Government withdraw all troops and allow us to fight it out ourselves?

Far from feeling that I have exaggerated the situation, I believe that civil war is not necessarily the only end to which we have to look forward under the Terms of the Treaty. So intense is local feeling at the moment that my colleagues and I may be swept off our feet, and contemporaneously with the functioning of the Treaty, Loyalists may declare independence on their own behalf, seize the Customs and other Government Departments and set up an authority of their own. Many already believe that violence is the only language understood by Mr Lloyd George and his Ministers.

*

During the next four years, when the boundary revision question was unresolved, Protestant fears and Catholic hopes were deeply stirred in many of the 'Border' areas, and a situation analogous to that of the seventeenth century was created. Sir James Craig refused to nominate a representative on the commission and threatened that, if an attempt were made to alter the boundaries of Northern Ireland, he would resign as Prime Minister and himself lead the defence of the threatened area. Eventually the British Government appointed a Belfast journalist, J. R. Fisher, to represent Northern Ireland, and he joined the Free State representative, Eoin MacNeill, and Judge Feetham of South Africa who acted as chairman. Southern political leaders expected that there would be substantial transfers to them, but a leak in the *Morning Post* of 7 November 1925, indicating that only minor changes were contemplated, caused such a furore in the Irish Free State that MacNeill resigned from the commission and the President of the Executive Council, William T. Cosgrave, sought immediate inter-governmental talks. The outcome was the tripartite treaty of 1925, whereby the governments of the United Kingdom, the Irish Free State and Northern Ireland agreed to leave the existing border unchanged (Document 25). A hopeful sign was the promise of Cosgrave and Craig 'mutually to aid one another in a spirit of neighbourly friendship' and to meet together in the future to consider matters of common concern.

DOCUMENT 25. TEXT OF THE AGREEMENT AMENDING AND SUPPLE-MENTING THE ARTICLES OF AGREEMENT FOR A TREATY BETWEEN GREAT BRITAIN AND IRELAND, SIGNED ON DECEMBER 3RD, 1925

Whereas on the 6th day of December, 1921, Articles of Agreement for a Treaty between Great Britain and Ireland were entered into; and

Whereas the said Articles of Agreement were duly ratified and given the force of law by the Irish Free State (Agreement) Act, 1922, and by the Constitution of the Irish Free State (*Saorstat Eireann*) Act, 1922; and

Whereas the progress of events and the improved relations now subsisting between the British Government, the Government of the Irish Free State and the Government of Northern Ireland and their respective peoples made it desirable to amend and supplement the said Articles of Agreement so as to avoid any causes of friction which might mar or retard the

further growth of friendly relations between the said Governments and peoples; and

Whereas the British Government and the Government of the
Irish Free State, being united in amity in this undertaking with
the Government of Northern Ireland, and being resolved
mutually to aid one another in a spirit of neighbourly comrade-
ship, hereby agree as follows:

1. The powers conferred by the proviso to Article XII of the
said Articles of Agreement on the Commission therein mentioned are hereby revoked, and the extent of Northern Ireland
for the purposes of the Government of Ireland Act, 1920, and
of the said Articles of Agreement should be such as was fixed
by Sub-section (2) of Section 1 of that Act . . . .

5. The powers in relation to Northern Ireland which by the
Government of Ireland Act, 1920, are made powers of the
Council of Ireland, shall be, and are hereby transferred to, and
shall become powers of the Parliament and Government of
Northern Ireland; and the Governments of the Irish Free
State and of Northern Ireland shall meet together as and when
necessary for the purpose of considering matters of common
interest arising out of or connected with the exercise and
administration of the said powers.

*

The *rapprochement* envisaged in 1925 did not materialize.
Despite the tripartite agreement, successive Dublin governments made the reunification of Ireland their primary aim,
while at the same time making little effort to win support for
their views among Ulster Protestants. In 1932 the coming to
power in the Irish Free State of Fianna Fail, and especially
De Valera's intervention in the political affairs of Northern
Ireland, where he was elected Member of Parliament for
South Down in the 1933 general election, inevitably provoked
a strong 'loyalist' reaction. In the 1937 Constitution De Valera
repudiated the tripartite agreement and formally laid claim to
Northern Ireland. Article 2 of the Constitution, which declared
the national territory to be 'the whole island of Ireland, its
islands and the territorial seas', antagonized most Ulster
Protestants and made the establishment of friendly relations
between the two parts of the country virtually impossible.

Relations between Northern Ireland and the other signatory of the tripartite agreement were more cordial, but friendship was tempered by caution and by the fear that at some time a British government might betray their interests. The guarantee in the Ireland Act 1949 that 'in no event will Northern Ireland or any part thereof cease to be part of His Majesty's dominions and of the United Kingdom without the consent of the Parliament of Northern Ireland' was intended to calm Unionist fears. But for most of his history the Ulster Protestant has felt threatened, and at the moment has an almost pathological fear of absorption into an Irish Republic. He now believes that his best—indeed his only—safeguard against that is the political institutions he acquired in 1920.

Understanding the complexities of the Northern Ireland problem becomes somewhat easier if one keeps these facts in mind. Threatened from within and without, the Government was strongly tempted to identify with the Protestant majority. Protestants were loyal to the regime and consequently it was better to keep all political, social and economic influence in their hands. This involved discrimination against Catholics, and the justification advanced for this was that Catholics were 'disloyal' and wished to destroy the state. Lord Brookeborough, Prime Minister of Northern Ireland 1943–63, was a prominent advocate of this form of discrimination and even after the civil rights movement had begun he would still attempt to justify it (Document 26). But the result of the policy was to alienate one-third of the population and to make it impossible to secure a democratic consensus for governing the country.

DOCUMENT 26. EXTRACTS FROM AN INTERVIEW WITH LORD BROOKEBOROUGH (*Irish Times*, 30 OCTOBER 1968)

Have the persistent allegations of discrimination against Catholics in the North worried you?

Yes; one doesn't like the idea. But I would like to make this plain. The Nationalists always say there is discrimination against the Roman Catholics. Well, there is no discrimination against Roman Catholics *qua* Roman Catholics, because they worship in a different way. What there is, is a feeling of resentment that most, and let me emphasise the word most, that most Roman Catholics are anti-British and anti-Northern

Ireland. This is nothing to do with religion at all. But there is this feeling of resentment that here is a man who is out to destroy Northern Ireland if he can possibly do it. That, I think, is it. They say why aren't we given more higher positions? But how can you give somebody who is your enemy a higher position in order to allow him to come and destroy you?

Are you not talking in terms of what might have been true in the 1920s?
No, I'm sure it still holds. I'm perfectly certain that if they got a chance they would push Northern Ireland into the Republic.
Is it not the democratic right of anyone in Northern Ireland to be a Nationalist and an anti-partitionist?
Yes, absolutely his democratic right.
And therefore to expect completely equal treatment from the state?
Well, it's very difficult to answer that, but surely nobody is going to put an enemy where he can destroy you?
Even if he is going to use constitutional methods to do it?
No. I wouldn't.

(ii)

In *The Government of Northern Ireland* (Allen & Unwin, 1936), Nicholas Mansergh wrote:

> Parties in Ulster emphasize traditional religious and racial antagonisms in order to exact a rigid loyalty from their supporters. They intensify a sectarian bitterness which civilised opinion deplores; and in so doing they force the judgement of the electors into the service of their prejudices. Needless to say, the parties have done no more than derive the fullest possible advantage from an existing situation. In every society there is a conflict of wills. The parties exist for the purpose of securing a decision between them. The main criticism, therefore, that one would direct against the operation of the party system in Northern Ireland is not that it fails to permit of nice shades of distinction in public opinion—for that were outside its function—nor yet that it fosters a bellicose spirit, though indeed the pugnacity of the respective parties might, with advantage, be restrained—but that it subordinates every vital issue, whether of social or economic policy, to the dead hand of sectarian strife.

H   93

The largest of the parties to which Professor Mansergh refers is the Ulster Unionist Party, which, until Stormont was prorogued in March 1972, dominated the political life of Northern Ireland and provided all of its governments. Historically it has close links with the Conservative Party and its members at Westminster normally take the Conservative whip, but Unionism is more pragmatic in its approach to economic and social questions than its British counterpart and has readily adopted the welfare legislation of the Labour governments. Where it differs from all British political organizations is in its sectarian character. It is essentially a Protestant party and all its leaders have been members of the Orange Order, a society whose *raison d'être* is the preservation of Protestant ascendancy in the province. Lord Craigavon, the first Prime Minister of Northern Ireland, boasted that 'Ours is a Protestant Government and I am an Orangeman'. His successor, Lord Brookeborough, branded Catholics as disloyal subjects who should not be employed (Document 26), and brusquely told his critics: 'They [i.e. the Catholics] have less to complain about than the US Negroes and their lot is a very pleasant one compared with that of the nationalists in, say, the Ukraine.'

Such statements (most of which belong to the 1930s) appear shocking today and few Unionist politicians would attempt to justify them. They were, to some extent, a product of the religious bigotry which has plagued the province for centuries, but they did contain a degree of political calculation and are all the more culpable for that. In a society divided politically on religious lines, the Protestant vote, if held intact, sufficed to give the Unionists a permanent hold on office. Consequently the Orange Order played a vital role in keeping the two communities apart and in ensuring that all Protestants united in voting for the party which guaranteed them power and privilege. Fear and insecurity played their part as well, especially the fear that the province might one day be absorbed into an Irish Republic dominated by their traditional enemies. For generations the British link had been regarded as the best safeguard against this, but in recent years it became apparent that Northern Ireland was growing apart from the rest of the United Kingdom, which had little sympathy for the outmoded attitudes and prejudices of its people. Some Unionists responded to this situation by attempting to break out of their sectarian framework and suggested that Catholics should be invited to join the party; but the Orange Order imposed its veto and the project was dropped. To date, the Unionist Party has never nominated or elected a Catholic Member of Parliament (Document 27).

In contrast to Unionism, Nationalist politics in Northern Ireland have been disorganized and fragmented, for it was difficult to hold a party together which could never hope for a share of political power and obviously had little influence with the Government. While there was still doubt about the future of Northern Ireland, the representatives of the Catholic minority refused to take their seats in Parliament. But in 1925 two Nationalists came in and by 1927 their number had risen to ten. They could hardly be called a party, rather were they a loose association of members, whose long-term objective was the reunification of Ireland but whose present role was to act as spokesmen in Parliament for the Catholic minority. They had no organization at constituency level, but depended on their followers flocking to the polling booths at election times much as they went to church on Sundays. They concentrated on the seats they could win, and it was said that 'Constituencies were like dioceses and MPs, like bishops, answerable to no one and answering no one'. In Document 28 Professor McCracken argues that the Nationalists, by declining to participate more fully in the government of the province, had put themselves in an impossible position. There was little incentive for them to participate: not many Unionists were prepared to share power with them or to take them into their confidence. Apart from that, frustrated constituents sometimes forced Nationalist members to withdraw from Parliament or transferred their support to more militant representatives.

In the periods 1936–9 and 1956–62 the IRA was active, but its campaigns were largely confined to raids for arms and attacks on military installations. Coupled with these military activities was intense political activity by Sinn Fein to obtain support in Nationalist areas (Document 29), and the party obtained nearly 25 per cent of the votes cast in Northern Ireland at the Westminster elections of 1955. The two Sinn Fein candidates elected for Mid-Ulster and Fermanagh–South

Tyrone were serving gaol sentences for their part in a raid on Omagh military barracks. The votes they obtained were evidence, not so much of support for physical force, as of the extent to which traditional Nationalists had been alienated from the regime.

The National Democratic Party, formed in 1965, tried to break with this sterile form of politics and to provide Nationalists with more realistic policies. But in the late 1960s many Catholics had lost faith in the ability or willingness of the regime to reform itself and were determined to destroy it.

Between the Unionists and the Nationalists stood the tiny Labour Party, attempting to bring Catholics and Protestants together in pursuit of their common interests. Outside observers, noting that Belfast is an industrial centre comparable with the strongholds of socialism across the water, are surprised that the Labour movement has not made greater progress there. But among the working class as elsewhere in Northern Ireland the line of political division is not economic or social but religious, and nowhere is sectarianism stronger than among the industrial workers of Belfast. Trade unions are strong also, but they have little influence on political attitudes. The communal strife of the late 1960s posed great problems for the Labour Party, anxious not to be caught on the sectarian rack, and, at the time Stormont was prorogued, it had only a single MP, Mr Vivian Simpson (Document 30).

DOCUMENT 27. EXTRACTS FROM *Northern Ireland: Fifty Years of Self-Government*, BY MARTIN WALLACE (DAVID & CHARLES, 1971)

(a) The character of Unionism was established by its early struggles, and has been little modified by the passing years. There is a defensive element, a siege mentality expressed in such negative slogans as 'No Surrender' and 'Not an inch'. This is particularly marked in the three western counties of Fermanagh, Tyrone and Londonderry, perhaps reflecting the fact that there is a concentration of Protestant settlement along the western border with areas of Catholic dominance immediately to the east. It is marked also in those Protestant working-class districts of Belfast which abut on the Catholic 'ghetto' of

West Belfast, possibly dating back to the influx of workers during the industrial revolution of the nineteenth century. . . .

There has always been a strong element of fear in Unionism. There is fear of Roman Catholicism, fear of coming under an Irish parliament dominated by Catholics. Unionist politicians have not hesitated to encourage and play on these fears, as a means of maintaining the solidarity of the Protestant vote and of concentrating political struggles on a single issue; provided that the electorate divided according to religious beliefs, success seemed assured. Inevitably, though, there has been an accompanying fear of betrayal; Ulster has its own word for traitor, 'Lundy', recalling a seventeenth-century governor of Londonderry who was prepared to yield the city to Catholic James II. There was a sense of betrayal in 1916, when men of the Ulster Volunteer Force—who had retained their identity as a British army division—suffered heavy casualties through inadequate support at the Battle of the Somme.

Distrust of the Liberal Party has, in recent years, tended to be transferred to the British Labour Party; it has been fostered for a political objective, the election of Unionist MPs who accept the Conservative whip at Westminster. Moreover, Northern Protestants are capable of distrusting their own leaders. The early leaders abandoned three Ulster counties—not to mention three other provinces—and accepted a form of home rule in 1921. Under economic pressure, they yielded much of Northern Ireland's financial independence. In 1965, Captain O'Neill seemed to abandon traditional Unionism by receiving the Prime Minister of the Republic of Ireland, Mr Sean Lemass, at Stormont. In 1969, following serious civil disorders, Major Chichester-Clark's administration seemed to be accepting the dictates of the British Government in matters nominally within Stormont's jurisdiction. Unionism has always had an uncompromising appearance, but the reality has been somewhat different, and this has always left the governing party vulnerable to criticism from Protestant extremists.

(b) In December 1959, the question of Catholic membership of the party was raised at a Young Unionist political school at Portstewart, County Londonderry. In a speech, Sir Clarence Graham, Chairman of the standing committee of the Ulster

Unionist Council, said he did not rule out the possibility that the day might come when many members of the Nationalist Party would wish to join the Unionist Party. Answering a question, he said he saw no reason why a Catholic should not be selected as a Unionist parliamentary candidate. Mr Brian Maginess, the Attorney-General, made a speech in which he called for greater toleration and co-operation between all sections of the community. In the ensuing and rather confused controversy, both men were widely criticised in Unionist circles, much of the criticism being based on an assumption that 'Roman Catholic' and 'nationalist' were necessarily synonymous. However, the Unionist executive committee issued a statement which could be interpreted as tacit support for their views. It pointed out that:

The policy and aims of the Unionist Party remain unchanged and are as laid down by Edward Carson and James Craig, namely:
(1) To maintain the constitutional position of Northern Ireland as an integral part of the United Kingdom and to defend the principles of civil and religious liberty;
(2) To improve social standards and to expand industry and agriculture; and
(3) To welcome to our ranks only those who unconditionally support these ideals.

Within a few days, the grand master of the Grand Orange Lodge of Ireland, Sir George Clark, made a speech asserting that under no circumstances would the suggestion that Catholics could be admitted to membership of the party be countenanced or accepted by the Orange Order. He said:

I would draw your attention to the words 'civil and religious liberty'. This liberty, as we know it, is the liberty of the Protestant religion. In view of this, it is difficult to see how a Roman Catholic, with the vast differences in our religious outlook, could be either acceptable within the Unionist Party as a member or, for that matter, bring himself unconditionally to support its ideals. Further to this, an Orangeman is pledged to resist by all lawful means the ascendancy of the Church of Rome, abstaining from uncharitable words, actions and sentiments towards his Roman Catholic brethren.

He added that it was possible that many Catholics might wish 'to remain within the Commonwealth', and that the way was open to them to support the Unionist Party through the ballot box. Sir George's views were not contradicted by the Party, and the controversy petered out after the Prime Minister, Lord Brookeborough, said that the Portstewart speeches had been quite unnecessary and that those concerned were 'charging at windmills and beating their heads against a wall about an issue which did not exist and which probably will not arise'.

DOCUMENT 28. EXTRACTS FROM 'THE POLITICAL SCENE IN NOR-THERN IRELAND 1926–1937', BY J. L. MCCRACKEN, IN *The Years if the Great Test 1926–39*, EDITED BY FRANCIS MACMANUS (MERCIER PRESS, CORK, 1967)

The truth is the parliamentary representatives of the minority had put themselves in an impossible position. Whether they were, like [Joseph] Devlin, in the tradition of the old home rule party of John Redmond or whether they were out and out Republicans their basic aim was to secure a united Ireland. In other words they wanted to undermine the regime that had been established in the North by the Act of 1920. That being so they could not play the role of an opposition in the traditional British manner; the relations between government and opposition which existed in Britain could not exist in the North even though the Northern parliament was modelled on the British one . . . .

Certain consequences followed from this situation. It enabled—indeed it almost obliged—Unionists to appropriate loyalty and good citizenship to themselves and to use the national flag as a party emblem; it led, at least in the popular mind, to the identification of Catholicism with hostility to the state; it detracted from the effectiveness of opposition criticism of the government even on issues which had no bearing on the constitutional question; and it encouraged irresponsibility, rashness and a narrow sectarian approach on the part of some Nationalist members. The Nationalists would undoubtedly have been more weighty as an opposition, they would probably have better served the interests of the minority and indeed of the whole community, they might have contributed to a better understanding between North and South if they had been prepared, even as a short term policy, to accept fully and frankly the constitutional position as they found it—as De Valera did when he entered the Dail in 1927.

DOCUMENT 29. MANIFESTO ISSUED BY THE IRISH REPUBLICAN ARMY, 12 DECEMBER 1956

Oglaigh na hEireann
(Irish Republican Army)

To the Irish People   General Headquarters
    Resistance to British rule in occupied Ireland has now entered a decisive stage. Early today, Northern units of the Irish Republican Army attacked key British occupation installations.

Spearheaded by volunteers of the Irish Republican Army, our people in the Six Counties have carried the fight to the enemy. They are the direct victims of British Imperialism and they are also the backbone of the national revolutionary resurgence.

This is the age-old struggle of the Irish people versus British aggression. This is the same cause for which generations of our people have suffered and died. In this grave hour, all Irish men and women, at home and abroad, must sink their differences, political or religious, and rally behind the banner of national liberation.

We call on Irish men in the British Armed Forces to stand by the motherland and refuse to bear arms against their countrymen. We call on members of the RUC and B-Special Constabulary to cease being tools of British Imperialism and either stand on one side or join us in the fight against tyranny. We warn them that should they reject this plea they will be adjudged renegades by the Irish people and treated accordingly by the Resistance Movement . . . .

The whole of Ireland—its resources, wealth, culture, history and tradition—is the common inheritance of all our people regardless of religious belief. The division of this country by

Britain, and its subjection to British control in the north and to British economic domination in the south, must now be ended forever. It is up to this generation of Irish men and women to receive for all time our unity, independence and freedom from foreign domination. The alternative, if the present situation continues, is extinction as a nation.

*

This manifesto is a good example of the Republican myth that Ireland was partitioned in the interests of 'British Imperialism' and that if the 'occupying forces' were withdrawn the country would soon be reunited. Events in Northern Ireland over the past few years have shown how little validity there is in this view.

DOCUMENT 30. EXTRACTS FROM *Ireland Since the Famine*, BY F. S. L. LYONS (WEIDENFELD & NICOLSON, 1971)

It might have been expected, in view of the industrial revival during the war and of the attempts to develop industry after it was over, that a strong Labour party would emerge as the principal alternative to Unionism. It is true that the membership of the trade union movement did increase very considerably. By the early sixties there were about 200,000 trade unionists, about ninety per cent of whom belonged to unions which had their headquarters in Britain. Since some of these unions also had members in the Republic there was here, one would have thought, a nucleus around which might have developed that working-class solidarity which James Connolly had striven for in the past and which, correctly, he had anticipated would be one of the first casualties of partition. But such solidarity proved hard to achieve. This was partly . . . because of divisions within the Irish movement as a whole, but partly also because the stature of the northern unions was diminished by the reluctance of the Northern Ireland government either to repeal the obnoxious Trade Union Act of 1927, or to recognise the Northern Committee of the Irish Congress of Trade Unions. With the advent to power of Captain O'Neill, these obstacles were at last removed and the way was cleared for somewhat easier relations between organised labour and the authorities.

Nevertheless, this improved status of the trade unions was not reflected in the improved status of Labour as a political force. On the contrary, the electoral showing of Labour candidates for the local parliament continued to be extremely poor. The reason for this was essentially the same as the reason for their poor showing before the war. In a society where the fundamental cleavage was religious and political, the concept of a workers' party dedicated to the overthrow of capitalism still seemed to many working-men to be peripheral, even irrelevant. Consequently, after the war as before it, Labour candidates were apt to come forward with qualifying epithets— 'Commonwealth' Labour, 'Republican' Labour, 'Eire' Labour and so on—which pointed firmly to their attitude towards partition, the presumption being that this was what really interested the electors. In an effort to counteract this fissi-parous tendency the Northern Ireland Labour Party took two important steps in 1949. On the one hand, it made clear that it wished to be a party on the lines of the British Labour party and to be associated with that party. And on the other hand, it put all its eggs in the basket of constitutionalism. Following the declaration of the republic in the south (April 1949), a Labour conference in the six counties passed the following resolution: 'That the Northern Ireland Labour Party believes that the best interests of Northern Ireland lie in maintaining the consti-tutional links with the United Kingdom'. But the chill wind that blew across northern politics in that bleak year was unkind to the delicate plant of Labour orthodoxy. In the general election which was Stormont's immediate reaction to Mr Costello's Republic, all nine Labour candidates were defeated. They did no better in 1953, but in 1958 and 1962 managed to secure four seats, though even these were likely to remain precarious so long as the central preoccupation of northern politics continued to be with issues that had little to do with the role of Labour in modern society.

(iii)

It is often overlooked by those who consider the community and political problems of Northern Ireland that from its establishment the state has been plagued by unemployment, caused partly by the decline of some of the traditional industries and partly by a decline in the numbers employed in agriculture. In addition, the Government, because of the restricted powers allowed to it by the Government of Ireland Act 1920, never had sufficient financial resources to develop the potential of the area or to provide adequate standards of housing or amenities for its people. This was what made the controversy about jobs and housing so bitter, for, had there been a level of employment and housing similar to that prevailing in the rest of the United Kingdom, the temptation to reserve these for 'your own side' would not have been so great.

Unemployment has been the greatest of all problems. An unforeseen difficulty was the raising of a tariff barrier by the Irish Free State, which cut off Londonderry, Strabane and Newry from their hinterlands and turned them into industrial 'black spots'. In 1925–6 nearly a quarter of the insured workers in the province were unemployed and that average was maintained until the outbreak of the Second World War. There were 'hunger marches' in the 1930s in which Catholics and Protestants combined, but working-class solidarity even in distress could not be maintained for long, and in the sectarian riots of 1935 in Belfast 11 people were killed and over five hundred injured.

The standard of housing was low. Between 1919 and 1939 the total of all types of dwellings built in Northern Ireland was 50,000, the vast majority by private enterprise. A similar number was destroyed in the air raids of the Second World War, and thus the province entered the post-war period with the same stock of houses that it had in 1914. Some rural district councils criminally neglected their responsibilities. For example, in Co. Fermanagh not a single labourer's cottage was built in the inter-war period. Those built in other areas were primitive and 87 per cent were without running water or sanitation. In towns conditions were little better—in Omagh, the capital of Co. Tyrone, raw sewage went straight into a river that was liable to overflow after heavy rainfall. As Document 31 shows, there was concern about the conditions under which the Northern Ireland working classes lived, but the Government did not have the financial resources to change these and was unable to persuade the United Kingdom to come to its help.

The Second World War is the great divide in the economic and social history of Northern Ireland. Employment shot up through activity in engineering and shipbuilding, and from the need to provide food; but the number out of work never fell below 20,000. The impetus gained during the war was never completely lost and the Government attracted new industries to the province by making generous grants towards the cost of buildings, plant and fuel. Between 1945 and 1967 it paid out £140 million in direct grants to industry and helped to create 61,000 jobs; but so rapid was the decline in the traditional industries (such as linen) and in the numbers engaged in agriculture, that the difficult problem of unemployment was not resolved. This unemployment was not evenly spread, and areas in the south and west of the province, usually having a majority of Catholics, had more than their fair share. The people of Derry, Strabane, Newry and other Nationalist towns believed that the location of industry, with government aid, had less to do with economic factors than with the political affiliations of the population.

British standards of social welfare were also introduced and largely paid for out of the British Exchequer. The province would no longer have to put up with poor housing, inadequate hospitals and schools, poverty and squalor. This increased the dependence of the Stormont Government on British aid; but, even more important, it opened a wide gap between the social welfare systems of Northern Ireland and the Irish Free State and did more to reinforce partition than any other single event since 1921.

On the other hand, free education for all up to university level produced a generation of young Catholics who were impatient to change the sectarian politics they had inherited. In the course of time some of these formed a professional élite, which was less ready to accept a position of social and political inferiority than had been their predecessors. It was members of this Catholic middle class which in 1964 founded the Campaign for Social Justice in Northern Ireland and began an agitation, not only for the ending of discrimination in jobs and housing, but also for a share of political power and in decision-making. Revolutions invariably occur at times of rising expectations when people regard themselves as relatively rather than absolutely deprived; and it was this section of the Catholic population which put in train the changes that are still going on.

DOCUMENT 31. EXTRACTS FROM *The Government of Northern Ireland: Public Finance and Public Services, 1921–1964*, BY R. J. LAWRENCE (OXFORD UNIVERSITY PRESS, 1965)

(a) In 1941, when Belfast slum-dwellers were driven out of their bomb-damaged houses to find refuge elsewhere, the Moderator of the General Assembly of the Presbyterian Church was moved to uncommon frankness. After describing how inexpressibly shocked he was by the sight of the people he saw walking the streets after the 'blitz', he said, 'I have been working nineteen years in Belfast and I never saw the like of them before. If something is not done now to remedy this rank inequality there will be a revolution after the war'. At the same time Belfast City Council became gravely concerned about the people's health. Tuberculosis was rife and caused almost half of all deaths in the age group 15–25. Infant mortality, excessive when compared with that in English industrial centres, was higher in 1940 than for twenty years past. In January 1941, when the Government grant for maternity and child welfare was running at only 21 per cent instead of a permissible 50 per cent, the Council began to press for more assistance.

In September of the same year a special committee appointed to examine the city's health services invited a former deputy Chief Medical Officer of the English Ministry of Health (Dr T. Carnwath) to make an independent investigation. He found that in its personal medical services Belfast fell far short of what might reasonably have been expected in a city of its size and importance. The existence of the poor law medical service and conflict with the Government on finance meant that the Council were not quite certain what they were doing, whether it was worth doing, or whether they were the people to do it. Even so, evacuation of children revealed to social workers a striking disparity between conditions in the city and the countryside. 'During the war', said a woman MP, 'I discovered that maternity and child welfare services were practically non-existent throughout Northern Ireland'. And the personal habits of evacuated slum-dwellers were such that (in the words of an official report) 'the shock to householders who granted them sanctuary was second only to the shock they had received on learning of the disaster which had befallen Belfast'. Finally, in country areas war made local people acutely aware that land drainage (of importance for food output) and fire services were primitive or non-existent.

(b) Originally it was an integral part of the plan to make both parts of Ireland distinct and self-sufficient financial units. From her own revenue (mainly transferred taxation collected on her soil and reserved taxation imputed to her) Ulster was expected to finance her own services and make an imperial contribution. She is no longer required to do this because governments in London and Belfast have gradually bent the financial framework of the constitution. The post-war financial agreements enable Stormont to vote money at the expense of the United Kingdom taxpayer. Moreover . . . Britain gives assistance that is not revealed in Northern Ireland's accounts. The Ulster farmer gets subsidies borne on the Vote of the United Kingdom Ministry of Agriculture (though agriculture is a transferred service), and manufacturing industry in the province has had special treatment. Since, therefore, Northern Ireland is no longer compelled to be self-sufficient, it seems rather pointless to try to compute her revenue.

It can easily be argued that this transformation is no more than just. The Ulsterman has accepted parity of taxation and equality of insurance contributions; the farmer helps to feed the nation; the industrialist and the worker earn foreign exchange. In every field persons in Britain and Ulster contribute on more or less the same terms; and in many areas of Great Britain, as in Northern Ireland, it is certain that Exchequer spending exceeds revenue.

At the same time, the existence of a separate legislature and system of public accounts also makes it possible to argue that Ulster has been treated, not with justice, but with generosity. Financial assistance from the United Kingdom during the three financial years 1961–63 averaged £45m a year . . . . In addition a memorandum produced by the Home Office in May 1963 showed that the province enjoyed special measures to encourage industrial development at a cost to the United Kingdom taxpayer of some £15m a year. About half of this was a charge on the provincial Exchequer and represented, not a direct payment from the United Kingdom, but a larger reduction in the imperial contribution than equity might warrant. But all of it was special in the sense that comparable expenditure in Britain was on a smaller scale or non-existent . . . . So, to put the matter roughly, if Ulster were independent and had to pay for her own defence and for diplomatic, consular and other 'imperial' services, she would either have to cut domestic spending by some £50m a year or raise that sum by taxation. Either course would be catastrophic.

*

Professor Lawrence's figures refer to 1963. The British Government's discussion paper, *The Future of Northern Ireland* (October 1972), said: 'The combined total of special payments, subsidies, and loan advances from the National Loans Fund, is estimated to amount to around £300 million in the current year, of which loan advances represent an amount of the order of £100 million'. It warned:

> In a world of growing inter-dependence, where even the aspirations of major sovereign powers can only be fully met by their participation in wider associations and communities, a small area such as Northern Ireland cannot, without the gravest consequences for its own citizens, make its way alone. Even if it were feasible for Northern Ireland so to reduce its expenditures as to be able to live within its own real means—and such reduction would greatly lower the standards of life and of services enjoyed by the whole community—it would remain dependent upon external investment and external trade, and upon its standing and credit-worthiness in the European and the wider international communities.

(iv)

Throughout the whole period of Stormont's existence, the relationship between the governments of Dublin and Belfast was one of the most controversial issues in Irish politics. The

Government of Ireland Act 1920 had attempted to solve the 'home rule' problem by setting up two Irish parliaments within the United Kingdom, one for the north and one for the south. To foster close co-operation between the two administrations, the Act established a Council of Ireland, representative of each, to deal with common problems, and also provided for the union of the two parliaments in the event of Northern Ireland agreeing to that. This constitutional settlement was unacceptable to the majority in southern Ireland, and it was with their representatives that the British Government signed the Anglo-Irish Treaty 1921 whereby the Irish Free State was given dominion status. As signed, the Treaty applied to the whole of Ireland, but Northern Ireland was provided with an opportunity of opting out and retaining its existing status. This it did immediately. In 1925 the 'Border' between Northern Ireland and the Irish Free State was confirmed by an agreement between the governments of London, Dublin and Belfast (Document 25). As part of that agreement the Council of Ireland was abolished before it met, and thereafter there were no formal links between the two parts of the country.

With the advent to power of De Valera, who had never accepted the 1925 agreement, partition became a political issue and relations between the Irish Free State and Northern Ireland deteriorated. In 1937 the promulgation of a new constitution, laying claim to the whole of Ireland, antagonized the Unionist majority in the north, and the fact that the south remained neutral during the Second World War appeared to justify the widening gulf between Belfast and Dublin. In 1949 the promulgation of a Republic of Ireland, outside the Commonwealth, and the beginning of a world-wide campaign to force Britain to withdraw from the north, prompted Westminster, in an effort to quell Unionists' fears, to pass the Ireland Act 1949, which guaranteed that there would be no change in the constitutional status of Northern Ireland without the consent of its parliament.

Nevertheless, propinquity did force the two Irish governments to co-operate to a limited degree on matters of common concern, such as cross-border traffic, hydro-electricity, pest control and fisheries. There had, however, been no meeting of the respective heads of government since Sir James Craig and

William T. Cosgrave had met when signing the 1925 agreement. The question of recognition of Northern Ireland was the stumbling-block. All political parties in the Republic were committed to the ending of partition and none dared risk abandoning 'the national aim'. But in July 1963, Sean Lemass, who had succeeded De Valera as Taoiseach, went some way towards ending this impasse. Speaking at Tralee he said:

We recognise that the Government and Parliament there [Northern Ireland] exist with the support of the majority of the Six County area—artificial though that area is. We see it functioning within its powers and we are prepared to stand over the proposal that they should continue to function with these powers, within an all-Ireland constitution, for so long as it is desired to have them. Recognition of the realities of the situation have never been a difficulty with us.

We believe that it is foolish in the extreme that in this island and amongst people of the same race there should persist a desire to avoid contacts, even in respect of matters where concerted action is seen to be beneficial. We would hope that from the extension of useful contacts at every level of activity, a new situation would develop which would permit of wider responsibilities in accord with our desires . . . . The solution of the problem of partition is one to be found in Ireland by Irishmen, and, as we move towards it, we can be sure that there is no power or influence anywhere which can prevent its implementation, when the barriers of misunderstanding and suspicion, which have sustained it, have been whittled away.

This speech represented a complete volte-face on the part of the southern government. Gone was the idea that Britain was perpetuating 'the Border', and instead there was an appreciation of the apprehensions of Ulster Protestants. It was against this background that Terence O'Neill, Prime Minister of Northern Ireland, invited Sean Lemass to Belfast in January 1965. By passing through the gates of Stormont, the southern premier gave at least *de facto* recognition to the Unionist regime.

Document 32 gives a moderate Unionist's version of relations between the two parts of Ireland over the past fifty years, and is interesting as illustrating the caution with which any Unionist politician had to speak on this most sensitive of issues.

DOCUMENT 32. EXTRACTS FROM AN ADDRESS BY MR TERENCE O'NEILL, PRIME MINISTER OF NORTHERN IRELAND, TO THE COMMONWEALTH PARLIAMENTARY ASSOCIATION, AT WESTMINSTER, 4 NOVEMBER 1968 (QUOTED IN *Ulster at the Crossroads*, EDITED BY JOHN COLE, FABER, 1969)

Ulster accepted [the Government of Ireland Act 1920] and determined to work it. She had never sought a Parliament of her own, but accepted it as part of a general settlement retaining the link with Britain. The South did not accept it. Even the establishment of the Irish Free State, retaining very tenuous links with the Crown, involved a bitter Civil War in the South. And by slow degrees a State was created there whose policies and outlook were entirely alien to the majority of Ulster people.

However, from 1922 onwards the country which is now called the Irish Republic and was then known as the Irish Free State, had complete control of its own destiny. It had a Government responsible to a parliamentary majority and with a legitimate claim to make agreements on behalf of its people. And now I come to a point which is often conveniently forgotten. In December 1925, the Governments in London, Dublin and Belfast concluded an Agreement, freely entered into on all sides. The Preamble expressed a desire 'to avoid any causes of friction which might mar or retard the further growth of friendly relations' between the Governments and peoples of the three Parties, and the Agreement, which was confirmed by each Parliament, confirmed the boundary line between North and South as enacted in 1920. Those who are interested will find Westminster's confirmation in the Ireland (Confirmation of Agreement) Act, 1925.

The point I want to make is that the lawfully constituted Government of the Irish Free State accepted, in free agreement, both the Border and the existence of a legitimate Parliament and Government in Northern Ireland.

The Dublin Government was headed in those days by a wise, modest and responsible statesman, Mr Cosgrave, and I have little doubt that his policies would have led in time to steadily improving relationships between North and South. Unhappily for the future of North–South relations, he was succeeded in 1932 by Mr De Valera—by a new party with new policies. I realize I am speaking now of one who is President of a friendly country, and who in his venerable age has come to be acknowledged as one of the most remarkable and enduring political figures of our time. But in him, the mystic and visionary have always been to the forefront. Because he had a dream of an Irish-speaking Ireland, he ignored the fact that the vast majority of his people spoke only English. Because he had a vision of Ireland united, he could not see that there were people who had loyalties of another kind. Under his leadership Eire closed its eyes to the realities of the situation, ignored the Agreement of 1925, and promulgated in 1937 a new Constitution laying claim to the whole island of Ireland, including the area within the jurisdiction of the Northern Ireland Government.

Moreover, by defaulting on its treaty obligations to the British Government, the Government of Eire initiated the so-called 'trade war', and erected on the Border a high tariff barrier. This, I emphasize, was no part of the settlement of 1920. The British Isles could have retained—and indeed did for the first period after partition—the characteristics of a Customs Union. It was Eire, not Northern Ireland or the United Kingdom, which gave to the Border the nature of an international customs frontier. For many years now, most goods passing from Eire to the North have continued to come into the United Kingdom duty-free. Not so, however, trade passing in the other direction. The manufactures of many Ulster firms, including those which have a natural hinterland in the South, have been excluded by insuperable tariffs or other forms of protection. In time, the Anglo-Irish Trade Agreement will end this situation, but as of today it still exists.

Is it surprising that such attitudes were resented in Northern Ireland? Is it remarkable that when we also had to endure physical violence from IRA terrorism, strongly based in the South, people in Northern Ireland took the view that these people were not interested in friendship or co-operation, but in imposing a settlement on us by force or other forms of coercion? Eire's neutrality in World War II did nothing to bridge the deep gulf of sentiment and tradition. And finally in 1948—with De Valera out of power, and a new Coalition Government in office—there came the declaration of an Irish Republic, and the final, irrevocable breach with Britain and the Commonwealth.

When that occurred, the Northern Ireland Government of the day very properly pressed for a clarification of its constitutional position from Mr Attlee's Government. This clarification was given, in two respects, and there should be no ambiguity about its nature.

It is not often that an Act of Parliament makes a solemn declaration on a major constitutional issue; but when it does so, the declaration of Parliament is, in my view, uniquely serious and binding. So may I read to you Section 1 (2) of the Ireland Act, 1949.

'It is hereby declared that Northern Ireland remains part of His Majesty's dominions and of the United Kingdom and it is hereby affirmed that in no event will Northern Ireland or any part thereof cease to be part of His Majesty's dominions or of the United Kingdom without the consent of the Parliament of Northern Ireland.'

That declaration is not only solemn and binding, but it is also realistic. For how could a basic change be made in the constitutional status of Northern Ireland against the will of those who have been chosen to represent its people in its own parliament?

But the matter does not end there, for in addition to the statutory declaration of Northern Ireland's territorial integrity Mr Attlee pronounced a wide-ranging guarantee of her right to constitutional self-determination. He said in the House of Commons on 28th October 1948:

The view of H.M. Government has always been that no change should be made in the *constitutional status* of Northern Ireland without Northern Ireland's free agreement.

Mr Harold Wilson was a member of the Government which gave that pledge, and on at least three occasions—the latest on Wednesday, 30th October 1968—he has affirmed it. The

Conservative Party also accept it as a pledge binding any Conservative Government. The very clear inference is that there ought not to be any major change in constitutional arrangements affecting Northern Ireland which would be unacceptable to it. And I really feel I ought to make this clear beyond all possible doubt. If the United Kingdom Government and the United Kingdom Parliament were to make a declaration tomorrow in favour of a United Ireland, it would achieve really nothing practical within Ireland. The choice must clearly be between a union by coercion—which I suggest to you is even more unthinkable now than it was in 1912; a union by consent —and let there be no doubt that we in Ulster do *not* consent to it; or an acceptance of the position as it actually exists. Do not be deceived by the slogans demanding that England should get out of Ireland . . . .

Now what is our attitude today, to the Irish Republic on one hand and Great Britain on the other?

In 1965, in spite of the continued unwillingness of Southern politicians to face up to the actual position in Ulster, I decided to take the initiative of meeting the then Dublin Prime Minister, Mr Sean Lemass. I knew he was a hard-headed realist, prepared to recognize the realities of the situation, and I regarded our meeting as a *de facto*, if not *de jure* recognition of Northern Ireland. We agreed from the start to set political and constitutional issues on one side, and concentrate instead upon promoting economic and other forms of practical co-operation —in tourism, in power supply and so on. This was the basis— the sensible, realistic basis—of my two meetings with Mr Lemass and my subsequent two meetings with his successor, Mr Lynch. I knew, of course, that they retained in their hearts the wish for a united Ireland but they, too, knew that I retained my loyalty to the United Kingdom. What I must emphasize is that, from my point of view, the object of such talks was to promote a decent, sane neighbourly relationship. Canada is no less an independent country and a member of the Commonwealth because of her friendly links with America.

But if such a relationship is to flourish, it demands sensible restraint and common prudence. You cannot go on talking business with someone who comes blundering into your back garden, kicking over the plants. Mr Lynch can have a friendly relationship based on mutual respect, or he can have the luxury of allowing himself to intervene in the domestic affairs of Northern Ireland and the United Kingdom. He really cannot have both . . . . We do not intervene in the domestic affairs of the South of Ireland. No terrorist bands from the North have sought to coerce the South. Leave us in peace, and there will be peace—peace in which the Governments in Ireland, North and South, may get on with the things that really matter. For our part, let me declare in conclusion that as long as I am Prime Minister it will be my aim, and that of my Administration, to build in Ulster a just and prosperous society, in which all its citizens may play a full and equal part.

PART IV

Revolution and Change

(i)

The installation of Terence O'Neill as Prime Minister in 1963 inaugurated a new era in Northern Ireland politics. He was the first Unionist leader who aspired to secure Catholic support for the regime. He sought to remove 'the Border' from Ulster politics by an exchange of visits with Sean Lemass, Taoiseach of the Irish Republic. He stimulated research and discussion on a wide range of economic and social issues, and bluntly told his followers that 'Unionism armed with justice will be a stronger cause than Unionism armed merely with strength'. He visited Catholic schools and hospitals and thereby caused Protestant Ultras to fear that their traditional ascendancy was being put at risk. During these years, also, the ecumenical movement began to win adherents in the province, and the Union Jack at half-mast on Belfast City Hall, on the occasion of Pope John XXIII's death, symbolized for many the betrayal of the fundamentalist Protestantism they cherished. Their spokesman was the Rev. Ian Paisley, a Free Presbyterian minister of tremendous energy, who railed against the 'Romeward' trend of Protestantism and devoted his considerable talents to the overthrow of Terence O'Neill and the reversal of his policies.

Catholics, apart from a very small middle-class group, treated the Prime Minister's overtures with caution, for they suspected that what he described as 'bridge-building' between the communities was only a more subtle means of making permanent the partition of Ireland. They required more concrete evidence of change in the form of jobs, houses and appointments to public boards than O'Neill was able to provide. His position was difficult, for attitudes in Northern Ireland

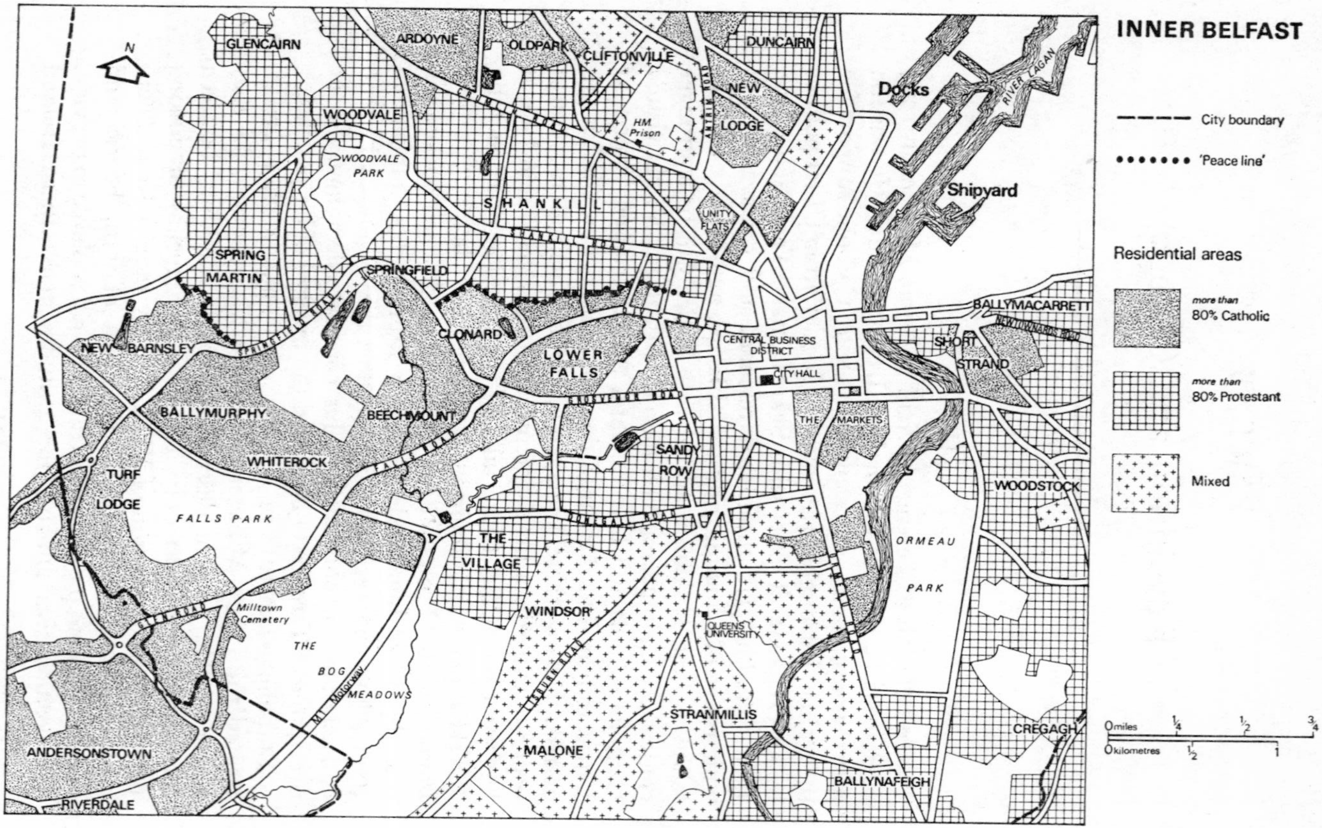
INNER BELFAST
City boundary
'Peace line'
Residential areas
more than 80% Catholic
more than 80% Protestant
Mixed
0 miles 1/4 1/2 3/4
0 kilometres 1/2 1
N
GLENCAIRN
ARDOYNE
OLDPARK
CLIFTONVILLE
DUNCAIRN
NEW LODGE
WOODVALE
HM Prison
WOODVALE PARK
SHANKILL
UNITY FLATS
Docks
Shipyard
RIVER LAGAN
SPRING MARTIN
SPRINGFIELD
CLONARD
LOWER FALLS
BALLYMACARRETT
NEWTOWNARDS ROAD
CENTRAL BUSINESS DISTRICT
CITY HALL
SHORT STRAND
NEW BARNSLEY
BALLYMURPHY
BEECHMOUNT
THE MARKETS
SANDY ROW
WHITEROCK
TURF LODGE
FALLS PARK
THE VILLAGE
WOODSTOCK
ORMEAU PARK
WINDSOR
QUEENS UNIVERSITY
Milltown Cemetery
THE BOG MEADOWS
M1 Motorway
STRANMILLIS
MALONE
BALLYNAFEIGH
CREGAGH
ANDERSONSTOWN
RIVERDALE
CRUMLIN ROAD
ANTRIM ROAD
SHANKILL ROAD
SPRINGFIELD ROAD
FALLS ROAD
GROSVENOR ROAD
DONEGALL ROAD
LISBURN ROAD

Map 2 Inner Belfast

change very slowly, and he was obliged publicly to defend Unionists, even when their actions (for example, in local authorities in Fermanagh and Tyrone) fell far short of generally accepted standards of social justice. After his retirement in 1969 he revealed the constraints under which any Unionist leader had to work, and frankly admitted:

I had won the trust of the Catholics as no previous Prime Minister had ever been able to do, but I was unable to restore to them the rights which small-minded men had removed from them during the first few years of Northern Ireland's existence.

The early years of O'Neill's administration saw the growth of the Civil Rights Association. Unlike the traditional Nationalist organizations, it ignored 'the Border' and demanded the same standards of equality and justice as prevailed in the rest of the United Kingdom. Its programme, too, was one which the British people could understand and sympathize with: one man, one vote in local elections; the end of discrimination in the allocation of houses and jobs; the repeal of the Special Powers Act; and the disbanding of the Ulster Special Constabulary. At the outset the movement's leaders came from a small group of Catholic professional and university-educated people, but gradually it attracted support from a wide spectrum of political opinion, including Irish republicans, whose activities had been curtailed in 1967 by regulations framed under the Special Powers Act. Because of this republican involvement, the Northern Ireland Government sought to project the Civil Rights Association as a front for subversive organizations, and used the forces of law and order in an attempt to suppress what the Cameron Commission described later as a perfectly legitimate reformist movement (Document 33).

On 5 October 1968, the outside world first learned of the explosive situation in Northern Ireland. During a civil rights march in Derry City, held in defiance of a ban imposed by the Minister of Home Affairs, William Craig, the RUC baton-charged the crowd in a crude and brutal operation. TV coverage of the incidents shocked people in the rest of the United Kingdom, but the Northern Ireland Government was unmoved, and Terence O'Neill warned that 'neither internal violence nor attempts to engineer outside pressure' would accelerate change in the province. But so strong was public feeling that the British Government was forced, almost against its will, to concern itself with the internal affairs of Northern Ireland. In conjunction with the Stormont administration, it agreed on a programme of reform which was announced on 22 November: Londonderry Corporation, which was totally unrepresentative, was to be replaced by a development commission; a fair system of house allocation was to be recommended to local councils; machinery for investigating citizens' grievances against central and local government was to be created; the adoption of universal adult franchise would be considered when local government was reorganized; and those sections of the Special Powers Act which conflicted with Britain's international obligations would be repealed as soon as circumstances allowed. These measures did not meet all the demands of the civil rights movement, but they were a substantial step forward, and, if implemented, would improve the position of Catholics in society.

Protestant Ultras reacted strongly to what they regarded as 'concessions' to their enemies. At Armagh on 30 November and during the People's Democracy march from Belfast to Derry in January 1969, they attempted to suppress the civil rights movement by the threat or use of violence. At Burntollet Bridge, outside Derry, where the marchers were attacked by a crowd armed with batons and stones, there appeared to be collusion between some members of the Ulster Special Constabulary and the Protestant mob. During the weekend which followed a group of RUC men entered the Catholic Bogside area of Derry shouting sectarian slogans, batoning people on the streets and causing a good deal of damage to their homes. These incidents provoked a wave of sympathy for the Catholics and created an embarrassing situation for the British Government.

In an effort to gain control of events Terence O'Neill made a dramatic appeal to the people on 9 December 1968, asking their support for what he described as 'a continuing programme of change to secure a united and harmonious community'. He warned his followers that the government had little choice in the matter:

Mr Wilson made it absolutely clear to us that if we did not face up to our problems the Westminster Parliament might well decide to act over our heads. Where would our Constitution be then? What shred of self-respect would be left to us? If we allowed others to solve our problems because we had not the guts—let me use a plain word—guts to face up to them, we would be utterly shamed.

Some Unionists were angered by talk like this, and blamed the Prime Minister for the problems that now beset the province. His most severe critic was William Craig, Minister of Home Affairs, and two days after the broadcast O'Neill was forced to dismiss him from the Cabinet. Two other Ministers, Brian Faulkner and William Morgan, were also unhappy at O'Neill's handling of the situation, and, when he insisted on setting up the Cameron Commission to investigate the causes of unrest in Northern Ireland since 5 October 1968, they resigned from the Government. A week later twelve Unionist backbenchers called for a meeting of the parliamentary party to discuss a change of leadership. In the hope of thwarting their plans, and at the same time gaining popular support for his policies, O'Neill decided to hold a general election. The gamble failed. Most of his opponents were returned, and the Unionist party was clearly divided into pro-O'Neill and anti-O'Neill factions. Outside Parliament Protestant extremists campaigned against him and a terrorist group sought to dislodge him by blowing up electricity pylons and water mains. They succeeded when on 28 April 1969 he resigned in favour of Major Chichester-Clark; but before stepping down, Terence O'Neill announced that the Cabinet had accepted the principle of 'one man, one vote' in local government elections.

The change of Prime Minister did not bring peace, and, after a summer of tension, communal disorder became widespread in August 1969. The most serious eruption took place in Derry following a march of the Protestant Apprentice Boys, when there were clashes between the Catholics and the RUC. Fearing an 'invasion' similar to that which had taken place in January, the people of the Bogside erected barricades to protect themselves from the police, flew the tricolour of the Irish Republic on the tall Rossville Street flats, repudiated the authority of the Stormont Government and proclaimed the area within the barricades as 'Free Derry'. Using CS gas and water-cannon, the RUC repeatedly tried to break into the Bogside, but eventually, exhausted and demoralized, they were forced to withdraw. The Government had no choice but to appeal to Westminster for assistance and British troops entered 'Free Derry' where they were greeted as deliverers.

By supplying troops the British Government had directly involved itself in the affairs of Northern Ireland. The Irish Government was involved as well; for as pictures of the Derry incidents flickered across television screens in the south, strong feelings had been aroused. The Taoiseach, Jack Lynch, announced that he was establishing Irish Army field hospitals on the Donegal border and seeking talks immediately with the British Government:

> Recognising, however, that the re-unification of the national territory can provide the only permanent solution for the problem, it is our intention to request the British Government to enter into early negotiations with the Irish Government to review the present constitutional position of the Six Counties of Northern Ireland.

That statement changed the whole character of the struggle, and on the night of 14 August, in Belfast, incensed Protestants surged into the Falls and Ardoyne intent on crushing what they saw as a conspiracy to overthrow 'their state'. But it was the action of the RUC which came in for most criticism, for, believing themselves to be involved in a Republican uprising, they fired indiscriminately wherever they saw a crowd (Document 34). The people of the Falls and Ardoyne defended themselves as best they could (the Provisional IRA was not then in existence), but in the course of three days seven people were killed and 500 homes burnt down, most of them Catholic. A contingent of 6,000 troops was rushed to Northern Ireland, and along a 'peace line' of corrugated iron they were given the distasteful task of containing the Protestants and Catholics of Belfast in their ghettos.

Military intervention on this scale had its political implications. These were made clear in the Downing Street Declaration of 19 August 1969, issued after a meeting between ministers of the United Kingdom and Northern Ireland governments (Document 35). A more extensive programme of reform was imposed upon the Unionists, and the GOC Northern Ireland was made responsible for the internal security of the province. A committee, chaired by Lord Hunt, advised that the RUC be disarmed and that the 'B' Specials be replaced by a new defence regiment which would be part of the British Army (*supra* Part II, section iii). The Home Secretary, James Callaghan, came to Northern Ireland to assure Unionists that 'the Border' was not an issue and to assure Catholics that there would be no delay in putting through reforms. Before he returned to London on 29 August he announced that there would be a new Housing Executive to build and allocate dwellings, a Minister of Community Relations, and working parties to consider how to prevent discrimination in employment or incitement to religious hatred.

Things could never be the same again after August 1969. Terence O'Neill assessed the position accurately when he wrote:

> What I think everyone failed to understand is that you cannot have a situation where Catholic houses are burnt down and Catholics shot in the street, and then say 'Here are some reforms, let's forget about the past'.

In the Falls and Ardoyne great fear and passion had been aroused, and many Catholics believed that the Unionists had neither the will nor the capacity to make the changes the British Government proposed. Left-wing movements, like the People's Democracy led by Michael Farrell, did not want to reform Northern Ireland but to destroy it. The 'Border' issue had surfaced in a significant way during the Derry riots, and there were signs that the IRA had begun to revive in traditionally republican areas. The fears of the Protestants had been aroused as well. In the Shankill and East Belfast, and in the Border areas of Fermanagh and Tyrone, many Unionists were convinced that British politicians (with little distinction of party) were prepared to betray them. The powers of Stormont had been curtailed, the 'B' Specials had been disbanded and the RUC placed under a City of London police officer, Sir Arthur Young. The influence of the Rev. Ian Paisley (he was returned as an MP to both Westminster and Stormont) and of

William Craig increased in the Protestant ghettos, and the once-powerful Unionst Party began to disintegrate. There was a lack of trust on all sides and no basis for lasting peace.

DOCUMENT 33. EXTRACTS FROM *Disturbances in Northern Ireland*, REPORT OF THE CAMERON COMMISSION, 1969 (BELFAST, HMSO, CMND 532)

The Civil Rights Association maintained that it was non-sectarian and concerned only with obtaining reforms and changes in the law which it sought and always by peaceful and non-violent means. It is undoubtedly the case that it has been the policy of the Association to refuse to permit the display of provocative symbols and banners, in particular the Republican Tricolour, at any demonstration that it organised or author-ised; it is also undoubted that on no occasion were weapons carried by demonstrators acting under Civil Rights Association auspices. The use on 5 October of placards and banner poles as missiles by certain demonstrators—mainly young Socialists who had come specially from Belfast—was an exception to this generality, and an illustration of the inefficiency with which that demonstration was organised and conducted and of the absence of any effective Civil Rights Association con-trol . . . .

The great majority of the Council of the Association are Roman Catholics, and the same applies to the membership of the body itself. This is not surprising, as the greater part of the matters on which the Civil Rights Association concentrates are concerned with grievances or complaints which relate to Roman Catholic sections of the community.

Thus it is apparent that here is an organisation of some substance, with a formal constitutional structure, means of co-operation with affiliated local associations with identical objects, and with a definite programme of reforms sought within the framework of the Constitution. It is dedicated to a policy of non-violence and is non-sectarian in origin and pur-pose. While it has within its membership those whose aims and objects are far different and more radical than those of the Association itself, and who would not exclude the use of violence if they thought it necessary or desirable to achieve their aims, the Association so far has been able to maintain its avowed policy of non-violent protest and agitation within the limits of the law. So far, it has obtained and still obtains the support of many who are neither Catholic nor interested in constitutional changes, violent or otherwise, and it is this ballast of moderate and earnest men and women on its Council and among its membership which has enabled the Association to maintain its originally designed course. But here is an instrument, already constituted and organised, which could without any excessive difficulty be successfully infiltrated by those whose intentions are far other than peaceful and constitutional. We have already commented on the presence of IRA sympathisers and members within the Association and of their acting as stewards on the occasions of marches or demonstrations. At the same time there is little doubt that left wing extremists of the type already closely associated with the control of People's Democracy would be ready to take over, if they could, the real direction of the Civil Rights Association and divert its activities from a reformist policy to a much more radical course which would not exclude the deliberate use of force and the provocation of disorder as an instrument of policy.

DOCUMENT 34. EXTRACTS FROM *Ulster 1969: The Fight for Civil Rights in Northern Ireland*, BY MAX HASTINGS (GOLLANCZ, 1970).

There were on the streets of Belfast four forces, closely engaged and beyond the reach of serious central direction. First, the Catholics; then the 'B' Specials, all armed with revolvers, rifles or sub-machine-guns; the RUC; and the Protestants from the Shankill, who began to mount heavy petrol-bomb attacks on houses and factories on the fringes of the Falls area. The RUC had by now convinced themselves that they faced something approaching a Catholic revolt. Fantastically, in Great Britain their senior officers had permitted the calling out of armoured cars mounted with heavy machine-guns. Many RUC men also had 9mm Sterling sub-machine-guns as personal weapons. There was the absolutely clear feeling among the police that they faced a direct threat. After the first gunfire, every time shots were heard, from whatever direction, the police would loose off burst after burst of sub-machine-gun fire at something —or nothing. And the armoured cars began to career the length of the Falls Road emptying belts of heavy calibre ammunition in the direction of any supposed threat.

In the silence and darkness broken only by gunfire, crackling flames from the fires, and faint shouts, there were a handful of Catholic snipers operating; also, without doubt, some Protestants. But even with field glasses, it was only half a dozen times that one caught a glimpse of a muzzle flash from a rooftop or a figure silhouetted against the skyline. Two police were hit in Dover Street, and carried to the shelter of the personnel carriers behind the police lines. But even with a finely sighted rifle, it would have been very difficult to make effective return practical against snipers that night. They moved too fast, there were not many of them, and they were small and only occasionally visible targets. The police embarked on a rampage of machine-gun fire that shattered every observer that witnessed it. Shots were believed to have come from Divis Flats: the police replied by hosing fire in the direction of the flats. An armoured car sprayed the buildings with heavy machine-gun fire, sending chips flying off the concrete parapets, and causing havoc within . . . .

On the street corners, the battle still raged. 'B' Specials with their revolvers shot out the street lights—oblivious to the danger of richochets—in the hope of making themselves poorer targets, then leaned around the streets with cigarettes dangling from their lips. Senior officers—such as were to be seen—appeared to have neither plan nor will to impose any kind of fire discipline. At intervals, a policeman would lean around a corner to loose off a burst of fire, then duck once more. Still the armoured cars continued their relentless patrols, turrets swivelling and guns elevating and depressing as they sought a target. One car swung round behind the police line, and halted in shelter while the crew jumped down to drink tea supplied by a local Protestant. The gunner, in his shirt sleeves, harangued a group of police: 'You know, of course, Dr Paisley has been telling us this would happen these nine months, but none of us had the sense to listen.' It was a remark that explained much Catholic feeling towards the police.

DOCUMENT 35. TEXT OF A COMMUNIQUÉ AND DECLARATION ISSUED AFTER A MEETING HELD AT 10 DOWNING STREET ON 19 AUGUST 1969 (LONDON, HMSO, CMND 4154)

1. The United Kingdom Government reaffirm that nothing which has happened in recent weeks in Northern Ireland derogates from the clear pledges made by successive United Kingdom Governments that Northern Ireland should not cease to be a part of the United Kingdom without the consent of the people of Northern Ireland or from the provision in Section 1 of the Ireland Act, 1949, that in no event will Northern Ireland or any part thereof cease to be part of the United Kingdom without the consent of the Parliament of Northern Ireland. The border is not an issue.

2. The United Kingdom Government again reaffirm that responsibility for affairs in Northern Ireland is entirely a matter of domestic jurisdiction. The United Kingdom Government will take full responsibility for asserting this principle in all international relationships.

3. The United Kingdom Government have ultimate responsibility for the protection of those who live in Northern Ireland when, as in the past week, a breakdown of law and order has occurred. In this spirit, the United Kingdom Government responded to the requests of the Northern Ireland Government for military assistance in Londonderry and Belfast in order to restore law and order. They emphasise again that troops will be withdrawn when law and order has been restored.

4. The Northern Ireland Government have been informed that troops have been provided on a temporary basis in accordance with the United Kingdom's ultimate responsibility. In the context of the commitment of these troops, the Northern Ireland Government have reaffirmed their intention to take into the fullest account at all times the views of Her Majesty's Government in the United Kingdom, especially in relation to matters affecting the status of citizens of that part of the United Kingdom and their equal rights and protection under the law.

5. The United Kingdom Government have welcomed the decisions of the Northern Ireland Government relating to local government franchise, the revision of local government areas, the allocation of houses, the creation of a Parliamentary Com-

missioner for Administration in Northern Ireland and machinery to consider citizens' grievances against other public authorities which the Prime Minister reported to the House of Commons at Westminster following his meeting with Northern Ireland Ministers on 21 May as demonstrating the determination of the Northern Ireland Government that there shall be full equality of treatment for all citizens. Both Governments have agreed that it is vital that the momentum of internal reform should be maintained.

6. The two Governments at their meeting at 10 Downing Street to-day have reaffirmed that in all legislation and executive decisions of Government every citizen of Northern Ireland is entitled to the same equality of treatment and freedom from discrimination as obtains in the rest of the United Kingdom, irrespective of political views or religion. In their further meetings the two Governments will be guided by these mutually accepted principles.

7. Finally, the Governments are determined to take all possible steps to restore normality to the Northern Ireland community so that economic development can proceed at the faster rate which is vital for social stability.

(ii)

In the five years of the O'Neill government only three people had died from violence; none died in the civil rights demonstrations from the autumn of 1968 to the summer of 1969. Thereafter the situation changed radically, and guns gradually took the place of stones and petrol-bombs. In the riots of July and August eight people were killed and over 150 injured by gunfire, 500 houses were destroyed and nearly 2,000 families were forced to flee from their homes. On 15 August when the British troops arrived in Belfast the frightened Catholics welcomed them into their areas, although some time was to elapse before they took down the barricades from their streets.

This section is devoted to documents which attempt to show the causes and consequences of the change which took place in the relationship between the Army and the two communities of Northern Ireland during the subsequent twelve months. The British Government's strategy was to use the Army to hold the ring while the police force was being reorganized and the political reforms were being pushed through Parliament. Early in 1970 this strategy was under severe strain and, in frustration, the GOC, Sir Ian Freeland, warned that the Ulster politicians would have to show more energy in solving their problems, as the Army could not be expected to remain on the streets indefinitely. At the general election of June 1970 a Conservative Government under Mr Edward Heath came into office at Westminster. Many Catholics (and Protestants also) believed that Conservatives would be more amenable to Unionist pressure than the Labour Government had been. In reality that proved not to be so; but the fact that at this stage, the Catholics were suspicious of the Conservatives was a factor that should have been taken into account. Mr Maudling's decision to allow Orange marches close to the Catholic areas, and the imprisonment of Bernadette Devlin for her part in the defence of the Bogside against the RUC, convinced many Catholics that British policy was being gradually changed. On 26–7 June there was terrible rioting in Belfast, in which five men, all Protestants, were killed, and £500,000-worth of property was destroyed. The Unionists blamed the troops for their tenderness with Catholics, and they were further infuriated at allegations that two Dublin Government Ministers were involved in gun-running for the IRA. The Northern Ireland Security Council decided that what was required to prevent a slide into anarchy was a demonstration of Army toughness. This approach was first used in the Catholic Lower Falls on 3-5 July 1970. After a seizure of arms in Balkan Street, the customary offer of help by the local priests in dispersing the crowds was brusquely refused, a curfew was imposed and a house-to-house search began. It was the sort of operation Unionists had been demanding for months, and many Catholics were persuaded that the Army was being used by the Stormont Government to repress them. The *Sunday Times* 'Insight' Team identified the summer of 1970 as the time of decisive change, and argued that the decision to allow Orange parades and to search only Catholic areas constituted an irresponsible handling of an explosive situation. The loss of confidence by the Catholics in the Army's impartiality led eventually to the acceptance of the IRA as the only protector on whom they could rely (Documents 36 and 37(a)).

There were recriminations within the IRA because of their inability to help the Catholics of Belfast and Derry during the riots of August 1969. Since 1965 the Republican movement had concentrated on political and social issues and had ceased to train for guerrilla warfare. Even before the Northern Ireland troubles this development had its critics and a number of old-style IRA leaders seceded from the main body and formed the Provisional Army Council. After 'the Falls curfew' of 3–5 July 1970 hundreds of recruits joined the 'Provisionals' and a frantic search for arms began. It was not until 6 February 1971 that the IRA killed the first British soldier and from then on both sides were at war, with the helpless civilians in between (Document 37(b)). On 11 March three young off-duty Scottish soldiers were murdered on a lonely road just north of Belfast; and 6,000 shipyard workers marched through Belfast in protest against the British Government's unwillingness to penetrate the Catholic 'no-go areas' where the IRA found refuge. Overwhelmed by the task confronting him and under sharp criticism from his own party, Major Chichester-Clark resigned. He was succeeded by Brian Faulkner, who, as it turned out, became the last Prime Minister of Northern Ireland on 23 March 1971 (Document 38).

DOCUMENT 36. EXTRACTS FROM *Ulster*, BY THE *Sunday Times* 'INSIGHT' TEAM (PENGUIN BOOKS, 1972)

At 8.20 p.m. the Army invaded the [Falls] area. The local IRA opened fire on them. Among their targets were troops of the Black Watch and Life Guards, so new to Belfast that they had driven straight from the ferry when it berthed at Belfast docks. 'They were absolutely terrified', [Brigadier] Hudson admitted later. There was, in consequence, a good deal of gunfire from the Army. One official report puts the Army's expenditure of ammunition at fourteen rounds of the 7·62mm bullets from the troops' self loading rifles, and one ·303 round. This frugality simply does not accord with eye-witness accounts. Nor does it tally with the private log of one officer involved, which records *1500* rounds of 7·62 mm ammunition fired, seventeen rounds of ·303, and ten rounds of 9mm pistol ammunition. If his figures are correct, one would have to have a low opinion of Army marksmanship to believe that all this was fired, in accordance with policy, only at 'identifiable targets'.

The troops also deluged the area with CS. The matchbox houses provided no refuge from the choking clouds. Some of the canisters broke enough roof tiles in falling to smash into attics and fill the houses with smoke. There was no escape for the occupants: the streets outside were also saturated. 'The women were white-faced with panic', Father Murphy recalls. By 10 p.m. Freeland believed that the only way to stop widespread bloodshed was to get everyone off the streets. He declared a curfew over the whole Falls area, and he did not lift it until Sunday morning, thirty-five hours later . . . .

While the curfew lasted, the Army took the opportunity to conduct a house-to-house search of the whole area—and this obvious military course was also the consequence of a political decision. At the 1 July Joint Security Committee meeting, it had been agreed that when arms were found in a house, the entire street should be searched. Whether this was a genuine military judgement, or merely to introduce a punitive element, we cannot say. But the policy of more generalized arm searches was dear to Chichester-Clark's heart, and on his brief visit Maudling had suggested that the Army might do a little more to make Chichester-Clark's life easier. Normally, the military refused to consider 'area' searches on the grounds that the opprobrium incurred outweighed any advantage. But since they had incurred opprobrium anyway, Chichester-Clark might as well be given a leg-up.

Just as the soldiers had always prophesied, the returns were not large by Ulster standards—especially if it was considered as the arsenal of 20,000 people. The Army H.Q. log lists: twenty-eight rifles, two carbines, fifty-two pistols or revolvers, twenty-four shotguns, 100 'incendiary devices', twenty pounds of gelignite, and 20,000 rounds of ammunition. The weapons would just about have equipped a rather down-at-heel infantry company. The ammunition, on the other hand, would have supplied a couple of battalions.

For this haul, the Army paid a very high price. Four civilians were dead: one run over by the Army, and three shot. None of the dead was alleged to be connected with the IRA, but it is perhaps fortunate, in view of the volume of fire, that more people did not die.

Illegal confinement, summary search and exposure to unprecedented amounts of CS gas outraged large sections of the Falls Road population. Their conviction that the 'invasion' had been politically motivated was confirmed, as they saw it, when the Army drove two beaming Unionist ministers, Captains William Long and John Brooke, on a tour of the subjugated Falls.

DOCUMENT 37. EXTRACTS FROM *States of Ireland*, BY CONOR CRUISE O'BRIEN (HUTCHINSON, 1972)

(a) From the summer of 1969 to 1970, the British Army had maintained a position of something like impartiality, through a kind of balance of unpopularities. Catholics tended to object to its presence in principle, but felt the need for it in practice. Protestants approved its presence in principle but objected to its role in practice, as protecting Catholic 'no-go areas', in which the IRA could build up its strength unhampered by 'normal policing'. (There was some truth in this view of the British Army's role at this time, and it accounts for the IRA's intermittent interest in co-operating with the British Army.) But after the Falls Road search, the popularity of the Army among the Protestants naturally shot up. The Army searches on the Shankill in October had provoked a similarly favourable response among Catholics. But there was always something 'unnatural' and therefore brittle in Catholic approval of the British Army, and there was always the Republican influence, devoted to making the Army unpopular again. Among the Protestants, approval of 'our Army' was more natural and proved more stable—once Catholic hostility to the Army became reassuringly plain. For the soldiers, from the summer of 1970 on, Catholic areas were unfriendly, while Protestant areas—barring exceptional incidents—were friendly. So Catholics were clearly bad guys, Protestants (relatively) good guys. Soldiers remaining in this atmosphere for any length of time were likely to begin to 'understand' the Orange point of view, or at least to understand the value of Orange taunts ('Fenian bastard', etc.) as verbal weapons against Catholics. This was a highly satisfactory development from the IRA point of view.

When a lorry-load of British troops went through Catholic territory singing 'The Sash my Father Wore' they were making an essential IRA point far more effectively than the IRA themselves could do. For what the troops were singing, as Catholics heard it, meant: 'As long as we are here, the Orangemen will rule and the Catholics will get it in the neck' . . . .

The Catholic ghettos were growing markedly more anti-British, the Army markedly more anti-Catholic. The death roll at the end of 1970 was twenty. By the end of the following year it was to reach ten times that figure.

(b) Whether because of doctrinaire incapacity to accept the reality of growing Catholic–Protestant polarization, or because of an honourable unwillingness to exploit this trend, the IRA leadership was utterly unprepared for the crisis of mid-August 1969 in Derry and Belfast. The IRA had very few weapons and very few people trained and ready to use them. Their prestige in the ghettos went sharply down. People wrote on walls:

IRA I Ran Away

It was out of this debacle and the consequent discredit of the Sinn Fein–IRA leadership that the Provisional IRA grew. To what exact extent its growth was watered by the Dublin Government remains in some doubt. But the IRA had always been subject to splits—especially splits between right and left—and the situation after August 1969 was obviously of the kind that gives rise to splits. The people in the ghettos, after all, were asking for more guns and less Marxist gobbledygook. These people, under the pressure of an immediate fear and need, did not consider whether the men who came with the guns might come with other ideas than mere defence, or whether these other ideas might prove more dangerous and destructive to the people 'defended', than ever the Marxist gobbledygook could possibly have been, or the Protestant backlash was, in the presence of the British troops.

The formidable thing about the new IRA—the Provisionals —was its simple relevance to the situation. Any ordinary, patriotic Catholic, clinging to the dual pieties of his community, could identify with the Provisionals. There was no 'taint of Communism' about them, nothing puzzling or foreign at all. And there was no nonsense about them either. They were not forever telling people that the Protestant workers were really on the same side as ourselves, when anyone could see—especially in and after August 1969—that these same Protestant workers were out to kill us. The Provisionals weren't telling people to turn the other cheek if a misguided Protestant brother had a bash at them. There had been enough of that. If the Protestants wanted trouble now, they could have it. These Provisionals weren't like the old crowd—they were getting the guns and they were ready to use them.

They were indeed. But not just for the defence of the ghettos, which of course is what they emphasized in the beginning. Their real objective was the reconquest of Ireland. Here again their strength was in the simplicity of their idea. This was no complicated, fantastic scenario like the old Official one: Socialist revolutions, North and South, uniting Protestant and Catholic workers and all that nonsense. No: this was a straightforward thing—the idea was to complete the work of 1916–21, by driving the British out of the last corner of Ireland which they held. What about the Protestants? Well, what about them? Some Protestants were on our side, good Irishmen. Very, very few of them. Right. What about the rest? Well, if the rest of them felt they were British, let them. As long as they stuck to that, they could get what was coming to the rest of the British in Ireland. 1798 was over, and it was no use going on about it all the time.

We had nothing against Protestants *as* Protestants.

As the people they actually were, we had quite a lot against them.

Here again the Provisional conception was clear and laudable, in terms of certain traditions and ideals of the Catholic community. However, the idea of the reconquest—as distinct from that of the briskly conducted defence—was not only clear and 'laudable': it was also terrifying to anyone, especially any Catholic in Belfast, who thought clearly about the idea's implications. What kind of war would it be, in character and duration, which would compel, not merely the British, but the majority in the area directly concerned, to capitulate? And what would be the condition of the Catholic ghettos, the pivots of the guerrilla war, by the time the war was won?

The Provisional had no interest in raising such questions. And as Provisional strength in various ghettos increased—mainly through the appeal of their defensive capability—it became apparent that questions which the Provisionals had no interest in raising would not be likely to be raised in areas where the Provisionals were strong. To ask defeatist questions was 'anti-national'. And it was unhealthy to be anti-national in Ardoyne or Ballymurphy, and to a lesser extent in wider areas.

It was not through intimidation that the Provisionals established themselves in the ghettos, or rather it was through a reaction against *Protestant* (including police) intimidation that this happened. But once Provisionals had established themselves, intimidation or—in Provisional terms—a kind of underground martial law—became a fact. The partial breakdown, after August, of the old kind of policing—essentially the policing of Catholics by Protestants—meant that what 'law and order' was available inside the ghettos was to a considerable extent dispensed by the IRA. In these circumstances, very few people, in the areas so controlled, could be expected to speak out against those who controlled them. (A few people did, none the less.) No opinion poll is possible in such circumstances. My own guess is that a majority of Catholics welcomed the IRA, as *defenders*, in the aftermath of August, and that a majority of Catholics came to dislike the IRA's offensive campaign and dread its consequences.

DOCUMENT 38. EXTRACTS FROM *How Stormont Fell*, BY HENRY KELLY (GILL & MACMILLAN, DUBLIN, 1972)

On Tuesday 16 March [1971, Chichester-Clark] flew to London for a surprise visit to 10 Downing Street. There he had talks with Mr Maudling, with the Prime Minister, Mr Heath, and with the British Defence Secretary, Lord Carrington. He asked for more troops, not for repressive measures against Catholics, not to save his own political skin about which he cared very little, but because he could see no other way to end no-go areas. His view was that there would have to be quick military response to violence, a return to, at first, Army patrolling and eventually to joint Army–RUC patrols.

Some day, he hoped, the RUC would then be able to go it alone in Catholic areas. He told the English ministers that if they would not agree to these suggestions he would resign. They didn't believe him . . . .

On Friday afternoon there was a Cabinet meeting at Stormont Castle at which every member of the Cabinet impressed upon Chichester-Clark the need to stay in office. There was no-one, his colleagues promised him, who could take over with any confidence. Brian Faulkner, who had stood by the Prime Minister for the previous 18 months, was not particularly verbose on this aspect of the situation but he did basically seem to want Chichester-Clark to stay at this stage. He still retained the view, of course, that if he were Prime Minister himself there would be no problems at all. Late on Friday it was announced that Carrington and some officials would fly into Belfast the next day for more talks. On the Saturday morning a silent Carrington flew in, met the Cabinet, talked and listened and left equally taciturn. The Prime Minister resigned later that night. His resignation statement was careful and summed up the ideas behind his weeks and months of coaxing and arguing with the British. He pointed to the recurring anomaly between power and responsibility brought about by the relationship between Westminster and Stormont. The statement was in effect, though Chichester-Clark cannot have intended it to be so, a confession from a Unionist Prime Minister that Unionism had failed and that there was only one course open to the British: direct rule . . . .

The British Labour Government in August 1969 did not really carry through the logic of its own policy: if the Government of Ireland Act allowed the British government control over the armed forces and if the use of those forces came to be the only thing of political import in Northern Ireland then the situation could be changed in one of two ways.

Either, unthinkably, the British could give the Unionists a free hand in controlling the Army, or they could take away security powers completely. As the Army became more and more embroiled in Northern Ireland, as soldiers began to die and the civilian casualty list mounted alongside the rate of explosions and 'general incidents' this second—indeed only—choice would emerge clearly. It was there in 1969 but it was recognised by only a few. Certainly there was a tenable point of view to balance it: to have taken over in 1969 might have made things worse. It is easy to say now that this couldn't possibly have been the case, but those were emotionally-charged days and instant cures rather than long-term solutions were the order of the moment. But when the British troops walked into Belfast and Derry in 1969 it was a tragedy and an expensive one that a Secretary of State didn't walk in after them. The Unionist mind is for ever returning to those days and speaking of how the Prime Minister gave away Stormont's powers and sold out their security forces. The truth of the matter is that it was not the famous Downing Street meeting which brought about the involvement of the British Army on a wide scale but the involvement of the British Army which brought about the meeting . . . . If politicians, commentators, ordinary people are honest, they will admit that the introduction of troops was vitally necessary at that point if a full-scale civil and religious war was not to erupt. Once the Army was in, then, the questions raised by the outgoing Chichester-Clark became the vital ones but they were not tackled until the situation had gone out of control. The Thursday before he resigned, Chichester-Clark had used some prophetic words in the Commons at Stormont. He accepted that there had been much speculation about his continuing in office. 'There has been a good deal of speculation in recent days', he told MPs, 'about changes in personalities. However personalities may change, these facts of which I have spoken will not change. Anyone who comes to this Dispatch Box will have to face them just as I have done. And I ask the House to remember too that we do no service to Northern Ireland if we snuff out the present campaign in ways which merely make a resumption at some other time and with increased popular support, inevitable. Our aim is not just to defeat the present vicious conspiracy but to create conditions in which such men and such activities can never prosper again.' By 'snuff out' he meant internment.

(iii)

In his pamphlet *The Northern Ireland Problem* (United Nations Association, 1972) Professor Harry Calvert wrote:

The 1920 Act established provincial institutions of government in Northern Ireland on the British pattern. The constitutional scheme provided for the vesting of power, in these institutions, in the majority party on the English model. Because of continuing insecurity on the constitutional question and pure sectarianism, parties have continued to split on sectarian lines. The majority has always been the Unionist Protestant party linked with the Orange Order and to some extent a closed association. It, therefore, has always wielded power in these institutions of government; i.e. it has had a majority of members in the House of the Northern Ireland parliament, it has formed the government of Northern Ireland, in which all power is vested. Looking at the obverse side what this means is that, politically, the Roman Catholic in Northern Ireland counts for virtually nothing. It matters not how able he is, how dedicated he is, even how loyal he is. The government does not need the support of Catholic members of parliament. Unionist members of parliament normally do not need Roman Catholic votes. The Roman Catholic community has literally nothing to bargain with politically. And, politically, he who cannot bargain gets a very poor deal.

It was not until mid-1971 that the implications of this situation came to be fully realized. By then most of the reforms which had been promised in the Downing Street Declaration and in the subsequent communiqué of 29 August 1969 had reached the statute book: the 'B' Specials had been disbanded and the RUC placed under the control of a Police Authority; commissioners for the investigation of citizens' grievances had been appointed; a statutory body was given responsibility for the building and allocation of houses, and a fundamental reorganization of local government was taking place. In any circumstances it would take years for legislation of this sort to show practical results; but the Catholics were not prepared to wait, even if they had trusted the Unionist government, which they did not. What they feared was some paper arrangement, which would satisfy Westminster and deceive the outside world but which would leave them no better off. They were especially critical of the failure to deal with discrimination in employment or to secure a better balance in the higher ranks of the civil service, and among the local government officers. Apart from that, the reforms had enhanced the powers of central government, and the majority of Catholics on the new statutory boards would sit as nominees of the Stormont Government rather than as representatives chosen by their own communities. Consequently Catholics stepped up their demands to a level which would involve changing the system. The Home Secretary, Reginald Maudling, understood the strength of their argument. 'The normal process of the elective democracy worked well in Britain', he said, 'so long as the party in power could be defeated in an election and the party in opposition had a reasonable chance to become the government, . . . but one must recognise that there are different circumstances in a country where the majority does not change.' And he added: 'It is reasonable and desirable to see how it is possible to broaden the basis of government in Northern Ireland and certainly to avoid a situation where a man of talent who can serve his country is debarred from doing so solely by religious beliefs.'

Mr Brian Faulkner went some distance towards meeting Catholic demands for a share in policy-making when, on 22 June 1971, he proposed to establish three new parliamentary committees to deal with social services, industrial development and environmental matters. At least two of the committees would have Opposition MPs as salaried chairmen. He said: 'Short of asking the Opposition to run the country, this is the best means of participation for them.' The six civil-rights MPs who had come together in 1970, under Gerry Fitt and John Hume, to form the Social Democratic and Labour Party (SDLP), at first responded favourably to Faulkner's proposal. But the shooting of two Catholics by the Army, in Derry, early in July and the resentment caused by the British Government's refusal to hold an independent public inquiry, destroyed any hope that Faulkner's proposal might have had. In response to strong public pressure the six SDLP MPs withdrew from Stormont, announcing that they would establish an alternative assembly. At a press conference in Belfast on 16 July 1971 they issued a party statement criticizing the Conservative Government's handling of Northern Ireland's affairs over the previous twelve months and expressing the opinion that there could be no hope for peace in the province until the system of one-party rule established in 1920 had been brought to an end (Document 39).

DOCUMENT 39. EXTRACTS FROM A STATEMENT ISSUED BY THE SOCIAL DEMOCRATIC AND LABOUR PARTY, 16 JULY 1971

The Parliamentary party of the SDLP issued a statement earlier this week in which it demanded an impartial inquiry into the deaths of two young men in Derry resulting from British Army action and in which we made it clear that in the event of failure by the authorities to agree to our demand we would take a certain course of action. Our demand has not been met and we have therefore no alternative but to pursue the course of action that we have already outlined in our earlier statement . . . . We have now been driven to the point when we have been faced with a clear choice: either to continue to give credibility to the system which in itself is basically unstable and from which derives the unrest that is destroying our community, or take a stand in order to bring home to those in authority the need for strong political action to solve our problems and to prevent any further tragic loss of life which derives from the instability of our political institutions. The deaths in Derry were a final but important straw. If as responsible public representatives we were unable to obtain action on an issue such as this—an issue which has outraged our constituents—what role is there for us in the present parliamentary system? If British troops had shot unarmed civilians dead in a riot situation in the streets of Birmingham what would have been the reaction of the British public? Would there have been an inquiry? Human life has been seriously devalued by violent elements in our society. We find it intolerable that it should be devalued by those charged with the responsibility of solving our problems. By doing so they play straight into the hands of those same violent elements. The actions of both the British Government and their Army in the Northern Ireland situation on this issue tend to confirm our increasing suspicions about the role of the Army completely in the present situation. These suspicions date from the arrival in power of the present [i.e. Conservative] administration.

These suspicions are instanced by the military action in the curfew of the lower Falls a few short weeks after they came to power; instanced by the proposals for a full-time battalion or battalions of the UDR; instanced by the unquestioning acceptance of the truth of Army public statements; instanced by the admitted policy of virtual internment by using the normal legal process, and instanced by the obviously decreasing political control of the military under the new British administration. Then we had the 'shoot to kill on suspicion' policy announced by Mr Faulkner, a policy now confirmed despite the subsequent denials that there had been any change. Then we have the obvious and increasing lack of consultation between the British Government and the Opposition leaders in marked and stark contrast to the previous administration, which, without prejudice to either side, sought our view, continually. The attitude of the present administration in Whitehall on this matter is either due to deliberate policy or to sheer carelessness, either of which is unpardonable in the serious situation in which we find ourselves.

Is it any wonder that we feel that the role of the military has changed from being that of impartial keepers of the peace to that of shoring up and supporting a particular individual in the office of Prime Minister? Has the British Government even yet faced the logic of its presence in Northern Ireland? Public memories are short but the memories of those who suffer are not. We would recall the circumstances of the intervention in August 1969 when the Army came to the streets to impose law and order and a reform programme was forced on Stormont.

What did that intervention mean other than that the Northern Ireland system itself had failed to produce the basis for peace, justice and stability? Now, two years later, having refused to face the logic of the situation, the British Government, without the slightest constitutional guarantee, asks us to believe that the chief architects of our injustice-ridden society—the Unionist party—are the people who can govern us towards a solution within the same system . . . .

All these have led us to the point of questioning the sincerity and determination of the British Government to solve the problem . . . . In so far as we can detect any definite policy it would appear to be the maintenance of Stormont in its present form carrying out minimum civil rights reforms and involving the Opposition only to a point when the Unionist right-wing would not be alienated. In other words, British policy is still governed as it always has been, except for a few short months in 1969, by the threat of a right-wing backlash. There can be no solution till the right-wing is confronted. The present policy, such as it is, has never had any chance of success, and has now been totally shattered by our decision to withdraw from the present parliamentary system and set up an alternative assembly. By so doing we will bring home to the world the reality of the Northern Ireland situation, which is that Stormont is, and always has been, the voice of Unionism. The assembly which we propose will be the voice of non-Unionists. There can be no solution which does not take account of both, and it would be our hope for this community that such account is taken sooner rather than later.

*

From Mr Faulkner's installation as Prime Minister in March 1971, the Provisional IRA had intensified its bombing of public buildings and business premises, culminating in the destruction of the huge new *Daily Mirror* printing works just outside Belfast on 17 July. Four days earlier the tenth British soldier had been killed. Mr Faulkner had used internment during previous IRA campaigns, and, as violence increased, he asked the British Government to approve of its use again. At first the Government hesitated, but because it could think of no other way of dealing with the IRA, it finally gave approval. Before dawn on 9 August the Army and the RUC swooped on the poor streets of Belfast, Derry, Newry, Strabane and other Catholic areas, and by that evening nearly 400 people had been detained. The intensity and scale of the Catholic reaction to internment took the British Government, the British Army and the British public by surprise. Vehicles were hijacked, factories and houses were burnt down and Belfast echoed with explosions and machine-gun fire. By 11 August twenty-three people were dead (one of them a priest shot while administering the last rites) and hundreds of families fled from one part of the city to another in a desperate search for safety and peace (Documents 40–2). Charges of brutality in the interrogation of detainees caused so much public disquiet that the Home Secretary was forced to set up a committee of inquiry, under Sir Edmund Compton. Their report found most of the allegations proved, but chose to regard them as 'ill-treatment' rather than 'physical brutality'. Such semantic quibbling infuriated Catholics and did little to win their support for the Army in its struggle with the IRA (Document 43).

The Protestants were infuriated as well. They saw the centre of towns and cities turned into battlefields, while the 'no-go' areas of Belfast and Derry provided safe havens for the snipers and bombers. Concessions to Catholics appeared only to increase their demands, and many feared that the British Government might ultimately betray what they described as their 'Protestant heritage'. In the early months of 1972 the right-wing Unionist, William Craig, harnessed this Protestant resentment in the Ulster Vanguard: an umbrella movement comprising the Orange Order (at least in Belfast), the Apprentice Boys, the Ulster Special Constabulary Association and the Loyalist Association of Workers. At Vanguard demonstrations a para-military uniformed force (later to become the UDA) paraded, and Craig told his audience: 'We are determined to preserve our British traditions and way of life. God help those who get in our way.' Violence and sectarian murders of the most bestial kind occurred daily, and the Stormont Government, fearful now of a threatened Protestant 'backlash', could exercise little influence or control. Even before the shock of 'Bloody Sunday' (30 January 1972), when thirteen Catholics were shot by paratroopers firing on a demonstration in Derry, the British Government must have realized that exceptional measures were called for, if there was to be any prospect of ending the spiral of violence. After some hesitation, Brian Faulkner was summoned to London to be told that the United Kingdom Government wished control of security in the province to be in Westminster's hands. The Unionist Cabinet objected to the transfer and threatened to resign if that were done. The Prime Minister, Edward Heath, refused to be intimidated, and on 24 March 1972 announced that all legislative and executive powers exercised by Stormont would be transferred to the United Kingdom Government which would be represented in Northern Ireland by a Secretary of State. This was an extremely courageous decision: it was an admission that the constitutional settlement of 1920 had failed, and committed the British Government to devising a new one 'ensuring for the minority as well as the majority community an active, permanent and guaranteed role in the life and public affairs of the Province' (Document 44).

DOCUMENT 40. EXTRACTS FROM *Ulster*, BY THE *Sunday Times* 'INSIGHT' TEAM (PENGUIN BOOKS, 1972)

(a) The Army had supposed that internment—despite it being a 'distasteful weapon', as Tuzo [General Harry Tuzo, then GOC Northern Ireland] publicly called it—could at any rate be made to work. Senior soldiers had foreseen that it would provoke a surge of violence and a further estrangement of the Catholic community from the governing authorities; but they had expected that the surge could be contained and would soon fall back.

They were appalled by the intensity of the Catholic reaction. They had foreseen rioting, but not warfare. The bald arithmetic tells the story. In the four months before internment—April to July 1971—four soldiers were killed, no policemen and four civilians. In the four months after it—August to November—thirty soldiers were killed, eleven members of the RUC and the Ulster Defence Regiment, and seventy-three civilians. Stormont stolidly maintained that without internment things would have been worse. It could only be a matter of assertion.

Still more serious for the survival of Northern Ireland as a governable state was the depth and permanence of the Catholic community's estrangement from the regime. By mid-December, 1,576 people had been arrested by the Army under the Special Powers Act. That meant almost the same number of households—virtually all of them Catholic—which had experienced the actual shock of the arrest, often in the early hours of the morning and often without much personal tenderness displayed: households which were thereafter without the member who was in many cases their main source of livelihood, and which had no idea how long the deprivation would last.

The fact that of those 1,576 no fewer than 934 had (by mid-

December 1971) already been released did little to ease this rising mass of resentment. To the families and friends of the released men, it only indicated a chilling carelessness about the way the lists had been drawn up; and the released men themselves seldom came back as tolerant of the régime as they had gone in.

(b) By the end of 1971 the signs of Catholic alienation from the régime were everywhere. Opposition MPs were not at Stormont. Most non-Unionist members of local councils and public bodies—even of the Derry Commission—had withdrawn from public work. An alternative assembly had met twice at Dungiven: it was not quite a parallel with the separatist beginnings of the Dail in 1919, but it was a deliberate sign from Catholic leaders that they saw no prospect of their community being governed from Stormont again. Over 20,000 Catholics, many of them members of the growing Catholic middle class, were taking part in a civil disobedience campaign: it mainly meant not paying rent and rates. The Stormont Government felt obliged to pass a Payments for Debt (Emergency Provisions) Act, which allowed sixteen different kinds of social security benefit to be withheld and set against the rent debt.

No appeal was possible. There was a certain justice in the measure, but families which had not saved the money they had withheld now found themselves grindingly poor. Again, the effect was widespread Catholic resentment.

Some shuffling of the cards seemed indispensable—some redistribution of power which would make non-Unionists feel that their lives were not wholly in the hands of the Unionists and provide them with governing authorities whom they could respect, or at least tolerate.

The Unionist answer was that it had been done: the redistribution of power had been contained in the reforms begun in 1968 and 1969, and now coming to completion.

DOCUMENT 41. EXTRACTS FROM THE LETTER OF A BELFAST GIRL, AGED 11, TO THE BBC PROGRAMME, 'YOUR OWN VOICES' (1971), PRINTED IN *Community Forum*, VOL. 3, NO. 1, 1973 (THE NORTHERN IRELAND COMMUNITY RELATIONS COMMISSION)

I lay awake all that night. I lay in horror, afraid and sobbing. I heard cries of fear and shots all around me. I thought of my friends out of the next street. Would any of them be killed? Would they be burned out? Everyone in our family was downstairs, except me and my younger sisters. The next morning it was quiet. Then a man came around crying out: 'Leave at once!' Some men tried to hold off the invaders. Others dumped women and children into cars and drove them as far away as they could. I was taken to someone's house—someone I didn't know, but I didn't care, as long as I was safe. Then I began to fret, because my mother and father and the rest of my family were somewhere else. Four days later I found out where the rest of my family were, and we went back to our street. It was quiet. Because no one else was there. It was black, ugly, and ghastly. It was burnt out shells of houses. Two days later we were moved to the house we have now.

Maybe we'll be safe.

DOCUMENT 42. EXTRACTS FROM *Children in Conflict*, BY MORRIS FRASER, SENIOR REGISTRAR IN PSYCHIATRY AT THE ROYAL BELFAST HOSPITAL FOR SICK CHILDREN (SECKER & WARBURG, 1973)

(a) With the establishment of Long Kesh internment camp and, as towards the end of 1971, total arrests reached several hundred, there was added to earlier stresses the fear that the father could be interned . . . . Consequently, few Catholic mothers have been able to watch the Army coming up their streets at night without at least a momentary pang of anxiety.

An Army swoop must, of course, be unexpected; it is often dramatic, and—at least for a child—always frightening. The mother's fear for her husband's safety is very quickly communicated. A ten-year-old patient said: 'They came up the street at five in the morning, breaking windows. They jumped on our stairs and broke them. I screamed and jumped under the bed. A man I know is interned. I feel sorry for his girl and boy, who are at school with me. When I heard about it yesterday I couldn't stop crying.

'They might take my dad; they would come in the middle of the night. I often can't sleep for thinking about it and have to go into his room and see if he's still there. He hasn't done anything wrong, but neither had the others.

'The last time they came in they took some men away and as they were leaving they shouted "We'll be back for the rest tomorrow".'

Soldierly banter, perhaps, but the result was intense separation-fear in this child, as it is in many others.

(b) Una, aged eight, was admitted to hospital towards the end of 1971, apparently unconscious. After being put to bed she woke up and began to shout incoherently about guns and bombs, and said that her father was going to be killed. She screamed, then lapsed into unconsciousness again. This pattern of waking, screaming, then becoming inaccessible continued for some hours. All physical investigations were negative; in due course she responded to sedation and was transferred to the child psychiatry unit.

She lives in a working-class Catholic district; her father has been active in an 'illegal organisation' for the past two years. Shortly after the outbreak of the disturbances, the father of one of her school friends was shot dead by the Army. From that time she began to have screaming or crying fits if she heard gunfire or explosions or, later, any loud noise.

On the night of admission her father had gone out. At about midnight there were several bursts of gunfire unusually near, then the house was shaken by an explosion. Una screamed 'Daddy!' then her limbs went rigid and she fell.

DOCUMENT 43. EXTRACTS FROM *Report of the enquiry into allegations against the security forces of physical brutality in Northern Ireland arising out of events on the 9th August, 1971*, THE COMPTON REPORT (LONDON, HMSO, CMND 4823)

Interrogation in Depth

The persons supervising the operation commented as follows:

Hooding

It was confirmed that the detainees were required to be kept fully hooded except when interrogated or in rooms by themselves. This meant, therefore, that hooding was confined to journeys outside the centre or movement within it and to the periods when complainants were held jointly or at the wall. We were told that in fact some complainants kept their hoods on when they could have removed them if they wished.

Noise

It was confirmed that while the detainees were held together pending interrogation or between interrogations, they were subjected to a continuous hissing noise, or electronic 'mush', loud enough to mask extraneous sounds and prevent effective oral communication between detainees. The noise was neutral, i.e. no music or speech sounds were intruded.

Posture on the Wall

It was confirmed that from time to time pending and between interrogations, the detainees were made to stand against a wall in a required posture (facing wall, legs apart, leaning with hands raised up against wall) for anything between 4 and 6 hours, except for periodical lowering of the arms to restore circulation . . . . It was confirmed that detainees attempting to rest or sleep by propping their heads against the wall were prevented from doing so. If a detainee collapsed on the floor, he was picked up by the armpits and placed against the wall to resume the approved posture . . . .

We find from our inspection of the records kept at the time of this operation that the men were at the wall for periods totalling as follows:-

Mr Auld 43½ hours
Mr Clarke 40 hours
Mr Donnelly 9 hours
Mr Hannaway 20 hours
Mr McClean 29 hours
Mr McGuigan 14 hours
Mr McKenna 30 hours
Mr McKer 15 hours
Mr McNally 13 hours
Mr Shivers 23 hours
Mr Turley 9 hours

We were told that the interrogatees were not made to stand at the wall in the required posture throughout. As stated above, the period of standing was 4–6 hours at a time. At other times they would have been sitting against the wall . . . .

Sleep

It was confirmed that it was the general policy to deprive the men of opportunity to sleep during the early days of the operation.

Food and Drill

The records we examined showed that bread and water was offered at 6 hourly intervals from 12.30 on the 11th August until the morning of the 15th August, when the diet began to be increased to normal rations . . . .

It will be noticed that while we are asked to investigate allegations of physical brutality, our conclusions are in terms of physical ill-treatment. Where we have concluded that physical ill-treatment took place, we are not making a finding of brutality on the part of those who handled these complainants. We consider that brutality is an inhuman or savage form of cruelty, and that cruelty implies a disposition to inflict suffering, coupled with indifference to, or pleasure in, the victim's pain. We do not think that happened here.

DOCUMENT 44. EXTRACTS FROM A SPEECH BY THE PRIME MINISTER, MR EDWARD HEATH, TO THE HOUSE OF COMMONS, 24 MARCH 1972

At a meeting which my right honourable friends the Home Secretary, the Lord President, the Defence Secretary and I had with the Prime Minister and the Deputy Prime Minister of Northern Ireland on 22 March, we made it plain that in the British Government's view new and more radical measures were necessary, if there was to be any prospect of breaking out of this deadlock.

We made three main proposals. First, in the hope of taking the Border out of the day-to-day political scene, and as a reassurance that there would be no change in the Border without the consent of a majority of the people of Northern Ireland, we proposed plebiscites on this issue.

Second, we proposed that a start be made on phasing out internment. Third, we were concerned about the present division of responsibility for law and order between Belfast and Westminster, whereby control remains largely with the Northern Ireland Government while the operational responsibility rests mainly with the British Army, and therefore with the United Kingdom Government. This responsibility is not merely domestic; it is a matter of international concern as well.

We were also well aware that the control of law and order was a divisive issue in Northern Ireland, and we thought that there would be advantage in seeking to take it out of domestic politics in Northern Ireland, at any rate for a time. We therefore told the Prime Minister and Deputy Prime Minister of Northern Ireland that we had reached the conclusion that responsibility for law and order in Northern Ireland should be transferred to Westminster.

The first two of our proposals were in principle acceptable to the Northern Ireland Government. But Mr Faulkner told us that his Government could not accept proposals for the transfer of responsibility for law and order from Stormont to Westminster. At a further meeting, yesterday evening, he confirmed, after having consulted his Cabinet, that this was its unanimous view, and that if any such proposals were implemented it would entail the resignation of the Northern Ireland Government.

The United Kingdom Government remain of the view that the transfer of this responsibility to Westminster is an indispensable condition for progress in finding a political solution in Northern Ireland. The Northern Ireland Government's decision, therefore, leaves them [i.e. the UK Government] with no alternative to assuming full and direct responsibility for the administration of Northern Ireland until a political solution to the problems of the Province can be worked out in consultation with all those concerned.

Parliament will, therefore, be invited to pass before Easter a Measure transferring all legislative and executive powers now vested in the Northern Ireland Parliament and Government to the United Kingdom Parliament and a United Kingdom Minister. This provision will expire after one year unless this

Parliament resolves otherwise. The Parliament of Northern Ireland would stand prorogued but would not be dissolved. The present Prime Minister of Northern Ireland has agreed to continue in office until this legislation is passed. The increased burden which this transfer of responsibilities will entail means that it will no longer be possible for my right honourable friend, the Home Secretary, to discharge these duties in addition to his many other responsibilities. A new office of Secretary of State for Northern Ireland is, therefore, being created. My right honourable friend, the Lord President, is to be appointed to this office together with the necessary junior Ministers. He will be empowered by the new legislation to appoint a Commission of persons resident in Northern Ireland to advise and assist him in the discharge of his duties. It will be our objective to invite to serve on this Commission a body of persons fully representative of opinion in Northern Ireland . . . .

A reduction of tension is the essential first step in the process of reconciliation. We believe that requires we should make a start in the process of bringing internment to an end. We intend within the next few weeks to set free, subject to safeguards where appropriate, those internees whose release is no longer thought likely to involve an unacceptable risk to security. The Secretary of State for Northern Ireland will establish a procedure to review each case personally. If the measures we have taken lead to a reduction in terrorist activity, it will be possible to consider further releases; but this must depend on a clearly established improvement in the security situation. Thus in the matter of internment, as in the next matter to which I shall refer, we are giving effect to our proposal which we put to the Northern Ireland Government and which in principle they accepted.

This Government, and their predecessors, have given solemn and repeated assurances that the position of Northern Ireland as a part of the United Kingdom will not be changed without the consent of the people of Northern Ireland. We have decided that it would be appropriate to arrange for the views of the people of Northern Ireland to be made known on this question, from time to time. We, therefore, propose in due course to invite Parliament to provide for a system of regular plebiscites in Northern Ireland about the Border, the first to be held as soon as practicable in the near future and others at intervals of a substantial period of years thereafter . . . .

We hope that this arrangement, while leaving open the possibility of a change in the status of the Province if the majority so wish, will both confirm that no such change will be made without their consent and provide, in the intervals between plebiscites, a greater measure of stability in the political life of Northern Ireland.

These are our immediate proposals. But they do not in themselves constitute a lasting solution for the problems of Northern Ireland. We remain determined to find a means of ensuring for the minority as well as the majority community an active, permanent and guaranteed role in the life and public affairs of the Province.

(iv)

If internment had outraged Catholics, the imposition of direct rule from Westminster left the majority of Protestants stunned and bewildered. That possibly explains why their reaction was not as violent as some had feared but was confined to a two-day general strike and an impressive loyalist demonstration at Stormont when Parliament met there for the last time. The Unionist Party, which had been put under intense strain by the events of the past three years, was thrown into confusion as groups within it began to reconsider their positions *vis-à-vis* Great Britain. William Craig, on behalf of Ulster Vanguard, demanded that the Northern Ireland Parliament be restored with full control over internal security; if this were not attainable, he favoured dominion status for the province, or in the last resort 'an independent British Ulster'. Vanguard had substantial working-class support and close links with the various para-military organizations and Tartan Gangs which proliferated at this time in the Protestant ghettos. The Democratic Unionist party, led by the Rev. Ian Paisley, pressed for total integration and a larger representation for the province at Westminster; but, as he found there was little support for his view that Northern Ireland should give up its Parliament, Paisley placed less emphasis on this aspect of his policy and more on the danger of 'a sell-out' to the Republic of Ireland.

What came to be known as 'official' Unionists (although Craig and his leading supporters remained within the party for some time after direct rule) stood by the proposals which Brian Faulkner had put to the British Government a few days before prorogation: parliamentary committees, replacement of the Special Powers Act by new emergency legislation under Westminster's control, a Bill of Rights and an Irish inter-governmental council to discuss matters of common concern to north and south. A number of Unionists, however, welcomed direct rule as providing the opportunity for a fresh start. Some transferred to the non-sectarian Alliance Party; others, while remaining Unionists, co-operated with the new administration and served on the Secretary of State's Advisory Commission.

The strategy behind 'the Heath initiatives' was to induce the alienated Catholic minority to participate in the working of the institutions of Northern Ireland, to scale down and eventually to end internment, and then, with the restoration of peace, to persuade the leaders of the Protestant and Catholic com-munities to agree on a new constitutional settlement, which would give each a fair share in the government and public life of the province. Under the Northern Ireland (Temporary Provisions) Act 1972, William Whitelaw, as Secretary of State, took over the administration and during his first six weeks in office over 200 internees were released. The response of the SDLP was generally favourable, but they did make it clear that until internment was ended they could not give the whole-hearted co-operation they wished. On the other hand, the decision of the Provisional IRA to continue their campaign of violence, and the increasing numbers of security forces killed by them during the early weeks of direct rule, made the conciliatory role envisaged for Mr Whitelaw very difficult. To add to his worries, Protestant extremists were infuriated by what they called 'the softly, softly approach' of the Army in Catholic areas, and Craig announced that those he represented would make the British Government's constitutional proposals unworkable. In London he told the Monday Club: 'We will go to any lengths, even to the use of force . . . and when we say force, we mean force.' The Ulster Defence Association and the Ulster Special Constabulary Association attempted to show that this was no empty threat. For five successive week-ends they brought the traffic of Belfast to a halt as they closed off streets with barricades made of hijacked buses and lorries, and on 27 May displayed their strength when 10,000 of them marched through the city in military formation.

The security situation never improved sufficiently, during the early months of 1972, for the constructive political discussions envisaged by the British Government to take place. The Unionists were sullen and unco-operative, and put all the blame for the deteriorating situation on the Whitelaw administration. The SDLP, afraid of being outflanked by more belligerently nationalist groups, were no more forthcoming, except to suggest that overtures might be made to the IRA for a cease-fire before it was too late. A fortnight before Stormont was prorogued Harold Wilson had met some Provisional IRA leaders in Dublin when they presented him with their peace terms:

1 An immediate withdrawal of British armed forces from the streets of Northern Ireland, coupled with a statement of intent on the eventual evacuation of HM forces and an acknowledgement of the right of the Irish people to determine their own future without interference from the British Government.

2 The abolition of the Stormont Parliament.

3 A total amnesty for all political prisoners in Ireland and England, both tried and untried, and for all those on the wanted list.

As Document 45 shows, the demands of both wings of the IRA were completely unrealistic and took no account at all of Protestant feelings. Nevertheless the United Kingdom Government, prompted by the SDLP, decided to negotiate with them and, as a result of an approach made by intermediaries, the IRA declared a cease-fire in Northern Ireland from midnight of 26 June 1972. On 7 July Provisional leaders, among them Sean Mac Stiofáin, Daithi O Conaill and Seamus Twoomey, met Mr Whitelaw and his staff in London (an RAF plane having been provided to fly them from Derry). The 'Provisionals' were unwilling to compromise, but the negotiations were cut short by the renewal of hostilities on 9 July. The pretext was a dispute over the allocation of houses in the

Lenadoon district of Belfast. Why did the IRA not stop when they were in a favourable position? John Whale of the *Sunday Times* has written: 'For any guerilla organisation, the greatest difficulty is to perceive when to exchange future prospects for immediate though lesser achievements.' By breaking the cease-fire and perpetrating atrocities such as that of 'Bloody Friday', 21 July, when twenty-two bombs exploded in Belfast, killing eleven people (two of them soldiers), the IRA made it impossible for the United Kingdom Government ever to negotiate with them again or to give them any say in determining Northern Ireland's future.

In the weeks after the renewal of hostilities Northern Ireland appeared to be on the verge of civil war. Between 9 and 16 July twenty-one civilians, eleven soldiers and one policeman met violent deaths, and 7,000 refugees sought shelter in the Republic of Ireland. People leaving their homes as a result of intimidation became a major social problem. In Belfast, Catholic districts like Andersontown, Ardoyne, Oldpark and Twinbrook, already overcrowded, began to encroach on Protestant areas which bordered them, thus starting off a new wave of communal riots, intimidation and sectarian murders. Probably at no time since the seventeenth century were the two Northern Ireland communities so hostile to one another as in the summer of 1972.

DOCUMENT 45. EXTRACTS FROM STATEMENTS MADE EARLY IN 1972 BY (a) SEAN MAC STIOFÁIN, CHIEF OF STAFF, PROVISIONAL IRA, AND (b) CATHAL GOULDING, CHIEF OF STAFF, OFFICIAL IRA, QUOTED IN *On Our Knees*, BY ROSITA SWEETMAN (PAN BOOKS, 1972)

(a) People say our campaign in Northern Ireland is sectarian. I deny that. It would have to be specifically anti-Protestant, but as many Catholic members of the UDR and the RUC have been shot as Protestants. They're shot because they're active agents of British Imperialism. They can resign and they'll be perfectly safe. The only Protestants we've deliberately killed have been members of the UVF who attacked Roman Catholic areas. In June 1970 eleven members of the UVF were killed, and we also killed some in internment week. This had to be done, otherwise more Catholics would have been killed, more houses burnt out. Targets like the EBNI [Electricity Board of Northern Ireland] are legitimate targets in a campaign such as ours. If the warning given had been acted on immediately there would have been no casualties. In the end all loss of life in Northern Ireland rests with the Unionists, and with the British Government. They've brought the present situation about. We've given our terms for a truce.

Our truce terms are: (1) That the British Army suspend all operations, withdraw from Catholic areas, pending their total withdrawal from the North. (2) That Stormont be abolished. (3) That a guarantee is given for the holding of free elections. (4) That all internees and political prisoners be released, North and South. (5) That compensation be paid to all those who've suffered as a result of British occupation.

People say, if the British Army is withdrawn from the North there'll be a Protestant backlash. We've been blackmailed with this threat for years. If it comes then we'll have to deal with it, but the best defence against it is a strong IRA . . . . What I think you would see if there was a declaration of intent to withdraw by the British, would be an exodus of the more bigoted elements in the North. I can't see any place for Craig and his type in a United Ireland. There would be no place for those who say they want their British heritage. They've got to accept their Irish heritage, and the Irish way of life, no matter who they are, otherwise there would be no place for them . . . . I think in the event of a British withdrawal you would see people like Paisley and Boal joining Dail Uladh, and we would be quite happy with that. We say, first, you must get the British out, then it's up to us to ensure that we get a Socialist Republic, not a 'gombeen' Republic.

(b) What we want is a democratization of the system in Northern Ireland—more democracy not less. We want representatives of the people to be the civil rights workers and people like Paisley and Boal. This means that the old political power blocs will be broken down. They are breaking down already. With civil rights guaranteed by some Bill of Rights the present regime couldn't continue, you can't have a dictatorship administering a democracy. Our aim is to develop the political and passive resistance of the people to the point where the administration just can't administrate any more.

I'm a physical force revolutionary. I'm not naive enough to think that we don't have to use guns. An armed proletariat is the only assurance that they can have the rule of the proletariat . . . .

The main function of the Official IRA in the North at the moment is to see that there is mass involvement. That the street committees and all kinds of civil resistance committees become kind of People's Soviets, actually administering the areas. We would like to see the local IRA units putting themselves at the disposal of these committees for the defence of the areas, to be the armed cadre of the people. In the case of the IRA administering law and order I don't think this should be done. I think the people should administer their own law and order and, if they want the IRA's help, they could call on them. In the end we won't have to go out and attack the British Army, but the British Army will have to come in and attack the people in these areas who are opposing the Establishment . . . .

The basic difference between us and the Provos is that they believe by uniting the Catholics North and South they can have a United Ireland, we say you can't. The middle class Catholics in the North are just as worried about retaining their stranglehold over the people as the middle-class Protestants are. They'd all love some kind of settlement so they can get back to the business of making money . . . .

I think some form of peace should be established. I don't mean the peace that will allow the establishment to continue its exploitation of the people, or the peace that will allow them to hunt down men on the run, but peace on *our* terms. These are: (1) an end to all repressive laws, such as the Special Powers Act. (2) The unconditional release of all internees, an amnesty for men on the run and release of political prisoners. (3) The withdrawal of the British Army to their barracks, pending their complete withdrawal from Northern Ireland. (4) A declaration of intent from the British Government that we in the Republican Movement will have the freedom to operate openly like any other political organization.

*

The people of Northern Ireland—both Catholic and Protestant —were shocked by the massacre of 'Bloody Friday', and the Government took advantage of the public mood. On 31 July the 'no-go' areas of both communities were simultaneously occupied by the Army, and a Special Task Force of RUC and military policemen was formed to deal with the sectarian murder squads that were operating from Shankill and East Belfast. In the latter area the arrest of a UDA leader provoked an attack on the Army, which fired back and killed two Protestants. The UDA was furious and one of its leaders, Tommy Herron, declared: 'The British Army and the British Government are now our enemies.' For some weeks the military feared simultaneous attacks from Protestant and Catholic guerrillas, and the Provisionals tried hard to make a link with UDA. Sectarianism was too strong for that.

In the political field the Secretary of State summoned an all-party conference at Darlington, on 25 September, to consider a form of government for Northern Ireland when direct rule came to an end. Only three parties came (the Unionist, Alliance and NILP) and to that extent the conference might be considered a failure. But other parties, including the SDLP, used the occasion to set out in detail their constitutional proposals (Document 46), and the British Government published these as annexes to its Green Paper, *The Future of Northern Ireland*. The Green Paper set out basic facts to be taken into account in a settlement and listed criteria that would have to be met. While repeating the guarantee that the status of Northern Ireland as an integral part of the United Kingdom would not be changed without the consent of the majority, the Government recognized that the problem had also an 'Irish Dimension' because the province was part of the island of Ireland (Document 47).

Exceptional measures were taken by the United Kingdom Government to ensure that the Green Paper was read by as many people as possible and summaries of its contents were distributed as supplements to the local newspapers. On the whole, the Green Paper was well received, although politicians tended to emphasize those parts of it which appeared to support their own points of view. Mr Whitelaw discussed the wide range of options listed in the paper with political parties, churchmen and community leaders, and gradually areas of agreement began to emerge. Almost all the parties agreed that Northern Ireland should have a single-chamber elected legislative assembly much larger than the old Stormont; that the Assembly should have a committee system (although there was disagreement on what the committees' powers should be); that there should be protection of fundamental human rights and freedoms; that there should be more co-operation between the two parts of Ireland, and some believed that there should be a permanent institution to facilitate this.

DOCUMENT 46. PROPOSALS BY POLITICAL PARTIES IN NORTHERN IRELAND FROM *The Future of Northern Ireland. A Paper for Discussion* (LONDON, HMSO, 1972)

Proposals of the Ulster Unionist Party (32 Members in the Northern Ireland House of Commons before prorogation. Leader, Mr Brian Faulkner)

(i) A unicameral Northern Ireland Parliament of 100 Members, elected by simple majority vote; five Parliamentary Committees, each covering the activities of a department, plus a Public Accounts Committee. Membership of Committees to reflect the strength of parties in Parliament and at least three to be chaired by Opposition Members.

(ii) An Executive to consist of a Cabinet comprising a Prime Minister and five or six Ministers each heading a department.

(iii) The Royal Ulster Constabulary and its Reserve to continue to be answerable to the Northern Ireland authorities, and to be responsible for intelligence gathering and the control of subversive activities (as far as possible) as well as for ordinary civil policing.

(iv) The Special Powers Act to be replaced by alternative emergency legislation, excluding the power to intern, with its operation dependent upon the declaration by the Northern Ireland Parliament of a state of emergency, and renewable for six months at a time by resolution of that Parliament. A system of Special Courts to deal with cases involving either widespread sectarian violence or widespread terrorist activity.

(v) A precise and comprehensive Bill of Rights, to equalise and safeguard citizens' rights, with provision for judicial review and enforcement.

(vi) A tripartite Declaration, analogous to the Agreement of 1925, by the Governments in London, Dublin and Belfast affirming the right of the people of Northern Ireland to self-determination. Inter-governmental discussion about co-operation in ending terrorism in Ireland, and review of extradition arrangements or declaration of a Common Law Enforcement Area in Ireland. If such action is taken, the formation of an Irish Intergovernmental Council, with equal membership from the Northern Ireland Government and the Government of the Republic of Ireland, to discuss matters of mutual interest, particularly in the economic and social fields.

Proposals of the Alliance Party (Three Members in the Northern Ireland House of Commons before prorogation. Leader, Mr Phelim O'Neill)

(i) A unicameral Northern Ireland Assembly elected by the Single Transferable Vote (STV) system of proportional representation at maximum intervals of four years, and divided into Committees according to the main functions. Chairman of Committees to be elected by the Assembly by proportional representation.

(ii) The Assembly itself to oversee executive functions through its Committees with management functions exercised by a Committee consisting of the chairman of the Assembly and the chairmen of its Committees.

(iii) The Royal Ulster Constabulary to be concerned only with serious crime and any police functions affecting security, and to be under Westminster control. An ordinary Police Force, to deal with parking, traffic control and offences, vandalism and minor crime, to be under the control of the Northern Ireland Assembly.

(iv) The Special Powers Act to be phased out as soon as possible, and the new Assembly to have no powers to enact any similar legislation. All security legislation (as also all legislative powers in relation to electoral matters) to be a Westminster responsibility.

(v) A Bill of Rights, guaranteeing to all citizens their fundamental human rights, and based on the Universal Declaration of Human Rights.

(vi) The Irish Republic not to be represented at talks on the political future of Northern Ireland but should accept a fair settlement. Extradition arrangements to be re-negotiated, to provide for extradition of persons charged with crimes of violence of a political nature. The formation of an advisory Anglo-Irish Council with representatives from Westminster, the Dail and the new Northern Ireland Assembly.

Proposals of the Northern Ireland Labour Party. (One Member in the Northern Ireland House of Commons before prorogation, Mr F. V. Simpson)

(i) A unicameral Northern Ireland Assembly of 100 Members, elected by proportional representation at maximum intervals of four years, with dissolution also possible by simple majority vote. A system of Departmental Committees of the Assembly elected on a proportionate basis.

(ii) Each Departmental Committee to constitute the legal entity formerly constituted by a departmental Minister.

(iii) Westminster to be responsible for the courts and judiciary, legislation on and licensing of firearms, emergency powers (which should accord with international obligations and conventions) and the power to raise, disband, arm, or control the criteria for recruiting of, any police force. The Northern Ireland Assembly, however, to retain management powers in relation to the police, including power to increase its strength and review the exercise of its functions.

(iv) Anything in the nature of Special Powers legislation to be a Westminster matter, but full account to be taken of the existence of a serious emergency in Northern Ireland.

(v) A Bill of Rights to give statutory expression to the Downing Street Declaration of August 1969 and acknowledge the Westminster Parliament's role as guarantor of civil, religious and political liberty in Northern Ireland. The position in Northern Ireland on such matters as the death penalty, race relations, homosexual practices, termination of pregnancy and divorce to be brought into line with that in the rest of the United Kingdom; all future legislation in the field of civil (and individual citizens') rights enacted at Westminster to be applied to Northern Ireland unless the Westminster Parliament determines otherwise; and the Westminster Parliament to reserve expressly the right to annul any provision made by the Northern Ireland Assembly which it resolves to affect adversely citizens' rights.

(vi) A consultative and deliberative Council of Ireland to be established.

Proposals of the Social Democratic and Labour Party (Six Members in the Northern Ireland House of Commons before prorogation. Leader, Mr Gerard Fitt)

(i) An immediate declaration by the United Kingdom that it would be in the best interest of all sections of the communities in both islands (i.e. Great Britain and Ireland) if Ireland were to become united on terms which would be acceptable to all the people of Ireland, and that the United Kingdom will positively encourage such a development.

(ii) Pending the achievement of unity, the establishment of an interim system of government for Northern Ireland under the joint sovereignty of the United Kingdom and the Irish Republic, who would reserve to themselves all powers relating to foreign affairs, defence, security, police and financial subventions and would be represented in Northern Ireland by Commissioners who would sign all legislation of a Northern Ireland Assembly or, if one or both considered it necessary, refer it for determination by a joint Constitutional Court.

(iii) The Assembly to consist of 84 Members elected by the STV system of proportional representation, with power to legislate in all fields including taxation, except those matters reserved to the joint sovereign powers.

(iv) An executive of 15 Members to be elected from the Assembly by proportional representation and to hold office through the duration of an Assembly except in the case of a 75 per cent adverse vote. A chief executive, elected by the executive, to allocate departmental responsibilities subject to the approval of both Commissioners.

(v) No representation for Northern Ireland in either the Westminster or the Dublin Parliament.

(vi) All powers of security to be under the direct control of a department headed by both Commissioners.

(vii) Creation of a new national Senate for the whole of Ireland, with equal representation from the Dublin Parliament and the Northern Ireland Assembly, the Parties from each being represented according to their strength, to plan the integration of North and South and agree on an acceptable constitution.

DOCUMENT 47. EXTRACTS FROM *The Future of Northern Ireland, A Paper for Discussion* (LONDON, HMSO, 1972)

The United Kingdom Interest

Division and disorder in Northern Ireland are liabilities both to that Province and to the United Kingdom as a whole; and in seeking to restore order and resume progress there the United Kingdom Government are serving both the national interest and the true interest of all the people of Northern Ireland. The United Kingdom Government has three major concerns in Northern Ireland. First, that it should be internally at peace—a divided and strife-ridden Province is bound to disturb and weaken the whole Kingdom. Second, that it should prosper, so as to contribute to and not detract from the prosperity of the whole. Third, that Northern Ireland should not offer a base for any external threat to the security of the United Kingdom. In pursuing these objectives, the Government will wish to consider at all times the views and interests in Northern Ireland and to take them as fully as possible into account. So long as Northern Ireland remains part of the United Kingdom, the United Kingdom Parliament must be the sovereign authority over all persons, matters and things in Northern Ireland, and the ultimate acceptance of that authority must be a necessary condition of the financial, economic and military assistance from which Northern Ireland benefits as a part of the United Kingdom. While such assistance continues, or may be required in the future, no Government could recommend a settlement to Parliament which did not give the Government an effective voice in the use to which it is put.

A recognition of the right of self-determination of the people of Northern Ireland does not exclude the legitimate interest of other parties. To say that it would be wrong to terminate the relationship between Northern Ireland and the rest of the United Kingdom against the wishes of a majority in Northern Ireland is not to say that it is for Northern Ireland alone to determine how it shall be governed as a part of the United Kingdom, since its association with Great Britain involves rights and obligations on both sides; it is to say that insistence upon membership of the United Kingdom carries with it the obligations of membership including acceptance of the sovereignty of Parliament as representing the people as a whole.

The Irish Dimension

A settlement must also recognize Northern Ireland's position within Ireland as a whole. The guarantee to the people of Northern Ireland that the status of Northern Ireland as part of the United Kingdom will not be changed without their consent is an absolute: this pledge cannot and will not be set aside. Nevertheless it is a fact that Northern Ireland is part of the geographical entity of Ireland; that it shares with the Republic of Ireland common problems, such as the under-development of western areas; and that, in the context of membership of the European Communities, Northern Ireland and the Republic will have certain common difficulties and opportunities which will differ in some respects from those which will face Great Britain. It is also a fact that an element of the minority in Northern Ireland has hitherto seen itself as simply a part of the wider Irish community. The problem of accommodating that minority within the political structures of Northern Ireland has to some considerable extent been an aspect of a wider problem within Ireland as a whole. Even if the minority had themselves been more disposed, and more encouraged than they were, to accept the settlement of 1920, they would still have been subject to those powerful influences which regard the unification of Ireland as 'unfinished business', declined to accept the institutions of Northern Ireland as legitimate, and were made manifest in the Irish Constitution of 1937. As long as such influences continue to exist they are bound to be a powerful factor to be taken into account in the search for stability in Northern Ireland. Moreover the problem of political terrorism, which has reached such proportions in Northern Ireland today, has always had manifestations throughout the island (although, of course, the great majority of those who wish to see the unification of Ireland do not advocate or approve of the use of violence to achieve it).

No United Kingdom Government for many years has had any wish to impede the realisation of Irish unity, if it were to come about by genuine and freely given mutual agreement and on conditions acceptable to the distinctive communities. Indeed the Act of 1920 itself, which has for so many years been the foundation of Northern Ireland's constitutional status, explicitly provided means to move towards ultimate unity on just such a basis; but the will to work this was never present. It is a matter of historical fact that this failure stemmed from decisions and actions taken, not only in Great Britain and Northern Ireland but in the Republic of Ireland also.

Whatever arrangements are made for the future administration of Northern Ireland must take account of the Province's relationships with the Republic of Ireland: and to the extent that this is done, there is an obligation upon the Republic to reciprocate. Both the economy and the security of the two areas are to some considerable extent inter-dependent, and the same is true of both in their relationship with Great Britain. It is therefore clearly desirable that any new arrangements for Northern Ireland should, whilst meeting the wishes of Northern Ireland and Great Britain, be so far as possible acceptable to and accepted by the Republic of Ireland which from 1 January 1973, will share the rights and obligations of membership of the European Communities. It remains the view of the United Kingdom Government that it is for the people of Northern Ireland to decide what should be their relationship to the United Kingdom and to the Republic of Ireland: and that it should not be impossible to devise measures which will meet the best interests of all three. Such measures would seek to secure the acceptance, in both Northern Ireland and in the Republic, of the present status of Northern Ireland, and of the possibility—which would have to be compatible with the principle of consent—of subsequent change in that status; to make possible effective consultation and co-operation in Ireland for the benefit of North and South alike; and to provide a firm basis for concerted governmental and community action against those terrorist organisations which represent a threat to free democratic institutions in Ireland as a whole.

The Way Forward

This is not the appropriate stage at which to form a final judgment on [the future shape of the administration of Northern Ireland], but in the view of Her Majesty's Government any firm proposals must meet the following criteria:

(a) In accordance with the specific pledges given by successive United Kingdom Governments, Northern Ireland must and will remain part of the United Kingdom for as long as that is the wish of a majority of the people; but that status does not preclude the necessary taking into account of what has been described in this Paper as the 'Irish Dimension'.

(b) As long as Northern Ireland remains part of the United Kingdom the sovereignty of the United Kingdom Parliament must be acknowledged and due provision made for the United Kingdom Government to have an effective and continuing voice in Northern Ireland's affairs, commensurate with the commitment of financial, economic and military resources in the Province.

(c) Any division of powers between the national and the regional authorities must be logical, open and clearly understood. Ambiguity in the relationship is a prescription for confusion and misunderstanding. Any necessary checks, balances or controls must be apparently on the face of a new constitutional scheme.

(d) The two primary purposes of any new institutions must be first to seek a much wider consensus than has hitherto existed; and second to be such as will work efficiently and will be capable of providing the concrete results of good government: peace and order, physical development, social and economic progress. This is fundamental because Northern Ireland's problems flow not just from a clash of national aspirations or from friction between the communities, but also from social and economic conditions such as inadequate housing and unemployment.

(e) Any new institutions must be of a simple and businesslike character, appropriate to the powers and functions of a regional authority.

(f) A Northern Ireland assembly or authority must be capable of involving all its members constructively in ways which satisfy them and those they represent that the whole community has a part to play in the government of the Province. As a minimum this would involve assuring minority groups of an effective voice and a real influence; but there are strong arguments that the objective of real participation should be achieved by giving minority interests a share in the exercise of executive power if this can be achieved by means which are not unduly complex or artificial, and which do not represent an obstacle to effective government.

(g) There must be an assurance, built into any new structures, that there will be absolute fairness and equality of opportunity for all. The future administration of Northern Ireland must be seen to be completely even-handed both in law and in fact.

(h) It is of great importance that future arrangements for security and public order in Northern Ireland must command public confidence, both in Northern Ireland itself, and in the United Kingdom as a whole. If they are to do so they must be seen in practice to be as impartial and effective as possible in restoring and maintaining peace and public order. In any situation such as that which obtains at present, where the Army and the civilian police force are both involved in maintaining law and order and combating terrorism, it is essential that there should be a single source of direct responsibility. Since Westminster alone can control the Armed Forces of the Crown this unified control must mean Westminster control. For the future any arrangements must ensure that the United Kingdom Government has an effective and a determining voice in relation to any circumstances which involve, or may involve in the future, the commitment of the Armed Forces, the use of emergency powers, or repercussions at international level.

The objective now must be to advance as rapidly as possible towards the preparation of a comprehensive new scheme for the government of Northern Ireland which will satisfy these fundamental conditions.

(v)

On 1 January 1973 the United Kingdom and the Republic of Ireland became member states of the European Economic Community and from then on the two governments co-operated more closely in the suppression of terrorism. The people of the Republic, terrified that murder and destruction should spill over the border into the south, offered little opposition when the Fianna Fail Government established special courts, without juries, to try those charged with subversive activities, or when the Offences Against the State (Amendment) Act was passed requiring IRA suspects to prove their innocence. Somewhat similar changes in the administration of justice in Northern Ireland were recommended in the Diplock Commission Report (Document 48), but many Catholics would maintain that the alternatives to internment introduced by the Detention of Terrorists Order 1972 and the Northern Ireland (Emergency Provisions) Act are differences of terminology rather than of process.

On 8 March 1973 a poll was held throughout Northern Ireland which showed a majority in favour of the province remaining part of the United Kingdom. Later in the month the Government's White Paper *Northern Ireland Constitutional Proposals* was presented to Parliament by the Secretary of State. The United Kingdom Government proposed to abolish the Northern Ireland Parliament and to replace it by an Assembly of about eighty members, elected by proportional representation for a fixed term of four years. A member of the Assembly would act as the political head of each department (for example, education, agriculture, etc.), and heads of departments would be assisted by committees whose membership would reflect the balance of political parties in the Assembly. Heads of departments would collectively form the Executive, and one of them, the Chief Executive, would be leader of the Assembly. The novel feature of the proposed constitution was the provision that the Executive could not be formed from a single party, if that party drew its support and its elected representation from one side of a divided community. There would continue to be a Secretary of State for Northern Ireland in the United Kingdom Government, and he would have to be satisfied that the

Executive fulfilled this requirement before any powers were devolved to the Assembly (Document 49).

Law and order had always been matters of controversy in Northern Ireland, and the United Kingdom proposed to make these 'reserved matters' under the control of Westminster. Safeguards against discrimination on religious and political grounds would be included in a Charter of Human Rights, and citizens discriminated against would have access to the courts for civil remedies.

The final section of the White Paper dealt with 'the Irish Dimension', and it was worded with great care, for, despite the guarantees that had been given to them, many Ulster Unionists were deeply suspicious of Britain's intentions in the long term. The Government confined itself to the statement that it favoured, and was prepared to facilitate, the establishment of institutional arrangements for consultation and co-operation between Northern Ireland and the Republic of Ireland (Document 49).

The White Paper stimulated intense political discussion, especially on the key issues of 'power-sharing' and the proposed Council of Ireland. In general, Protestant reaction was less favourable than Catholic. Mr Faulkner asserted that Unionists would not share power with those whose objective was a United Ireland and that there could be no co-operation with the Republic until its government recognized the right of the people of Northern Ireland to self-determination. He did not reject the proposals; instead he tried to convey the impression that the unsatisfactory aspects of the White Paper might be altered by negotiation with the United Kingdom Government, or by conventions agreed upon once the Assembly was in operation. The Rev. Ian Paisley and Mr Craig were more forthright: the proposals were unacceptable and they pledged themselves to make them unworkable. The SDLP gave the proposals a guarded welcome, but warned that constitutional changes would not of themselves solve the Northern Ireland problem. Without the end of internment and the creation of an acceptable police force to take the place of the Army, there would be no peace in Catholic areas and little hope of any political consensus emerging. The Alliance and Northern Ireland Labour Parties wholeheartedly welcomed the White

Paper but had an incredibly difficult task in attempting to gain support from an electorate that was polarized on religious lines.

DOCUMENT 48. EXTRACTS FROM *Report of the Commission to consider legal procedures to deal with terrorist activities in Northern Ireland,* THE DIPLOCK REPORT, 1972 (LONDON, HMSO, CMND 5185)

We are . . . driven inescapably to the conclusion that until the current terrorism by the extremist organizations of both factions in Northern Ireland can be eradicated, there will continue to be some dangerous terrorists against whom it will not be possible to obtain convictions by any form of criminal trial which we regard as appropriate to a court of law; and these will include many of those who plan and organize terrorist acts by other members of the organization in which they take no first-hand part themselves. We are also driven inescapably to the conclusion that so long as these remain at liberty to operate in Northern Ireland, it will not be possible to find witnesses prepared to testify against them in the criminal courts, except those serving in the army or the police, for whom effective protection can be provided. The dilemma is complete. The only hope of restoring the efficiency of criminal courts of law in Northern Ireland to deal with terrorist crimes is by using an extra-judicial process to deprive them of their ability to operate in Northern Ireland, those terrorists whose activities result in the intimidation of witnesses. With an easily penetrable border to the south and west the only way of doing this is to put them in detention by an executive act and to keep them confined, until they can be released without danger to public safety and to the administration of criminal justice.

Deprivation of liberty as a result of an extra-judicial process we call 'detention', following the nomenclature of The Detention of Terrorists (Northern Ireland) Order, 1972. It does not mean imprisonment at the arbitrary Diktat of the Executive Government, which to so many people is a common connotation of the term 'internment'. We use it to describe depriving a man of his liberty as a result of an investigation of the facts which inculpate the detainee by an impartial person or tribunal by making use of a procedure which, however fair to him, is inappropriate to a court of law because it does not comply with

Article 6 of the European Convention. Lawyers, particularly English and Irish lawyers, tend to assume that the only safe evidence on which to convict a man upon a criminal charge is that which is admitted and elicited in accordance with the technical rules of procedure which are at present used in English and Northern Irish criminal courts and are stricter in favour of the accused than those followed in the Courts of other countries in Europe. But in fact there may be material available to the security authorities which would carry complete conviction as to the guilt of the accused to an impartial arbiter of common sense, although it is based on statements by witnesses who cannot be subjected to questioning by lawyers on behalf of the accused or even produced for examination by the arbiter himself . . . .

It is now recognized by those responsible for collecting and collating this kind of information that when internment was reintroduced in August, 1971, the scale of the operation led to the arrest and detention of a number of persons against whom suspicion was founded on inadequate and inaccurate information. Such evidence as we have heard leads us to believe that the security authorities have learnt the lessons of this experience and that the danger of them recommending detention on inadequate evidence is now greatly reduced. We think, however, that it is a valuable safeguard against abuse of the power of detention that under the new Order the security authorities' case against a suspected terrorist has to be submitted to the consideration of some independent and impartial person or tribunal before any final decision to keep him in detention is reached. We have no reason to think that since the original Advisory Committee to hear applications for release from internment was first set up in September, 1971, there has been any intentional misuse of the powers of detention by the security authorities in Northern Ireland upon whose advice the Executive has to rely in taking the initial step. But those human beings charged with the task of suppressing terrorist organizations and preventing and detecting terrorist crimes are working under tremendous pressure, often in personal peril. It is only natural that occasional errors of judgment may be made as to the probative strength of the material inculpating a particular suspect. If these occur the best corrective is to bring

to bear upon the case fresh minds not subject to similar pressure
or perils . . . .

Nevertheless, however slight the risk of mistake by the Commissioners and the Detention Appeal Tribunal appointed under
the Detention of Terrorists (Northern Ireland) Order, their
proceedings must of necessity take place in private and the
reasons which in the current atmosphere of terror make it
impossible to call witnesses to testify in open court are likely to
deprive these tribunals too of the opportunity of questioning
the actual persons from whom information inculpating the
detainees was obtained, although they may have an opportunity, not available to an ordinary court of law, of learning
from those by whom information about the accused was
obtained, facts which bear upon the reliability of their sources
but which could not safely be disclosed in the presence of the
accused or his lawyers. Even these facts, however, must fall
short of disclosing the actual identity of the source. We recognize
that the procedures available to these tribunals can never
appear to be as complete a safeguard that none but the guilty
will be deprived of their liberty, as in the safeguard which is
provided by a public trial in a court of law, at which the actual
witnesses can be produced in person and their evidence tested
by cross-examination on behalf of the accused . . . .

[Changes in the administration of justice recommended:]
1. Trials of scheduled offences ('those crimes which are commonly committed at the present time by members of terrorist
organizations') should be by a Judge of the High Court, or a
County Court Judge, sitting alone with no jury, with the usual
rights of appeal.
2. The armed services should be given power to arrest people
suspected of having been involved in, or having information
about, offences and detain them for up to four hours in order to
establish their identity.
3. Bail in cases involving a scheduled offence should not be
granted except by the High Court and then only if stringent
requirements are met.
4. The onus of proof as to the possession of firearms and
explosives should be altered so as to require a person found in
certain circumstances to prove on the balance of probabilities

that he did not know and had no reason to suspect that arms
or explosives were where they were found.

5. A confession made by the accused should be admissible as
evidence in cases involving the scheduled offences unless it was
obtained by torture or inhuman or degrading treatment; if
admissible it would then be for the court to determine its
reliability on the basis of evidence given from either side as to
the circumstances in which the confession had been obtained.

6. A signed written statement made to anyone charged with
investigating a scheduled offence should be admissible if the
person who made it cannot be produced in court for specific
reasons, and the statement contains material which would have
been admissible if that person had been present in court to give
oral evidence.

*

The Northern Ireland (Emergency Provisions) Act 1973
implemented the above recommendations, but met strong
opposition, when passing through Westminster, from the
Labour Party and Mr Fitt, leader of the SDLP. At the
committee stage they carried an amendment, the effect of
which was that in trials of scheduled offences there should be
three judges, not one, if the accused was being tried without a
jury; but in the report stage the Government restored the
original clause.

The hearings of the commissioners, appointed under the
Detention of Terrorists (Northern Ireland) Order 1972 to
consider the evidence against persons upon whom an interim
custody order has been made by the Secretary of State, have
met with a great deal of criticism both from the lawyers who
have appeared for detainees and from civil rights organizations. A person whose case is referred to the commissioners is
given a written statement as to the nature of the terrorist
activity of which he is accused, not less than three days before
the hearing, and he is entitled to be represented by counsel or a
solicitor. In many cases, in order to protect the informer, the
charge has to be made in general or ambiguous terms; evidence
is frequently given by witnesses concealed behind curtains who
cannot be cross-examined; the accused and his counsel are
sometimes asked to withdraw when evidence of a material kind

is tendered to the commissioners, with the result that neither the detainee nor his counsel is aware of the specific offence for which he is being detained. The dilemma of the security authorities is obvious, because the lives of witnesses would be in jeopardy if their identity was known or suspected; nevertheless the procedures are open to serious objection and are regarded by many Catholics and some Protestants as a more sophisticated form of internment.

DOCUMENT 49. EXTRACTS FROM *Northern Ireland Constitutional Proposals*, 1973 (LONDON, HMSO, CMND 5259)

Conditions for devolution of powers

As soon as the Assembly has been elected, the Secretary of State will discuss with representatives of the parties how devolution on a basis of government by consent may take place. Hitherto, the executive dispositions in Northern Ireland have been made by the Governor under the Act of 1920 and in accordance with the current British constitutional conventions. But those conventions have been applied to Northern Ireland in a situation where:

(a) the same party has been the majority party after each General Election; and

(b) that party has never returned to Parliament in the course of half a century a member from the minority community which comprises more than a third of the population.

It is from this situation there flows the problem, as described in the Paper for Discussion, of 'binding the minority to the support of new political arrangements in Northern Ireland'.

Formation of the Executive

There is no future for devolved institutions of government in Northern Ireland unless majority and minority alike can be so bound. This is not to say that any 'right of veto' can be conceded to violent, subversive or unconstructive elements determined, if they can, to undermine any new system from the outset. But the Government does not believe that this is the wish of the overwhelming majority in either community. What has to be found—through their representatives—is a system of exercising executive power in Northern Ireland which is broadly acceptable to them. One important means of ensuring this will be more effective participation by the Assembly as a whole, through its structure of committees, in the development of policy; but it is the view of the Government that the Executive itself can no longer be solely based upon any single party, if that party draws its support and its elected representation virtually entirely from only one section of a divided community. The Executive must be composed of persons who are prepared to work together by peaceful means for the benefit of the community. Members of the Executive will be required to take an appropriate form of official oath or make an affirmation on taking up their appointment.

It is this central issue which, after the election of the Assembly, the Secretary of State will urgently discuss with its elected leaders. The objective of the discussions will be to seek an agreed understanding which the United Kingdom Government can with confidence recommend to Parliament as a fair and viable basis for the devolution of power. When the Government is satisfied:

(a) that the procedures of the Assembly and the proposed method of exercising executive powers will, taken together, be a reasonable basis for the establishment of government by consent (that is to say, with substantially wider support from the community as a whole than would necessarily be indicated by a simple majority in the Assembly);

(b) in particular, that executive powers will not be concentrated in elected representatives from one community only; and

(c) that any proposed arrangements will represent not just a theoretical framework for fair and acceptable government, but a system which can and will be worked effectively by those concerned,

it will seek the approval of Parliament for the devolution by subordinate instrument of extensive law-making powers to the Assembly, and for a broadly corresponding devolution of executive powers to a Northern Ireland Executive, which will be constituted in accordance with the arrangements that have been agreed.

Legislative powers

Whatever powers to legislate may be devolved upon a regional law-making authority in Northern Ireland, it must and will be made clear that such devolution does not diminish in any way the right of the United Kingdom Parliament to legislate for Northern Ireland, as for any other part of the United Kingdom, in relation to any matter whatever. In practice, it is to be expected that, in the context of an acceptable and smooth-running scheme of devolution, Parliament would legislate for Northern Ireland within the field of wholly devolved powers only in the most rare and exceptional circumstances or at the request of the Northern Ireland Executive; but there can be no room for ambiguity about the right to do so . . . .

Restraints upon devolved legislative powers

The constitutional bill will include a general provision to the effect that, in the exercise of any responsibilities devolved upon it, the Northern Ireland Assembly shall not have the power to make any law of a discriminatory character. This is one component of a complex of proposals designed to afford protections and safeguards amounting to a charter of human rights . . . .

The Bill will also provide that, in the exercise of powers devolved upon it, the Assembly may not impose upon any member of an appointed body, or upon any person paid out of public funds in Northern Ireland, as a condition of his appointment, service or employment, any requirement to make any form of oath or declaration save when such an oath or declaration is required in comparable circumstances in the rest of the United Kingdom . . . .

Law and order

The reservation of broad 'law and order' powers for the time being must not exclude Northern Ireland involvement in matters of great concern to its people; and, indeed, many of the practical problems in relation to policing and other matters cannot be solved without a high degree of public co-operation and goodwill. This interest will be fully acknowledged in the new structure in a number of ways. First, the Northern Ireland Executive will be invited to act as an advisory committee to the Secretary of State in relation to those responsibilities reserved to him. He will therefore have an opportunity to discuss matters of general public concern and interest with the elected leaders of the Northern Ireland community, and to take their views fully into account.

Second, democratic participation in restoring to all parts of Northern Ireland the full benefits of a normal police service is essential. The Police Authority, which will continue to have a statutory responsibility for the management of the police service, will be re-constituted following consultations with the Assembly so as to introduce into it an element drawn from elected representatives. In addition, the new District Councils which will come into being in October, will be able to form the basis of local committees with advisory responsibilities in relation to the policing of their districts. They could for example, invite the local police commander to attend meetings so that they could keep themselves informed of the way their district was being policed; they could explain problems and put forward suggestions; they could offer advice; they could help to promote recruitment; they could encourage local citizens to help prevent intimidation, vandalism, etc; they could provide links with tenants' associations and other groups whose co-operation was important to good relations in the district; and they could take special interest in such matters as road traffic and road safety . . . .

Relations with the Republic of Ireland

It is noteworthy that virtually all the Northern Ireland political parties have envisaged some sort of scheme for institutional arrangements between North and South which many described as a 'Council of Ireland', although there were different concepts of such a Council, and in some cases an emphasis upon conditions which would have to be met before it could operate successfully.

As far as the United Kingdom is concerned, it favours and is prepared to facilitate the formation of such a body. The constitutional proposals would permit the new Northern Ireland institutions to consult and co-ordinate action through a Council of Ireland. There are undoubtedly many matters of substantial mutual interest such as tourism, regional development, electricity and transport.

The widespread interest which exists in the idea of a Council is a firm basis for moving to a specific discussion of the matter. There have been arguments that the Government should at this stage, in consultation with the Republic of Ireland, write into the constitutional Bill for Northern Ireland a complete scheme for such a Council. These arguments are, however, unrealistic. If a Council is to be set up not merely as a statutory concept, but as a useful working mechanism in North–South relations, it must operate with the consent of both majority and minority opinion in Northern Ireland, who have a right to prior consultation and involvement in the process of determining its form, functions and procedures. There are clearly a number of different levels at which such a Council might operate, including the inter-governmental and the inter-parliamentary.

True progress in these matters can only be achieved by consent. Accordingly, following elections to the Northern Ireland Assembly, the Government will invite the Government of the Republic of Ireland and the leaders of the elected representatives of Northern Ireland opinion to participate with them in a conference to discuss how the three objectives set out in the Paper for Discussion may best be pursued, that is:

(a) the acceptance of the present status of Northern Ireland, and of the possibility—which would have to be compatible with the principle of consent—of subsequent change in that status;
(b) effective consultation and co-operation in Ireland for the benefit of North and South alike; and
(c) the provision of a firm basis for concerted governmental and community action against terrorist organisations.

The objectives are inter-related. If and when firm agreements are reached, consideration can be given to the means by which they should be formally adopted as between sovereign states. But, consistent with the principle of consent, the first stage clearly must be discussions involving all the parties.

*

The Northern Ireland Act, giving effect to the main proposals of the White Paper, became law on 18 July 1973. It repealed the Government of Ireland Act 1920, and abolished both the office of Governor and the Parliament of Northern Ireland. In place of the latter there was to be an Assembly of 78 members, elected under a system of PR from large constituencies having, according to population, five to eight members each. The Executive was not to exceed twelve members, of whom two (including a legal member) need not have been elected to the Assembly. If the Secretary of State for Northern Ireland fails to find an Executive fulfilling the terms of Clause 2 (1) (b) of the Act on 'power sharing', he may dissolve the Assembly and hold an election; but if by April 1974 an acceptable Executive has not been appointed, the constitutional scheme lapses, and then, presumably, either the province will be integrated with Great Britain or the present form of direct rule will be continued.

(vi)

Local government in Northern Ireland has been reorganized in accordance with the Macrory Report. The Housing Executive and Area Boards are responsible to the appropriate government departments for the administration of many of the functions hitherto carried out by the local authorities. Central government nominates a substantial proportion of the members of Area Boards and is thus in a position to ensure that the principle of 'power-sharing' extends downwards into local government. Community participation in the administration of their own areas was encouraged by the creation of twenty-six district councils, with responsibility for the environment and certain local services. The first elections to the new district councils were held on 30 May 1973. They were conducted under the system of proportional representation for multi-seat constituencies and thus provided an opportunity for the political parties to organize for the more important Northern Ireland Assembly elections of 28 June.

A feature of the elections was the rejection by the electorate of candidates sponsored by the Republican Clubs (Official Sinn Fein) or by militant Protestant organizations such as the UDA and the Loyalist Association of Workers. Another feature was the election of a single party, the SDLP, to represent the Catholic community. But perhaps the most significant feature of all was the further fragmentation of the Unionist Party between those who took a pledge to support Brian Faulkner's leadership and policies and a group led by two former Ministers, Harry West and John Taylor, who rejected the essential principles of the Constitution Act. This 'split' ensured that no party was returned in sufficient strength to control the Assembly and some form of coalition was necessary. The parties won seats as follows:

'Faulkner' Unionists	23
SDLP	19
Loyalist Coalition	18
'Unpledged' Unionists	9
Alliance	8
NILP	1

The 'Faulkner' Unionists, SDLP and Alliance could form an Executive which would have a substantial majority in the Assembly, and one which, in the words of the Constitution Act, was 'likely to be widely accepted throughout the community'. The Assembly met on 30 July, and, after a noisy debate, elected a presiding officer. Thereafter there was stalemate. Over the past four years the Unionist Party had shown a tendency to discard its leader whenever it got into difficulties, and there were signs that this operation was being contemplated again. A number of Unionist associations, particularly in the south and west of the province, had defied Mr Faulkner and elected members to the Assembly who were pledged to work for the restoration of a Stormont-type parliament with control of internal security and to reject any form of Council of Ireland. The Orange Order, which traditionally had played a key role in Unionist politics, rejected the United Kingdom's constitutional proposals and criticized the party leader for his ambiguous attitude. Consequently Mr Faulkner was chary of being involved in discussions on the formation of an Executive, while at the same time giving the impression that he was willing to serve. The SDLP members were in some difficulty also. Many of their constituents lived in areas where the Army and the IRA were at war, and were caught between two very ruthless adversaries. The priority, as the SDLP saw it, was to secure a reduction of violence to a level at which troops might be withdrawn and some form of policing put in their place. The trouble was that the RUC was regarded by many Unionists as 'our police force' and they would not tolerate its being changed in order to appease the Catholics. Paradoxically, security, which was no concern of the Northern Ireland Assembly, was one of the chief obstacles to the formation of an Executive. Mr Whitelaw was caught in the usual dilemma: any proposals he made to satisfy one party were almost certain to dissatisfy the other.

In an effort to break the stalemate Mr Heath came to Belfast on 28 August and told the party leaders that they must make the necessary compromise to form an Executive. When that was done the details of strengthening the RUC and making it into an acceptable and efficient force could be discussed with Westminster, the Secretary of State for Northern Ireland and the Police Authority. The tripartite conference on a Council of Ireland could then be held. In a public statement on 29 August Mr Heath warned that the British public and all British parties were growing impatient with the intransigence of Northern Ireland politicians (Document 50). A few days later, Mr James Callaghan, on behalf of the Labour Party, underlined the Prime Minister's message, and in the closing pages of his book, *A House Divided: the Dilemma of Northern Ireland* (Collins, 1973), warned:

> If, at any time, the Assembly and the Executive should be made unworkable through a deliberate refusal by the majority to play their part, then in my judgement the United Kingdom would be entitled to reconsider her position and her pledges on all matters. If a majority of the elected representatives of the Northern Ireland people are

in the end unwilling to accept the sovereignty of Westminster, then they have no right to demand either the help or the protection of the British Government.

DOCUMENT 50. STATEMENT BY THE PRIME MINISTER, MR EDWARD HEATH, TO THE PEOPLE OF NORTHERN IRELAND, ON A VISIT TO BELFAST, 29 AUGUST 1973 (*Irish Times*, 30 AUGUST 1973)

The Northern Ireland Constitution Act is now the law of the land and you have elected representatives. It is their task to form an executive to take over the powers which the Westminster Parliament has shown itself prepared to hand over to them . . . .

I am prepared to ask for the recall of the Westminster Parliament the very moment parties in the Assembly agree to form the Executive. In this I have the support of the two other party leaders at Westminster.

I realise full well that we are asking much of the parties of the Assembly to work together in the interests of the whole community of Northern Ireland. But I must tell you quite frankly that having taken the necessary steps to enable a resumption of the political life of Northern Ireland, the people of Britain will not understand any reluctance to take full advantage of it.

Although at the moment responsibility for security is being kept at Westminster, the Executive will of course be able to discuss these problems with the Secretary of State who is a member of the United Kingdom Cabinet, and surely the opportunity of working together over a wide field of other matters is one which the representatives in the Assembly should seize at once.

At the same time the Governments in Westminster and Dublin, together with the Northern Ireland Executive, can get on with working out the machinery, in the form of developing institutions, to meet the requirements of the Irish Dimension to which Her Majesty's Government has pledged itself.

Her Majesty's Government has kept faith with the people of Northern Ireland through these murderous years. The Constitution Act provides that in no event will Northern Ireland or any part of it cease to be part of the U.K. without the consent of the majority of the people of Northern Ireland voting in a poll.

We have maintained the security forces to protect all, regardless of politics or faith.

We pledged a plebiscite on the Border. That has been held and the decision taken.

We pledged the abolition of the Special Powers Act and the control of emergency powers by Westminster. That has been done.

We pledged the reform of judicial procedures to enable the criminals to be brought more speedily and more certainly to justice. That is now the law.

We have pledged a conference on matters of common interest to North and South. That pledge too will be honoured.

The rest now is in the hands of your representatives in the Assembly. Let us go to it in the cause of restoring peace to Northern Ireland and rebuilding a fair and prosperous future for her people.

(vii)

On his visit to Dublin on 17 September 1973, the Prime Minister, Mr Heath, in an interview on BBC television, made it clear that if an Executive were not formed and functioning in Northern Ireland by 30 March 1974, the Constitution Act would lapse and a political crisis of the utmost gravity would result. In such a situation there could be no reversion to the system of direct rule which had followed the suspension of Stormont. That had been tolerated by the Westminster Parliament as a temporary expedient only, and, if the present proposals failed, many people would believe that the only viable alternative was the total integration of Northern Ireland in the United Kingdom. The Prime Minister's remarks were probably intended to create a greater sense of urgency among Northern Ireland politicians whose dilatoriness in forming an Executive had irritated him, but their effect was the very opposite to that intended. Mr Faulkner's position was placed in jeopardy, as many Unionists, pledged and un-pledged alike, would prefer integration in the United Kingdom to power-sharing with the SDLP, if that alternative was now being offered to them by Mr Heath. In this they found common ground with the supporters of the Rev. Ian Paisley and Mr Craig, and they could by acting together in the Assembly precipitate the political crisis which the Prime Minister was trying to avoid.

The Taoiseach, Mr Cosgrave, with whom Mr Heath had just had a full day's conference, was taken by surprise, as the statement suggested a change in British Government policy. The Labour Party was even more surprised, and Mr Wilson wrote to the Prime Minister seeking a clarification of this breach of the bi-partisan agreement on Northern Ireland. At a meeting of the Commonwealth Parliamentary Association at Grosvenor House, London, on the following day, Mr Heath withdrew somewhat from his earlier position, and declared:

> We are looking for a means to get to grips with the fundamental problem of Northern Ireland. That is to enable its people to live and work together and be responsible for the peaceful management of their own affairs. In the longer term that is not something which Westminster can provide. We can provide the framework. But only the people of Northern Ireland and their elected representatives can take up the challenge, can themselves take on the responsibility of their own affairs . . . .
>
> They cannot be provided from outside. This is the basic reason why, as I said last night in Dublin, the essential thing is that those in Northern Ireland who really want to share power and really want to govern themselves should come together. This is what the people of Northern Ireland and the people of Great Britain want and are entitled to expect from elected representatives. This has been and will remain the policy of Her Majesty's Government. It is illusory to suppose that there are new policies or new options which enable the parties in Northern Ireland to escape from this fundamental reality.

But in the last resort, the Prime Minister said, there may be no alternative to integration. The Labour Party was still not satisfied and pressed for an unambiguous withdrawal by Mr Heath from the position he had taken up in the Dublin interview. The Prime Minister did so in a letter to Mr Wilson: 'If the provisions of the Act were to prove unworkable, we should be back to direct rule and a situation of the utmost gravity. There would have to be new discussions between the parties in Westminster and in the Westminster Parliament.'

In such a situation it is worthwhile to examine the options available to the United Kingdom Government. It is difficult to see direct rule as more than a temporary expedient to continue only until a more permanent settlement has been worked out. Its continuation for any length of time, without a diminution of violence, would strengthen the demands of the British people for the withdrawal of the troops, or indeed for the Government to wash its hands of the whole business. Such withdrawal, whether precipitate or phased, would be extremely dangerous and it is unthinkable that any British Government could contemplate it. If civil war followed, the Catholic minority would suffer and the South would inevitably be drawn in. In time violence could spill over into Liverpool, Glasgow and other towns with substantial Irish populations, where urban guerrillas could cause immense destruction and suffering. Apart from that, world opinion would be very critical of Britain if she tried to escape from a problem that her own colonial past had created.

Total integration has attractions for many Unionists: it would emphasize the British connection and considerably reduce their fear of absorption into the Irish Republic. But it is doubtful if this solution would find much support from any British party. The prospect of endless debates on the Irish Question in Westminster and the possibility of decisions on issues of vital importance to the British people depending upon the votes of Northern Ireland MPs are certain to deter any United Kingdom government from taking up this option. In any case, as Mr Heath has pointed out, integration does not tackle the fundamental cause of the Ulster problem, the inability of the two communities to live together.

Negotiated independence has been suggested as another solution. Mr Craig and Mr John Taylor have said repeatedly over the past twelve months that, if they cannot have the old Stormont system restored, they would prefer 'an independent British Ulster'. Some SDLP members have been attracted to this idea, and obviously have regarded the separation of the

province from the United Kingdom as a first step in the movement towards a united Ireland. But if the reluctance of
Unionists to share power with Catholics makes the present
proposals unacceptable, the minority are unlikely to fare better
in an independent Ulster. A negotiated settlement of this kind
would almost certainly involve a redrawing of the boundaries
of Northern Ireland, with Fermanagh, Tyrone, south Down,
south Armagh and Derry City going to the Republic of
Ireland. Some Unionists might as a last resort welcome this
and consider the creation of a Protestant redoubt in north-east
Ulster a satisfactory solution to the problem. But if this were to
succeed there would have to be considerable population
movements. There are nearly a quarter of a million Catholics
in Antrim, Belfast, north Down and north Armagh; more than
half of them in Belfast where the main trouble is. This solution
is just not practicable. Catholics, in particular, have a deep
attachment to the lands on which their families have lived for
generations and would not be prepared to abandon them. On
the other hand, the most hard-line and intransigent Unionists
are to be found in areas liable for transfer to the Republic: it
is difficult to imagine Mr West, Mr Taylor or Lord Brookeborough being enthusiastic about a solution that would make
them TDs in the Dublin Dail.

Perhaps the most desperate option of all would be UDI, in
which certain Unionists took the province, or as much of it as
they could control, out of the United Kingdom. The Green
Paper, *The Future of Northern Ireland*, has warned that no
British Government could be a party to such a settlement:

> It may be argued by some that if Northern Ireland was
> prepared to accept a drastic fall in the standards of living
> and services, it could in that sense be viable though at a
> high cost to all its people; but that is too limited a view.
> Such a form of government could not be viable in a much
> more fundamental sense, that of being a State commanding
> the loyalty of the overwhelming majority of its own
> citizens and the acceptance and respect of the inter-
> national community.

Almost certainly the United Kingdom and the Republic of
Ireland would put an embargo on trade with such a Northern

Ireland, and the new state would find itself isolated outside the European Economic Community. The suggestion that Northern Ireland could obtain financial assistance from Russia in exchange for bases may sound ludicrous; nevertheless it has been seriously considered by some supporters of Mr Craig. The province depends for its prosperity and social services on the economy of the rest of the United Kingdom, and if British capital and trade were withdrawn it would be utterly ruined.

There is no better solution to the problems of Northern Ireland than that described in the White Paper and implemented in the Constitution Act 1973. The United Kingdom no longer has any imperial or strategic reasons for wishing to remain in Ireland. Her paramount concern is to devise a settlement whereby the two communities in Northern Ireland can live together in harmony and trust, and under which the two parts of Ireland can co-operate for their mutual benefit. The guarantee in Section 1 of the Constitution Act that the status of Northern Ireland will not be changed without the consent of the people is absolute, but that does not preclude the United Kingdom from fostering good relations between north and south. Clearly all parties in the Republic would like to see Ireland united, but they have come to realize that this can be achieved only by consent. At the moment they would be satisfied with a political settlement in Northern Ireland which would enable the two communities to work closely together, and which would create a Council of Ireland with powers to evolve. As soon as Protestants and Catholics have learned to trust one another in Northern Ireland, the Irish Question will be nearer to a final solution; for as Mr Roy Bradford, Minister of Development in the last Unionist Government, has said, 'The fears and suspicions that separate Protestants and Catholics in the North are the fears and suspicions that separate the North from the South.'

Postscript

On 21 November 1973 the Unionist, SDLP and Alliance parties agreed to form an administration for Northern Ireland, with Brian Faulkner as Chief Executive and Gerry Fitt as his deputy. On the following day Mr Whitelaw told the House of Commons that their agreement to do so was conditional on the holding of a conference, representing the United Kingdom and Irish governments and the members of the Executive designate, to deal with the important matters of the status of Northern Ireland, a Council of Ireland, and the problems of law enforcement, extradition and internment. If agreement were reached on these matters, direct rule from Westminster would end, and the administration of the province would be entrusted to the Executive.

The proposed conference was held at Sunningdale, Berkshire, 6–9 December 1973. Before it met, William Whitelaw, the architect of the settlement, was appointed Secretary for Employment and was replaced in Northern Ireland by Francis Pym. The conference was presided over by the then Prime Minister, Mr Heath, and it required all his patience and skill to effect a compromise. The Ulster Unionist Council had agreed by a slender majority to support Mr Faulkner 'in his efforts to create a strong regional executive or government', but they made power-sharing with the SDLP contingent on the recognition of Northern Ireland as an integral part of the United Kingdom, and on the Republic of Ireland's co-operation in bringing terrorism to an end. On the other side, the SDLP declared that without the creation of a 'meaningful' Council of Ireland, and a commitment by the British government to phase out internment, they could not participate in the proposed Executive. After four days of hard bargaining, the delegates signed a communiqué to the effect that:

1. The Irish government 'fully accepted and solemnly declared that there could be no change in the status of Northern Ireland until a majority of the people of Northern Ireland desired a change in that status'.

2. There was to be a Council of Ireland, with a ministerial level, consisting of seven ministers each from North and South who would have executive power, and a consultative assembly, consisting of thirty members each from the Northern Ireland Assembly and the Dail. The latter bodies would determine the functions of the Council, but it was suggested that the Council of Ministers should be consulted on the appointment of police authorities in both parts of Ireland to secure maximum co-operation in combating crime and terrorism.

3. An Anglo-Irish Commission of Jurists would examine proposals for dealing with fugitive offenders and make recommendations.

4. The British government promised 'to bring detention to an end in Northern Ireland for all sections of the community as soon as the security situation permits'.

On 1 January 1974 direct rule came to an end, and the Northern Ireland Executive assumed responsibility for governing the province in accordance with the terms of the Constitution Act. Three days later the Ulster Unionist Council rejected Mr Faulkner's policy and he resigned as leader of the party. He continued as Chief Executive, but from then on the political structures so laboriously put together over the previous twelve months were placed under great strain. The government of the Irish Republic showed a surprising reluctance to declare unambiguously that they recognized Northern Ireland as part of the United Kingdom. Meanwhile 'the Faulkner Unionists' grew more fearful of the implications of the proposed Council of Ireland. On 16 January 1974 Mr Faulkner and Mr Cosgrave met at Baldonnel, near Dublin, in an effort to resolve their problems, but because of a law case challenging the constitutionality of the Sunningdale agreement, the Irish government felt unable to make the declaration the Unionists were demanding. The General Election for the Westminster parliament in February 1974 made matters worse, for the 'Loyalists', led by

Messrs Paisley, Craig and West (who had replaced Mr Faulkner as leader of the Unionists), decided to use the poll in Northern Ireland as a referendum on Sunningdale. Not a single Faulkner supporter was elected, and the 'Loyalists' won eleven of the twelve Ulster seats. Moderate Unionists regarded the results as a rejection of Sunningdale but not of power-sharing, and they began to withdraw from their previous qualified support for the Council of Ireland. All meetings between northern and southern ministers came to an end. On 13 March 1974, the Taoiseach, Mr Cosgrave, gave the long-awaited recognition of Northern Ireland as part of the United Kingdom, but by then it was too late to make any difference. On the following day *The Times* stated:

> The only way of preserving Sunningdale from either still-birth or final repudiation by the majority of Unionists, is to bring it in by stages, postponing to a better day the introduction of a Council of Ireland.

A month later, the Ulster Workers Council, which had substantial support from Protestant trade unionists, called a general strike which brought the industrial and commercial life of the province to a halt. Their aim was to have the Sunningdale agreement rejected and the Constitution Act 1973 repealed. In an effort to save the Executive, the SDLP agreed to a modified Council of Ireland, but their concession was nullified by Mr Wilson's ill-judged speech on television, which outraged the entire Protestant population. Faced with a break-down of essential services and conscious of the growing support for the strike among his followers, Mr Faulkner urged the Secretary of State, Mr Rees, to negotiate with the UWC on the political changes they required. When he refused, the Unionists resigned and the Executive collapsed on 28 May 1974. The Assembly was prorogued for four months and fresh constitutional discussions began. But attitudes have hardened, particularly among loyalists, and 'power-sharing' in the form envisaged by the United Kingdom Government will be difficult to achieve. Consequently, Northern Ireland now faces its most serious crisis since the troubles began in 1969.

Select Bibliography

The current conflict in Northern Ireland has produced a spate of books, pamphlets, surveys and official reports. The purpose of this bibliography is not to provide a comprehensive list of this literature but to give guidance to the student in search of further information. The official reports contain much useful material and should not be overlooked.

I GENERAL HISTORIES

BECKETT, J. C., *The Making of Modern Ireland 1603–1923*, Faber, 1966. A scholarly survey of the period since the Plantation of Ulster.

LYONS, F. S. L., *Ireland Since the Famine*, Weidenfeld & Nicolson, 1971. Massive and masterly study of Ireland since 1850. Part IV deals with Northern Ireland since 1920.

2 THE CONSTITUTION

CALVERT, H., *Constitutional Law in Northern Ireland*, Stevens & Sons, 1968.

PALLEY, C., *The Evolution, Disintegration and Possible Reconstruction of the Northern Ireland Constitution*, Institute of Irish Studies, Belfast, 1972. Examines changing relationship between United Kingdom and Northern Ireland following the disturbances of 1969. The most recent work.

3 WRITINGS 1968–73

AKENSON, D. H., *Education and Enmity. The Control of Schooling in Northern Ireland 1920–50*, David & Charles, 1973.

BELL, J. B., *The Secret Army*, Blond, 1970. The definitive history of the IRA.

BOULTON, D., *The UVF 1966–73*, Torc, 1973. Ulster's other secret army.

BOYD, A., *Holy War in Belfast*, Anvil, Tralee, 1969. Summary of riots over the past hundred years.

CALLAGHAN, J., *A House Divided: the Dilemma of Northern Ireland*, Collins, 1973.

DE PAOR, L., *Divided Ulster*, Penguin, 1970. An Irish Republican view.

DEVLIN, B., *The Price of My Soul*, Pan, 1969.

FITZGERALD, G., *Towards a New Ireland*, Charles Knight, 1972.

HARBINSON, J. F., *The Ulster Unionist Party 1882–1973*, Blackstaff Press, Belfast, 1973.

HASTINGS, M., *Ulster 1969; the Fight for Civil Rights in Northern Ireland*, Gollancz, 1970. Best account of early period.

HEZLET, A., *The 'B' Specials*, Pan, 1973. The case for the defence.

JACKSON, H., *The Two Irelands*, Minority Rights Group, 1972.

KELLY, H., *How Stormont Fell*, Gill & Macmillan, Dublin, 1972. Instant history.

MCGUFFIN, J., *Internment*, Anvil, Tralee, 1973. Only book on the subject.

O'BRIEN, C. C., *States of Ireland*, Hutchinson, 1972.

O'NEILL, T., *Ulster at the Crossroads*, Faber, 1969. Collection of political speeches.

ROSE, R., *Governing without Consensus*, Faber, 1971. Survey of political attitudes.

STUDY GROUP OF THE INSTITUTE FOR THE STUDY OF CONFLICT, *The Ulster Debate*, Bodley Head, 1972.

SUNDAY TIMES 'INSIGHT' TEAM, *Ulster*, Penguin, 1972.

WALLACE, M., *Northern Ireland: Fifty Years of Self-Government*, David & Charles, 1971.

4 OFFICIAL REPORTS

THE CAMERON REPORT 1969, *Disturbances in Northern Ireland*, Belfast, HMSO, Cmnd 532.

THE HUNT REPORT 1969, *The Advisory Commission on Police in Northern Ireland*, Belfast, HMSO, Cmnd 535.

THE COMPTON REPORT 1971, *Report of the inquiry into allegations against the security forces of physical brutality in Northern Ireland arising out of events on the 9th August 1971*, London, HMSO, Cmnd 4823.

THE SCARMAN REPORT 1972, *Violence and Civil Disturbances in Northern Ireland in 1969*, Belfast, HMSO, Cmnd 566.

THE WIDGERY REPORT 1972, *Report of the Tribunal appointed to inquire into the events on Sunday 30th January 1972, which led to the loss of life in connection with the procession in Londonderry on that day*, London, HMSO, HL101, HC 220.

THE DIPLOCK REPORT 1972, *Report of the Commissioners to consider legal procedures to deal with terrorist activities in Northern Ireland*, London, HMSO, Cmnd 5185.

The Future of Northern Ireland, A Paper for Discussion (the Green Paper), London, HMSO, 1972.

Northern Ireland Constitutional Proposals (the White Paper), London, HMSO, Cmnd 5259.

NORTHERN IRELAND CONSTITUTION ACT 1973, Chapter 36.

Index

Act of Union (1800), 3, 37, 43
Aldershot explosion (1972), 27
Alliance Party: formation of, 151, 156; proposals at Darlington conference, 158-9, 167; elected to Assembly, 178, 186
All-Party Committee (1949), 20
Andersonstown (Belfast), 116, 153
Anglo-Irish Agreement (1925), 16–17, 90–1, 110
Anglo-Irish Agreement (1938), 18
Anglo-Irish Commission of Jurists (1974), 187
Anglo-Irish Treaty (1921), 10, 15–16, 18, 49–50; terms of treaty, 54–5; effects on N. Ireland, 87–8, 108
Antrim, 3, 42, 49, 53, 73, 184
Apprentice Boys (Derry), 76, 119, 141
Ardoyne (Belfast), 116, 120, 133, 153
Area Boards, 177
Armagh, 3, 31, 37, 49, 53, 75, 80, 82, 84, 118
Armagh, south, 15, 16, 184
Army, British: intervention in N. Ireland, 120–1; the 'Falls curfew', 127–30; role in N. Ireland, 134–5; SDLP on, 138–9
Assembly, 165, 166–7, 172–4, 177–9, 187
Assembly elections (1973), 178–9
Asquith, H. H., 48
Attlee, Clement, 19, 112

Ballymurphy, 116, 133
Barnhill, John (Senator), 27
Barritt, D. and Carter, C. F., 6
Beckett, J. C., 12, 34, 42
Belfast: growth of industry, 3, 39, 40–2; religious ghettos, 42–3; riots (1886), 44–5; riots (August 1969), 74–6, 120, 123–4, 158; City Council, 105, 184; riots (1970), 126–8, 128–30, 135, 140; see also 6, 8, 47, 53
Belfast Telegraph, 8, 20
Black, Harold, 13, 14

'Bloody Friday', 153, 156
'Bloody Sunday', 22, 141
Bogside, 74, 118–20
Boyne, Battle of, 2, 4, 34
Border, the (of N. Ireland and Republic), 15–16, 19–20, 27, 89; Lynch on, 22, 120; De Valera on, 108; Lemass on, 109; O'Neill on, 110–13; Heath on, 180
Boundary Commission, 15–17, 50, 54–5, 88–91
Bradford, Roy, 185
Brooke, Capt. John, 130, 184
Brookeborough, Viscount (Sir Basil Brooke): on religious discrimination, 4, 92–3, 94; on Catholics in Unionist Party, 99
Brookfield Street (Belfast), 75
Brown, Rev. J., 38
'B' Specials see Ulster Special Constabulary
Buckingham Palace Conference (1914), 17, 48, 51
Burntollet Bridge, 73, 118
Butt, Isaac, 43–4; speech on Home Rule, 45–6

Cairncross, Neil, 13, 14
Callaghan, James (Home Secretary), 13–14, 58, 121, 179
Calvert, Harry, 59, 135
Cameron Commission Report: on 'B' Specials, 69–70; on RUC, 72–3; on religious discrimination, 80–6; on Civil Rights Association, 122–3
Campaign for Social Justice, 104
Carnwath, Dr T., 105
Carrington, Lord, 133, 134
Carson, Lord (Sir Edward Carson), 17, 47–8, 49, 50, 51, 56, 98
Carter, C. F., 6
Catholic Emancipation, 37, 38
Chamberlain, Austin, 68, 88
Chamberlain, Neville, 18
Chichester-Clark, Major James: becomes Prime Minister, 58, 97, 119;

introduces reforms, 121, 125–6; seeks more troops, 133–4; resigns, 128, 135
Churchill, Lord Randolph, 44
Churchill, W. S., 17, 68
Civil Authorities (Special Powers) Act (NI), 25, 142; provisions summarized, 76–8, 117; Faulkner proposes its replacement, 151, 157; Heath promises its repeal, 181
Civil rights movement, 25, 64; attitude of police to, 71, 72–3, 117; Cameron Report on, 122–3
Clark, Sir George, 98
Cole, John, 110
Collins, Michael, 16
Commissioner for Complaints, 126
Commonwealth Parliamentary Association, 110, 182
Community Relations, Minister of, 121
Community Forum, 143
Compton Report, 141; on physical brutality, 145–7
Connolly, James, 101
Conservative Party, links with Unionists, 44, 94
Constitution of Eire/Ireland (1937), 18, 21, 108, 111, 162
Constitution of N. Ireland (1920), 3, 10, 13, 49–50; Government of Ireland Act, 52–4, 59–61, 62, 87, 110
Constitution of N. Ireland (1973), 11, 22–3, 166–8, 172–7
Conway Street (Belfast), 75
Cooke, Rev. Henry, 37
Cosgrave, Liam, 16, 23, 182, 187, 188
Cosgrave, William T., 17, 90, 109, 110
Costello, John A., 102
Council of Ireland, 10, 12, 17, 49, 53, 108; ended (1925), 91, 108; proposals for new council, 11, 175–7, 179, 185, 186, 187, 188
Court of Human Rights (Strasbourg), 22
Coventry explosions, 24
Craig, William, 11, 25, 167, 182, 183–8; on relations with Westminster, 58; opposes reforms, 117–19, 122; threatens violence, 141; suggests UDI, 150, 183
Craigavon, Viscount (Sir James Craig), 4, 11, 17, 62, 65; on Boundary Commission, 68–9, 88–90, 94, 98, 108
Crumlin Road (Belfast), 75, 116
Cushendun, Lord, 39

Daly, Cathal B. (Bishop of Ardagh and Clonmacnois), 27
Dail Eireann, 10, 16, 18, 23, 24, 49, 187

Darlington Conference, 156
Defenders, 37
Democratic Unionist Party, 11, 150
Derry City (Londonderry), 6, 8, 16, 104, 117, 118, 135, 138, 140, 152, 184; see also Londonderry
Derry, Siege of, 2, 34
Derry, south, 15
Detention of Terrorists Order (1972), 166, 168, 170, 171
De Valera, Eamon, 16, 18–19, 20, 24, 91, 108–9, 111–12
Devlin, Bernadette, 127
Devlin, Joseph, 99
Devolution of powers (1973), 172–4
Dewar, M. W., 38
Diamond, Battle of (1795), 37
Diplock Report, 79, 166, 168–72
Direct Rule (March 1972), 147–50, 150–3, 182–3
Discrimination, 21; Cameron Report on, 80–6; in Londonderry Corporation, 82; in employment, 83–4; justification for, 92–3, 104–5, 117, 135–7
Document 2, 16
Donegal, County, 19, 31
Donegal, east, 17
Downing Street Declaration (August 1969), 59, 120, 125–6, 136, 159
Down, County, 3, 42, 49, 53
Down, north, 184
Down, south, 16, 18, 91, 184
Dublin, 10, 15, 17, 20, 21, 23, 39, 67, 158, 180, 181, 187
Dungannon, 74, 80, 81

Easter Rising (1916), 23, 48
Economic development of north-east Ulster, 40–2; after Second World War, 104
'Economic War', 18, 111
Education, 8–9; voluntary schools, 9; post-war reconstruction, 104–5
Election (1918), 9–10, 49
Election: February 1969, 119; June 1973, 178–9
Electoral law, 62, 64, 79, 82–3; see also Proportional representation
European Economic Community, 162, 166, 185
Executive (1973): formation of, 172–4, 177; Faulkner and, 178–9, 188

'Falls Curfew' (August 1970), 127–30, 133
Falls Road (Belfast), 25, 42, 43, 119, 123, 130
Farrell, Michael, 121

Faulkner, Brian, 78–9, 119; Prime Minister, 128, 139, 140–1; parliamentary committees, 137, 148, 157; attitude to Discussion Paper and Constitution Act, 168, 178–9; after election of June 1973, 179, 181–2, 186, 187, 188
'Faulkner' Unionists, 178–9, 187
Feetham, Judge, 90
Fenians, 23, 27, 43
Fermanagh, County, 3, 16, 17, 31, 49, 53, 62, 80, 83, 96, 103, 117, 121, 184
Fianna Fail, 16, 18–19, 91, 166
Financial relations with Great Britain, 106–7
Fine Gael, 16, 19
Fisher, J. R., 90
Fitt, Gerry, 137, 171, 186
'Flight of the Earls' (1607), 31
Franchise, parliamentary see Electoral law, Proportional representation
Fraser, Morris, 144
'Free Derry', 120
Freeland, Sir Ian (GOC N. Ireland), 127
Free Presbyterian Church, 115
Future of Northern Ireland (Green Paper), 13, 63, 66, 107, 156, 157, 161, 184

Gaelic Athletic Association (GAA), 5, 70
Gaelic League, 9, 70
George, D. Lloyd, 10, 11, 49, 50, 51, 52, 68–9, 87, 88, 89
'Ghettos' (Belfast), 42–3, 116
Gladstone, William, E., 40, 43, 44
Goulding, Cathal, 25, 153, 154–5
Government of Ireland Act (1920), 3, 10, 12, 13, 16, 49, 51, 52, 54, 55, 57, 63, 67, 88, 91, 99, 108, 110, 136, 163, 177
Graham, Sir Clarence, 97
Griffith, Arthur, 16, 24
Gun-running, 22, 48

Halifax, Lord, 24
Hankey, Sir Maurice, 69
Hanna, Rev. Hugh, 37
Hannaway, Kevin, 146
Hastings, Max, 64, 123
Hayes-McCoy, Professor, 27
Healy, Timothy M., 44
Herron, Tommy (UDA leader), 156
Heath, Edward, 22, 127, 133, 141, 147–50; visit to Belfast, 179; statement in Belfast, 180–1; visit to Dublin and subsequent controversy, 181–3, 186

Home Rule, 3, 10, 37, 40, 43, 44, 45–6, 47, 48, 49, 50, 51, 56
'Hooding' of prisoners, 145
Housing: discrimination in allocation, 84–5; standards of, 103; Housing Executive, 121, 177
Hume, John, 137
Hunt Report, 67, 71, 121

Imperial contribution, 107
Infant mortality in N. Ireland, 105
Internment, 24, 78–9; introduced (9 August 1971), 140, 142–3; physical brutality, 145–7; Heath promises end of, 149, 188
Interrogation, 145–7
Ireland Act (1949), 19, 92, 108, 112
Ireland, Republic of, 15, 19, 108, 110, 113
Irish Army, 22
'Irish Dimension', 23, 156, 162–4, 175–7, 180
Irish Free State, 11, 15, 16, 17, 54, 55, 87, 88, 90, 108
Irish Historical Studies, 31
Irish Republican Army (IRA), 5, 19, 22, 23–8, 43, 49, 67, 72, 75, 87, 95–101; formation of 'Provisionals', 128, 130–3; meet Harold Wilson, 152; 'ceasefire', 153

James II, 2, 34, 36, 97
Jenkins, Roy, 58, 61
Johnston, Dr Roy, 25
Jones, Thomas, 68, 69, 88

Kelly, Henry, 133–5

Labour Party (British), 19, 97, 182
Labour Party (N. Ireland), 96, 101–2, 156, 159–60, 167
'Law and Order', 148–9, 167, 174–5, 180
Lawrence, R. J., 105
Leeson Street (Belfast), 75
Legislative powers (Constitutional Proposals 1973), 174
Lemass, Sean, 20–1, 97; speech on N. Ireland (1963), 109, 113, 115
Lenadoon (Belfast), 153
Liberals, 44, 45, 47, 97
Linen, 41
Local Government: franchise and representation 81; religious discrimination, 80–4; reorganization, 177; elections (1973), 177
London, 21, 23, 65, 106, 110, 121, 158
Londonderry, 3, 31, 49, 53, 71, 73–4, 80–4, 96; see also Derry
Long, S. E., 38

Long, Captain William, 130
Long Kesh, 144
Loyalist Association of Workers, 141, 178
Loyalist Coalition, 178
Lynch, Jack (Taoiseach of Republic of Ireland), 16, 22–3, 113, 120
Lyons, F. S. L., 101

McClean, P. J., 146
McCracken, J. L., 95, 99
Mac Giolla, Tomas, 25
McGuigan, Francis, 146
McKenna, Sean, 146
McKerr, Gerald, 146
McNally, Patrick, 146
McNamara, Kevin (Westminster MP), 13
McNeill, Eoin, 90
Macrory Report, 85, 177
Mac Stiofáin, Sean, 26, 152, 153–4
Maginess, Brian, 98
Mansergh, Nicholas, 64, 93
Maudling, Reginald, 127, 133, 137
Maynooth, 15
Middlemas, Keith, 68, 88
Monaghan election (1883), 44
Montgomery, Hugh de F., 50
Moody, T. W., 31, 42
Morgan, William, 119
Morning Post, 17, 69, 90
Mountjoy, Lord Deputy, 30
Mulvey, Father A., 74

National Democratic Party, 96
Nationalism, Irish, 12, 38, 43–5, 56, 67, 95–6, 99–100
Ne Temere decree, 7
Neutrality, Irish in Second World War, 19, 111–12
Newark, Professor, on Special Powers Act, 77
Newry (Co. Down), 80, 81, 84, 104, 140
Northern Ireland Civil Rights Association see Civil rights movement
Northern Ireland Community Relations Commission, 143
Northern Ireland Constitution Act (1973), 177, 178, 180–1, 185, 187
Northern Ireland Constitutional Proposals, 8, 166–8, 172–7
Northern Ireland (Emergency Provisions) Act (1973), 166, 171–2
Northern Ireland Labour Party see Labour Party (N. Ireland)
Northern Ireland (Temporary Provisions) Act, 151
North-south relations, 21, 107–14, 175–7

O'Brien, Conor Cruise: on internment, 78–9; on British Army, 130–1; on IRA, 131–3
O Conaill, Daithi, 152
O'Connell, Daniel, 37
Offences against the State (Amendment) Act, 166
'Official' IRA (Gardiner Place), 26, 132, 154–5
O'Hanlon, Fergal, 25
Oldpark (Belfast), 116, 153
O'Neill, Hugh, Earl of Tyrone, 30
O'Neill, Terence (Lord O'Neill of the Maine), 7, 21, 78, 97, 101, 110; on north-south relations, 110–14; as Prime Minister, 115–19
'Operation Harvest' (1956), 24; IRA Manifesto, 100–1
'Operation Motorman' (1973), 156
'One man, one vote', 119
Omagh (Co. Tyrone), 80, 82, 84, 96, 103
Orange Order, 3, 4, 34, 37, 38–40, 44, 89, 94, 95; on Catholics in Unionist Party, 97–9, 127, 130, 141, 178
Orme, Stanley, 13
Oxford Union, 20

Paisley, Rev. Ian, 11, 115, 121, 124, 150, 154, 167, 182, 188
Parliament Act (1911), 47
Parliament of Northern Ireland, 53, 57–8, 62–3, 87
Parliamentary Committees, 137, 157, 158, 159
Parnell, Charles S., 3, 40, 44, 46–7, 56
Partition, 10, 15–17, 20, 49, 50–2, 111
Payment of Debts (Emergency Provisions) Act, 143
'Peace Line', 116, 120
Peep O'Day Boys, 37
Penal Laws, 2, 34–6
Peoples Democracy, 118, 121, 123
Plantation of Ulster, 2, 31–3
Police Act (NI), 72
Police Authority, 136
Political parties, 93–102
Proportional representation (PR), 62, 64, 177
'Provisional' IRA (Kevin Street), 26, 78; formation of, 128, 131–3; bombing by, 140–1, 151; 'cease-fire', 152–3, 188
Poverty in Belfast, 105–6
Pym, Francis, 186

Rebellion of 1798, 3, 37, 38
Redmond, John, 49, 51, 52, 56, 99
Rees, Merlyn, 188
Reform Programme (1968), 118

Relations between north and south, 15–23, 107–14, 175–7, 186
Republic of Ireland, 15, 16, 19, 21, 23, 27, 56, 97, 108, 113, 150, 162–3, 166, 175, 186
Republican Clubs, 178
Riots, 22, 74–6, 117, 123–4, 126–7; of 1886, 44
Rising of 1641, 2, 33
Robb, John, 27
Rose, Paul, 13
Rossville Street (Derry), 74, 119
Royal Irish Constabulary (RIC), 70
Royal Ulster Constabulary (RUC), 20, 24, 70–2, 142, 153, 157; Catholics in, 70–1; Cameron Report on, 72–3; and Civil Rights Association, 73; and 'loyalists', 73; Scarman Report on, 74–6; in Bogside, 120, 123–4, 134, 136
Russell, James L., 9
Russia, 185

Sandy Row (Belfast), 43, 116
Scarman Tribunal, 71, 74–6
Scotland, 10
Senior, Hereward, 38
Shankill Road (Belfast), 43, 119, 130, 156
Shipbuilding, 41
Shivers, Patrick, 146
Simpson, Vivian, 96, 159
Sinn Fein, 10, 23, 25, 26, 49, 52, 56, 67, 89, 95, 178
Social Democratic and Labour Party (SDLP): founded, 137; withdrew from Stormont, 138–40; see also 152, 156, 160–1, 167, 178–9, 181, 183, 188
Solemn League and Covenant (1912), 48, 50
Solly-Flood, General, 69
Somme, Battle of, 97
Special Powers Act (NI) see Civil Authorities (Special Powers) Act (NI)
States of Ireland, 78, 130
Stormont, 5, 9, 11, 12, 14, 18, 21, 58–9, 96, 104; prorogation of (1972), 22, 79, 121, 133–5, 141, 147–50, 183
Sunday Times 'Insight' Team, 127, 128–30, 142–3

Taylor, John, 11, 27, 178, 183–4
Textile industry, 41
This Week, 22
Tone, Theobald Wolfe, 27, 36, 37, 38, 43
Trade unions in N. Ireland, 6–7, 96, 101–2

Tralee (Co. Kerry), 22, 109
Treaty, Anglo-Irish (1921), 10, 15, 16, 49, 54–5, 87, 108
Tripartite Treaty (1925), 90–1, 110
Turley, Brian, 146
Tuzo, General Harry (GOC N. Ireland, 142
Twinbrook Estate (Belfast), 153
Twoomey, Seamus, 152
Tyrone, County, 3, 15, 16, 17, 31, 49, 53, 96, 103, 117, 121

Ulster at the Crossroads, 110
Ulster Debate, The, 12
Ulster Defence Association (UDA), 141, 151, 156, 178
Ulster Defence Regiment (UDR), 68, 142, 153
Ulster Special Constabulary, 67; Hunt Report on, 67–8; size and composition, 68–9; Cameron Report on, 69–70, 74, 117, 121, 123, 124, 136, 141, 151
Ulster Unionist Council, 11, 45, 48, 49, 51, 97–8, 186, 187
Ulster Unionist Party, 4, 13, 15, 63, 64–6, 94–5, 96–9, 122, 150, 156, 157–8, 178–9
Ulster Unionists, 3, 10, 11–13, 14, 15, 19, 47, 48, 52, 56, 152, 187, 188
Ulster Vanguard, 11, 141, 150
Ulster Volunteer Force (UVF), 48, 97, 153
Ulster Workers Council (UWC), 188
Ulster's Solemn League and Covenant (1912), 48, 50
Unemployment, 6, 7, 102–4
United Irishmen, 36–8
'Unpledged' Unionists, 178

Wales, 10
Wallace, Martin, 96
Welfare state in N. Ireland, 104
West, Harry, 11, 178, 184, 188
Westminster, 9–15, 22–3, 44, 57–60, 94, 97, 110; financial relations of N. Ireland with, 106–7; intervention (1969), 120–1, 141, 150, 159, 165, 180, 187
Westminster, Statute of (1931), 17, 18
Whitelaw, William, 151, 152, 156, 179, 186
William III (William of Orange), 2, 4, 34
Wilson, Harold, 59, 112, 119, 152, 182, 188
Wilson, Sir Henry, 69
Wright, Oliver, 59

Young, Sir Arthur, 72, 121